TOSEL UP⁺
HIGH JUNIOR

심화편

강남준 감수

김희영 이지혜 전민호 최부근 저

Contents

이 책을 추천하며...

　　다양한 측면에서 평가해야 할 언어능력을 획일적인 기준을 가지고 평가해 왔던 기존의 시험체계와 달리, TOSEL은 각 교과과정과 연령별 인지단계를 세심하게 고려한 평가방법이라는 측면에서 매우 객관적이고 합리적인 영어능력인증시험입니다.

　　다른 모든 교육평가에서와 마찬가지로 영어능력인증시험에서도 수험생의 다양성을 인정하고 그것을 평가기준에 반영하는 것은, 교육적 성과를 가장 정확하게 평가할 수 있다는 점에서 상당히 바람직하고 고무적인 일이라 할 수 있겠습니다.

　　Tosel UP+를 감수하면서 가장 흡족했던 부분은 학습서이면서도 피교육자를 최대한 배려한 교육적 가치가 돋보인다는 것입니다. 다시 말해 독자가 될 어린이와 청소년들에게 "수험서"가 주는 딱딱한 이미지와 부담감을 최대한 잊고 재미있게 접근할 수 있도록, 구성이나 내용 전개에 있어 최대한 흥미와 재미를 느낄 수 있도록 배려했다는 점에서 큰 장점을 가진 교재라 평가할 수 있었습니다.

　　이처럼 지나치게 학습적인 부분만 강조하여 독자들에게 부담과 피곤을 먼저 느끼게 하는 기존의 교재들이 간과한 부분을 보완하여 어린이와 청소년의 특성을 파악하고 그들의 눈높이에 최대한 맞춰 중요한 사항들을 자연스럽게 익히도록 한 부분에서 이 교재의 연구진과 편집자들의 노력을 읽을 수 있었습니다.

　　학습 내용뿐 아니라 학습의 주체가 되어야 할 학생들을 배려하는 교육적 가치를 담고 있는 이 교재가 부디 많은 독자들에게 사랑을 받고 수많은 학생들에게 값지고 알찬 열매를 가져다주기를 기대합니다.

숙명여자대학교 TESOL대학원

주임교수 강 남 준

Test of the Skills in the English Language의 약자로 비영어권 국가들의 영어사용자들을 대상으로 영어구사능력을 측정하여 그 결과를 인증하는 영어능력인증 시험제도입니다.

EBS 한국교육방송공사가 주관하는 영어능력인증 시험제도

TOSEL은 미국이 개발하고 주도하는 기존 영어능력시험에 응시함으로써 유출되는 막대한 로열티를 절감하고자 대한민국의 대학입학수학능력시험 출제위원을 역임한 교수들이 우리의 실정에 적합하게 개발한 시험이며, EBS 한국교육방송공사가 주관하는 영어능력인증 시험제도입니다.

영어사용자 중심의 맞춤식 영어능력인증 시험제도

TOSEL은 동일한 난이도와 문항형식으로 연령에 관계없이 획일적으로 평가하는 기존의 시험제도와 달리 각급 학교의 교과과정과 연령별 인지단계를 고려한 각 단계별 난이도와 문항형식으로 영어숙달 정도를 측정함으로써 영어사용자 중심의 맞춤식 영어능력인증 시험제도입니다.

평가 유형에 따른 개인별 장점과 단점 지적, 개인별 영어학습의 방향을 제시하는 성적분석 자료를 제공하여 영어능력에 대한 종합검진 서비스 제공

TOSEL은 평가유형에 따른 개인별 장점과 단점을 지적하고, 개인별 영어학습의 방향을 제시하는 성적분석 자료를 제공하여 영어능력에 대한 종합검진 서비스를 제공함으로써 영어사용자인 소비자와 영어능력평가를 토대로 영어 교육을 담당하는 교사 및 기관 인사관리자인 공급자를 모두 만족시키는 영어능력인증 시험제도입니다.

TOSEL은 대한민국의 공교육기관 및 각급 학교의 내신, 교내평가, 졸업인증, 입학전형 등에 활용되고, 기업체와 관공서의 신입사원 선발, 인사고과, 해외 파견요원 선발 능에 활용되어 여러 가지 영이능력인증 시험을 치러야 하는 부담을 덜어주고, 기존 영어 시험을 대체하는 영어능력인증 시험제도입니다.

TOSEL 평가의 기본원칙

TOSEL은 연령별 인지단계를 고려하여 아래와 같이 6단계로 나누어 평가합니다.

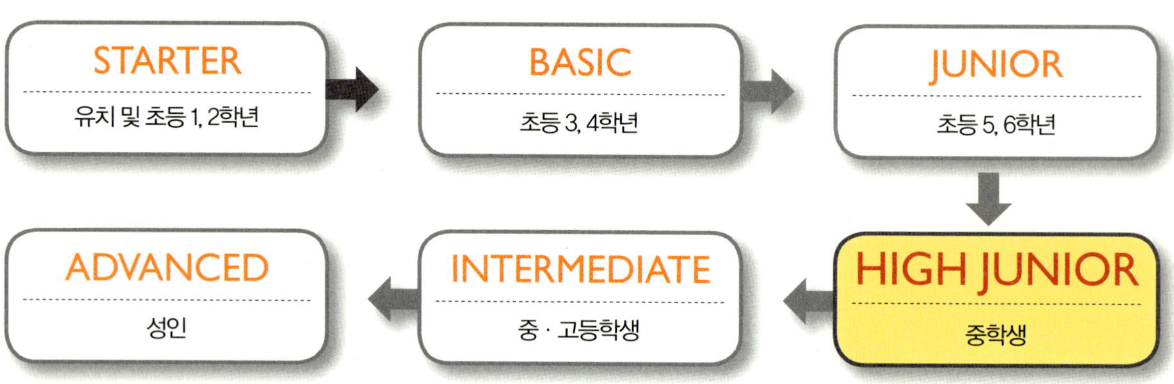

* 단, 응시지원자는 응시수준과 상관없이 지원 가능함.

TOSEL은 PBT(PAPER – BASED TEST)와 IBT(INTERNET – BASED TEST)를 통하여 간접평가와 직접평가를 모두 시행합니다.

대한민국 초등학교, 중학교, 고등학교 및 대학생과 직장인들의 업무수행능력, 국제적 공용어로서의 영어숙달 정도를 평가하여 그 결과를 공식 인증한다.

01 ··· 교육청 관내 초·중·고등학교 교내평가 및 수행평가 대행

02 ··· 대학교 신입생, 편입생 선발 시 특전 및 가산점 부여

03 ··· 대학교 졸업자격 영어인증시험 채택

04 ··· 대학원 신입생 선발 시 특전 및 가산점 부여

05 ··· 관공서 및 기업체 신입직원 선발 및 직원 외국어 능력 인사고과 평가시험 대체

정부기관/학술단체

교육과학기술부, 서울특별시

대학 및 대학원

고려대학교 법학전문대학원, 고려대학교, 국제디지털대학교, 경찰대학교, 경원대학교, 강원대학교 법학전문대학원, 한서대학교

특목중·고

민족사관고등학교, 한일고등학교, 청심국제중고등학교, 고양외국어고등학교, 과천외국어고등학교, 김포외국어고등학교, 명지외국어고등학교, 부산국제외국어고등학교, 부일외국어고등학교, 성남외국어고등학교, 인천외국어고등학교, 전북외국어고등학교, 대전외국어고등학교, 청주외국어고등학교, 강원외국어고등학교, 전남외국어고등학교

초등학교 및 중학교

청심국제중고등학교, 부산국제중학교, 계양중학교, 동양중학교, 문일중학교, 장평중학교, 중랑중학교, 한양중학교, 휘경중학교, 목포제일중학교, 동지여자중학교, 동지중학교, 전농중학교, 남산중학교, 금당중학교, 삼광중학교, 중동중학교, 용마중학교, 대저초등학교, 부산분포초등학교, 센텀초등학교, 안산경일초등학교, 서울신정초등학교, 서울석관초등학교, 대광초등학교, 서울정덕초등학교, 증약초등학교, 한양초등학교, 원주삼육초등학교, 춘천삼육초등학교, 화랑초등학교, 여도초등학교, 꿈의학교, 대구삼육초등학교

시험 유형별 구성

평가방식 : 연령별 별도 평가

구분	응시대상(수준)	구성
ADVANCED	고등(특목고 포함), 대학생, 성인	Section I : Listening Comprehension Section II : Reading Comprehension
INTERMEDIATE	중, 고등(국제중, 특목고 포함)	
HIGH JUNIOR	중학(국제중 포함)	
JUNIOR		Section I : Listening and Speaking Section II : Reading and Writing
BASIC	초등 1~6, 중학(국제중 포함)	
STARTER		

* Intermediate level의 Writing은 직접평가방식으로 이루어집니다.

배점 및 등급(Absolute Assessment + Comparative Assessment)

구분	ADVANCED	INTERMEDIATE	HIGH JUNIOR	JUNIOR	BASIC	STARTER
배점	990점	990점	100점	100점	100점	100점
등급	1~10등급으로 구성					

문항 수 및 시험 시간

구분	문항 수			시험시간		
	Section I	Section II	Total	Section I	Section II	Total
ADVANCED	70문항	70문항	140문항	45분	55분	100분
INTERMEDIATE	40문항	47문항	87문항	30분	60분	90분
HIGH JUNIOR	30문항	40문항	70문항	20분	40분	60분
JUNIOR	30문항	30문항	60문항	20분	30분	50분
BASIC	30문항	30문항	60문항	20분	30분	50분
STARTER	20문항	20문항	40문항	15분	25분	40분

HIGH JUNIOR 문항유형

유형	영역	문항 수	내용
Section I : Listening and	Part A. [Listen and Respond]	10	대화를 듣고 알맞게 응답하는 능력 측정
	Part B. [Listen and Retell]	10	대화를 듣고 내용을 파악하여 말할 수 있는지 측정
	Part C. [Listen and Predict]	5	담화를 듣고, 내용의 주인공이 할 수 있는 말로 적절한 표현을 예측할 수 있는지 측정
	Part D. [Listen and Speak]	5	대화에 참여하여 상대방의 말을 듣고 이해하여 적절히 응답할 수 있는지 측정
Section II : Reading and Writing	Part A. [Error Recognition]	5	영어의 규칙에 맞는 문장을 쓸 수 있는지 측정
	Part B. [Sentence Completion]	5	상황에 맞는 어휘나 구를 이용하여 올바른 문장을 쓸 수 있는지 측정
	Part C. [Reading and Logical Thinking]	5	글을 읽고 논리적 관계를 파악하여 글의 흐름에 가장 알맞은 어휘를 찾을 수 있는지 측정
	Part D. [Reading and Retelling]	15	다양한 주제의 지문을 읽고 내용을 정확히 이해 또는 유추하여 말할 수 있는지 측정
	Part E. [Read and Write]	10	다양한 주제의 지문을 읽고 내용을 정확히 이해하였는지, 읽은 지문을 정확히 요약할 수 있는지 측정/다양한 주제의 지문을 읽고 내용을 자신의 견해나 주장을 정확히 표현할 수 있는지 측정

HIGH JUNIOR 배점표

Section		Part		문항수	점수	합계 점수	시간
I	Listening and Speaking	A	Listen and Respond	10	1.6	15	20
		B	Listen and Retell	10	1.6	15	
		C	Listen and Predict	5	1.6	7.5	
		D	Listen and Speak	5	1.6	7.5	
II	Reading and Writing	A	Error Recognition	5	1.6	7.5	40
		B	Sentence Completion	5	1.6	7.5	
		C	Reading and Logical Thinking	5	1.6	7.5	
		D	Reading and Retelling	15	1.6	22.5	
		E	Read and Write	10	1	10	
Total				70	–	–	100	60

토셀 응시방법 안내

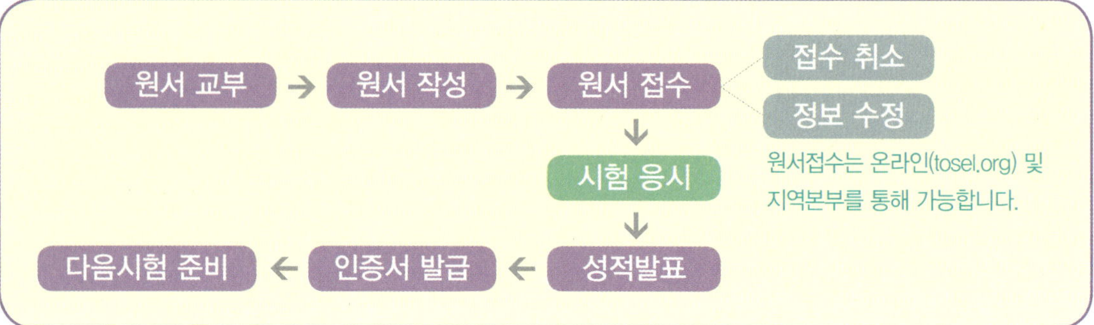

원서 교부

응시원서는 Tosel 홈페이지 내 [신청서 다운]에서 교부받을 수 있습니다.

원서 작성

원서를 교부받은 후에는 응시원서 기재사항을 기재하여 접수하시면 됩니다.

원서 접수

- 대리인 접수는 가능하나 전화접수는 불가능합니다.
- 접수된 응시료는 타인으로 대체가 불가능합니다.(환불 처리 후 타인으로 접수)
- 접수된 응시료는 환불규정에 따라 차등 차감하여 환불합니다.

응시자 유의사항

- **[TOSEL 홈페이지에서 OMR답안지 다운로드]**를 클릭하여 시험 전에 작성법 및 기표방법을 숙지하시기 바랍니다.

> 당 시험은 OMR Reader기가 수험자의 답안지를 판독한 결과에 따라 성적을 처리하며,
>
> 답안 작성 오류(잘못된 필기구 사용, 불완전한 마킹, 수험번호마킹오류)로 채점 불가능한 답안은 0점 처리되오니,
>
> 이점 유의하시기 바랍니다.
>
> OMR 마킹시 수험생 이름, 수험번호, 답안 이외의 공간에 낙서를 하여 OMR Reader기가 수험자의 답안지를
>
> 판독 못할 경우 채점이 불가능하므로 답안은 0점 처리되오니, 이점 유의하시기 바랍니다.

▶▶ 고사장 및 고사실 확인

- 고사장 및 고사실은 홈페이지를 통해 수험표 출력기간 동안 확인이 가능하오니 반드시 위치와 교통을
  미리 확인하시기 바랍니다.
- 일부 고사장의 경우 교통이 혼잡할 수 있으니 대중교통을 이용하시기 바랍니다.

▶▶ 준비물

- 필기구 : 컴퓨터용 사인펜, 수정테이프, 검정 볼펜(주관식 작성용)
- 신분증, 수험표

※ 모든 레벨의 경우 사진 및 신분증 미제출 / 미지참 시 시험 응시가 불가합니다.

▶▶ 응시료

- TOSEL – ADVANCED : 36,300원
- TOSEL – INTERMEDIATE : 33,000원
- TOSEL – HIGH JUNIOR : 29,700원
- TOSEL – JUNIOR / BASIC / STARTER : 24,200원

SECTION I

TOSEL
HIGH JUNIOR

LISTENING AND SPEAKING

PART A. Listen and Respond

PART B. Listen and Retell

PART C. Listen and Predict

PART D. Listen and Speak

 CD1 - Track 2

예제를 통해 Part A의 유형을 연습해 봅시다.

🔵 CD1 - Track 3

Mark your answer on your answer sheet. 답안지에 정답을 표시하세요.

W : How long will it take to get to your house?

M : Well, it's going to take about an hour by a train.

W : _______________________________

(A) That's enough for me. I am full.
(B) Oh, it's not close.
(C) I feel better. Thanks.
(D) Could you give me a ride?

W : 너희 집에 가는데 얼마나 걸리니?

M : 글쎄, 기차로 한 시간 정도 걸릴 거야.

W : _______________________________

(A) 그거면 충분해. 배불러.
(B) 오, 가깝지 않구나.
(C) 훨씬 낫다. 고마워.
(D) 나 좀 태워다 줄래?

정답 : (B) 'How long does it take to ~(~하는데 얼마나 걸리니?)'라고 시작하면 어떤 일에 걸리는 소요시간을 묻는 것입니다. 여자가 자신의 집까지 가는데 걸리는 소요시간을 말했으므로 남자는 그에 대한 의견을 밝히는 것이 자연스럽습니다.

＊ **give a ride** 태워다 주다

🔵 CD1 - Track 4

Mark your answer on your answer sheet. 답안지에 정답을 표시하세요.

M : Will you return the books to the library on your way back home from school?

W : I'm afraid I can't. I should go to the hospital to do volunteer work.

M : _______________________________

(A) The library is a perfect place for volunteer work.
(B) I didn't borrow any books from the library.
(C) You'd better hurry up to school.
(D) Just forget it. I will handle that.

M : 학교에서 집으로 오는 길에 도서관에 책을 반납해주겠니?

W : 안 되겠는걸. 자원봉사하러 병원에 가야 해.

M : _______________________________

(A) 도서관은 봉사활동을 하기에 정말 좋은 곳이야.
(B) 나는 도서관에서 책을 빌리지 않았어.
(C) 너는 서둘러 학교에 가는 것이 좋겠다.
(D) 괜찮아. 내가 반납해도 돼.

정답 : (D) 남자가 여자에게 도서관에 들러 책을 반납해 줄 수 있는지 묻자 여자가 사정이 있어 안 되겠다고 말합니다. 이런 경우라면 남자는 여자가 부탁을 거절한 데 대하여 무안하지 않도록 응수할 필요가 있겠군요.

＊ **return** 반납하다 / **volunteer** 자원봉사(하다) / **hurry up to** ~로 서둘러 가다

PART A. Listen and Respond 🔵 CD1 - Track 5

Directions *: In this part of the test, you will hear a short conversation. Then you will hear four possible answer choices. Each conversation and answer choices will only be played one time. Listen carefully and choose the most suitable response to the last statement. Then fill in the corresponding space on your answer sheet.*

1. Mark your answer on your answer sheet. 🔵 CD1 - Track 6

    (A)   (B)   (C)   (D)

2. Mark your answer on your answer sheet. 🔵 CD1 - Track 7

    (A)   (B)   (C)   (D)

3. Mark your answer on your answer sheet. 🔵 CD1 - Track 8

    (A)   (B)   (C)   (D)

4. Mark your answer on your answer sheet. 🔵 CD1 - Track 9

    (A)   (B)   (C)   (D)

5. Mark your answer on your answer sheet. 🔵 CD1 - Track 10

    (A)   (B)   (C)   (D)

6. Mark your answer on your answer sheet.   CD1 - Track 11

(A)   (B)   (C)   (D)

7. Mark your answer on your answer sheet.   CD1 - Track 12

(A)   (B)   (C)   (D)

8. Mark your answer on your answer sheet.   CD1 - Track 13

(A)   (B)   (C)   (D)

9. Mark your answer on your answer sheet.   CD1 - Track 14

(A)   (B)   (C)   (D)

10. Mark your answer on your answer sheet.   CD1 - Track 15

(A)   (B)   (C)   (D)

11. Mark your answer on your answer sheet.   CD1 - Track 16

(A)   (B)   (C)   (D)

12. Mark your answer on your answer sheet. CD1 - Track 17

    (A)   (B)   (C)   (D)

13. Mark your answer on your answer sheet. CD1 - Track 18

    (A)   (B)   (C)   (D)

14. Mark your answer on your answer sheet. CD1 - Track 19

    (A)   (B)   (C)   (D)

15. Mark your answer on your answer sheet. CD1 - Track 20

    (A)   (B)   (C)   (D)

16. Mark your answer on your answer sheet. CD1 - Track 21

    (A)   (B)   (C)   (D)

17. Mark your answer on your answer sheet. CD1 - Track 22

    (A)   (B)   (C)   (D)

18. Mark your answer on your answer sheet. CD1 - Track 23

      (A)   (B)   (C)   (D)

19. Mark your answer on your answer sheet. CD1 - Track 24

      (A)   (B)   (C)   (D)

20. Mark your answer on your answer sheet. CD1 - Track 25

      (A)   (B)   (C)   (D)

21. Mark your answer on your answer sheet. CD1 - Track 26

      (A)   (B)   (C)   (D)

22. Mark your answer on your answer sheet. CD1 - Track 27

      (A)   (B)   (C)   (D)

23. Mark your answer on your answer sheet. CD1 - Track 28

      (A)   (B)   (C)   (D)

24. Mark your answer on your answer sheet.   CD1 - Track 29

    (A)   (B)   (C)   (D)

25. Mark your answer on your answer sheet.   CD1 - Track 30

    (A)   (B)   (C)   (D)

26. Mark your answer on your answer sheet.   CD1 - Track 31

    (A)   (B)   (C)   (D)

27. Mark your answer on your answer sheet.   CD1 - Track 32

    (A)   (B)   (C)   (D)

28. Mark your answer on your answer sheet.   CD1 - Track 33

    (A)   (B)   (C)   (D)

29. Mark your answer on your answer sheet.   CD1 - Track 34

    (A)   (B)   (C)   (D)

30. Mark your answer on your answer sheet.　CD1 - Track 35

  (A)   (B)   (C)   (D)

31. Mark your answer on your answer sheet.　CD1 - Track 36

  (A)   (B)   (C)   (D)

32. Mark your answer on your answer sheet.　CD1 - Track 37

  (A)   (B)   (C)   (D)

33. Mark your answer on your answer sheet.　CD1 - Track 38

  (A)   (B)   (C)   (D)

34. Mark your answer on your answer sheet.　CD1 - Track 39

  (A)   (B)   (C)   (D)

35. Mark your answer on your answer sheet.　CD1 - Track 40

  (A)   (B)   (C)   (D)

36. Mark your answer on your answer sheet.   CD1 - Track 41

    (A)   (B)   (C)   (D)

37. Mark your answer on your answer sheet.   CD1 - Track 42

    (A)   (B)   (C)   (D)

38. Mark your answer on your answer sheet.   CD1 - Track 43

    (A)   (B)   (C)   (D)

39. Mark your answer on your answer sheet.   CD1 - Track 44

    (A)   (B)   (C)   (D)

40. Mark your answer on your answer sheet.   CD1 - Track 45

    (A)   (B)   (C)   (D)

다음의 어휘들을 익히고 Checkups에 기록해 보세요.

	489 Intensive Words		Checkups		
			1st	2nd	3rd
1	appropriate	[형] 적절한 [동] 유용하다, 전유하다			
2	swarm	[명] (곤충) 떼			
3	frustrate	[동] 좌절시키다			
4	aggression	[명] 공격, 침략			
5	applause	[명] 박수			
6	pessimism	[명] 염세주의			
7	substance	[명] 실체, 본질			
8	scratch	[동] 할퀴다, 긁다			
9	refine	[동] 정제하다, 세련되게 하다			
10	resign	[동] 사임하다, 물러나다			
11	adapt	[동] 적응시키다, 개조하다			
12	intellect	[명] 지성, 지능			
13	interrupt	[동] 가로막다, 방해하다			
14	disguise	[동] 위장, 변장하다 [명] 위장			
15	premier	[명] 수상 [형] 최고의, 제위의			
16	incline	[명] 경사 [동] 마음을 돌리다, 기울이다			
17	compliment	[명] 칭찬 [동] 칭찬하다			
18	reserve	[동] 따로 남겨두다, 예약해놓다 [명] 비축			
19	startle	[동] 깜짝 놀라게 하다			
20	opponent	[명] 적수, 반대자			
21	lightning	[명] 번개, 벼락			
22	synonym	[명] 동의어			
23	bachelor	[명] 학사			

489 Intensive Words		Checkups		
		1st	2nd	3rd
24	clown	[명] 광대		
25	wreck	[명] 난파 [동] 난파시키다, 난파하다		
26	creep	[동] 기다, 포복하다		
27	adjourn	[동] 연기하다, 휴회하다		
28	aquarium	[명] 수족관		
29	banish	[동] 추방하다, 떨쳐버리다		
30	choke	[동] 질식시키다, 억제하다		
31	conspiracy	[명] 음모, 공모		
32	deplete	[동] 격감시키다, 고갈시키다		
33	enhance	[동] (질, 능력 등을) 높이다, 강화하다		
34	feat	[명] 위업, 공(적), 묘기		
35	illuminate	[동] 조명하다, 비추다		
36	intangible	[형] 손으로 만질 수 없는		
37	longitude	[명] (지리) 경도		
38	morale	[명] 사기, 의욕		
39	overt	[형] 명백한, 공공연한		
40	queue	[명] 땋은 머리 [동] 줄을 서다		
41	wrath	[명] 분노, 화		
42	sanitary	[형] 위생의, 위생적인		
43	stagnant	[형] 흐르지 않는, 발달이 없는		
44	torment	[명] 고뇌 [동] 괴롭히다		
45	verify	[동] 증명하다, 확인하다		

예제를 통해 Part B의 유형을 연습해 봅시다.

 **Example 1**   🎧 CD1 - Track 47

M : Do you want special packing for the present?
W : Yes. It's for my mother's birthday.
M : Okay, then choose the wrapping paper and a card.

Q : Where are they?
   (A) at a restaurant
   (B) at home
   (C) at a clothing shop
   (D) at a gift shop

M : 선물에 특별한 포장을 하기를 원하시나요?
W : 네. 어머니께 드릴 생일 선물이거든요.
M : 좋습니다, 그럼 포장지와 카드를 골라보세요.

Q : 그들은 어디에 있습니까?
   (A) 레스토랑에
   (B) 집에
   (C) 옷가게에
   (D) 선물가게에

정답 : (D) 여자가 선물가게에서 어머니의 생일선물을 구입하고 있습니다. packing이나 wrapping paper가 힌트가 됩니다.

* **packing** 포장 / **wrapping paper** 포장지

Example 2   🎧 CD1 - Track 48

W : The printer is driving me crazy!
M : Wha's the matter?
W : A piece of paper is stuck in here, but I can't get it out.

Q : What is the woman doing?
   (A) buying a printer
   (B) fixing a paper jam
   (C) driving a car
   (D) consulting a doctor

W : 프린터 때문에 미치겠네요!
M : 무슨 문제인데요?
W : 종이 한 장이 여기에 걸렸는데, 뺄 수가 없네요.

Q : 여자는 무엇을 하고 있습니까?
   (A) 프린터 구매
   (B) 종이 걸린 것 고치기
   (C) 자동차 운전
   (D) 의사에게 진찰을 받는 중

정답 : (B) 여자가 프린터 안에 걸린 종이 한 장을 빼내지 못해서 전전긍긍하고 있습니다. 여자의 마지막 말을 놓치지 말아야 합니다.

* **fix** 고치다 / **paper jam** 프린터나 복사기 안에서 종이가 나오다 걸려서 빠지지 않는 것 / **consult(=see) a doctor** 의사에게 진찰을 받다 / **be stuck** 걸리다, ～에 빠지다

PART B. Listen and Retell CD1 - Track 49

Directions *: In this part of the test, you will hear a short conversation. Each conversation will be followed by a question. The conversations are not in print and will only be played one time. Listen carefully to each conversation and answer the questions in your test booklet. Then fill in the corresponding space on your answer sheet.*

1. How much will the man pay? CD1 - Track 50

    (A) 5 dollars

    (B) 6 dollars

    (C) 7 dollars

    (D) 8 dollars

2. Why was the woman absent from the math class? CD1 - Track 51

    (A) She overslept in the morning.

    (B) Her clock was running slow.

    (C) She didn't set the alarm clock.

    (D) She had a misunderstanding about the time of the class.

3. Why is the man so excited? CD1 - Track 52

    (A) There will be a lot of snow.

    (B) He is admitted to attend the school.

    (C) Tomorrow is the school anniversary.

    (D) School will be closed for days.

4. What is Peter's occupation? CD1 - Track 53

    (A) a painter

    (B) a reporter

    (C) a writer

    (D) a mechanic

5. What day of the week is it today? CD1 - Track 54

    (A) Monday

    (B) Tuesday

    (C) Wednesday

    (D) Thursday

6. What is the woman doing? CD1 - Track 55

    (A) She is asking the way to a telephone booth.
    (B) She is looking for her daughter.
    (C) She is choosing a shirt to buy.
    (D) She is having her daughter getting an audition.

7. Where are they? CD1 - Track 56

    (A) at the snack bar
    (B) in the library
    (C) in the street
    (D) at the movie theater

8. What time of year is it? CD1 - Track 57

    (A) Spring
    (B) Summer
    (C) Fall
    (D) Winter

9. What is the man's favorite subject? CD1 - Track 58

    (A) art
    (B) science
    (C) social studies
    (D) physical education

10. What will the woman bring to the party? CD1 - Track 59

    (A) potato chips
    (B) tuna sandwiches
    (C) Korean rice cakes
    (D) a bunch of flowers

PART.B

11. How old is the man? CD1 - Track 60

(A) nineteen
(B) twenty
(C) twenty-one
(D) twenty-two

12. When is the woman able to meet the man? CD1 - Track 61

(A) Saturday morning
(B) Saturday afternoon
(C) Sunday morning
(D) Sunday afternoon

13. What does the woman want to do for her vacation? CD1 - Track 62

(A) going camping
(B) staying at home
(C) doing something special
(D) traveling to a wonderful place

14. Where is the woman? CD1 - Track 63

(A) at an auto repair shop
(B) at a laundry
(C) at a hospital
(D) at a computer repair center

15. What will the man buy? CD1 - Track 64

(A) black sneakers
(B) red sneakers
(C) blue sneakers
(D) black high-top sneakers

16. What does the woman think of the bag? CD1 - Track 65

    (A) She doesn't like the pattern.
    (B) The colors are not what she wants.
    (C) It is too expensive.
    (D) It is old-fashioned.

17. What do they think of the new shopping mall? CD1 - Track 66

    (A) It is responsible for the traffic jam.
    (B) Its price policy is very attractive.
    (C) It contributes to the local economy.
    (D) Many local stores are closing due to it.

18. What is the problem with the woman's printer? CD1 - Track 67

    (A) The printer doesn't work well.
    (B) The black ink cartridge is leaking.
    (C) The printer is running out of black ink.
    (D) The black ink doesn't dry well on the paper.

19. How will the man go to the airport? CD1 - Track 68

    (A) by airport bus
    (B) by taxi
    (C) by subway
    (D) on foot

20. What is the problem with Andy? CD1 - Track 69

    (A) He does not wash himself well.
    (B) He is not diligent about his household chores.
    (C) He does not apologize for his fault.
    (D) He always makes the same old excuses.

21. What is the woman doing?   CD1 - Track 70

  (A) looking for a person
  (B) preparing for a reception party
  (C) selling computer equipment
  (D) having a job interview

22. When did the boy graduate from middle school?   CD1 - Track 71

  (A) yesterday
  (B) last Tuesday
  (C) last Wednesday
  (D) last Thursday

23. How is Linda feeling?   CD1 - Track 72

  (A) envious
  (B) delighted
  (C) frightened
  (D) confused

24. What is Brian most likely to do next?   CD1 - Track 73

  (A) erase the additional zero off the paper
  (B) report the theft to the police
  (C) find Jeff and bring him over to the boss
  (D) contact the bank and cancel the transfer

25. What are they most likely to do next?   CD1 - Track 74

  (A) go to a coffee shop
  (B) say good-bye to each other
  (C) exchange their phone numbers
  (D) have a little more talk on the spot

26. Where are they?   CD1 - Track 75

    (A) at a restaurant
    (B) at a clothing shop
    (C) in a wedding hall
    (D) in a hospital

27. What is the woman doing now?   CD1 - Track 76

    (A) buying a suit
    (B) cooking
    (C) writing a report
    (D) preparing for a job interview

28. What are they talking about?   CD1 - Track 77

    (A) chemistry
    (B) the future city
    (C) recycling of waste
    (D) separate garbage collection

29. Why did the man visit the woman?   CD1 - Track 78

    (A) to buy one more bucket
    (B) to get a refund on the bucket
    (C) to fix the bucket
    (D) to exchange his purchase

30. How much did the man pay for his bike?   CD1 - Track 79

    (A) 340 dollars
    (B) 300 dollars
    (C) 280 dollars
    (D) 260 dollars

31. Where is Pamela?   CD1 - Track 80

    (A) a beauty salon

    (B) a clothing store

    (C) a gallery

    (D) a fitness center

32. What are they doing?   CD1 - Track 81

    (A) booking a flight

    (B) packing up for a trip

    (C) searching for lost flight tickets

    (D) choosing gifts in a shop

33. What is the man doing?   CD1 - Track 82

    (A) pumping chemicals into the river

    (B) watching a movie

    (C) working in a factory

    (D) reading a newspaper

34. What are they talking about?   CD1 - Track 83

    (A) a birthday party

    (B) a birthday gift

    (C) how to keep a cat

    (D) one reason for the allergy to cats

35. What does the man want to do for Sue?   CD1 - Track 84

    (A) preparing for the meeting

    (B) mailing the letters

    (C) getting some aspirin

    (D) taking her to a hospital

36. From what time can the woman enter the exhibition on Saturday? CD1 - Track 85

    (A) 10 a.m.
    (B) 12 p.m.
    (C) 2 p.m.
    (D) 5 p.m.

37. What will the speakers do next? CD1 - Track 86

    (A) prepare for the presentation
    (B) take an exam
    (C) go to the park
    (D) play with a puppy

38. Where is the woman? CD1 - Track 87

    (A) in the police office
    (B) in the classroom
    (C) in the stationery store
    (D) in the lost and found

39. Which will the man most likely take? CD1 - Track 88

    (A) a subway
    (B) a bus
    (C) a taxi
    (D) a train

40. What is the woman's plan? CD1 - Track 89

    (A) to give up school
    (B) to buy a car for commuting
    (C) to move in the school dormitory
    (D) to rent a room near the school

다음의 어휘들을 익히고 Checkups에 기록해 보세요.

	489 Intensive Words		Checkups		
			1st	2nd	3rd
46	expectant	[형] 예상되는, 예비의			
47	trace	[명] 흔적, 발자국 [동] 추적하다			
48	restore	[동] 제자리로 돌리다			
49	deduce	[동] 연역(추론)하다			
50	occupy	[동] 차지하다			
51	resist	[동] 저항하다			
52	inquire	[동] 질문하다, 심문하다			
53	descend	[동] 내려가다, 전해지다			
54	crude	[형] 날것의, 가공하지 않은			
55	shelter	[명] 피난처, 은신처			
56	prosecute	[동] 기소하다, 구속하다			
57	recognize	[동] 인정하다, 인지하다			
58	intervene	[동] 훼방 놓다, 간섭하다			
59	herbivore	[명] 초식 동물			
60	airsick	[형] 비행기 멀미하는			
61	decline	[명] 경사, 내리막, 감퇴			
62	complement	[명] 보충물 [동] 보충하다			
63	conserve	[동] 보호하다, 보존하다			
64	insurance	[명] 보험			
65	opposite	[형] 정반대의 [명] 정반대물			
66	stammer	[동] 말을 더듬다			
67	anonymous	[형] 무명의, 익명의			
68	streak	[명] 줄, 선 [동] 줄을 긋다			

	489 Intensive Words		Checkups		
			1st	2nd	3rd
69	acrobatics	[명] 곡예, 교예			
70	resume	[명] 이력서 [동] 요약하다			
71	nurture	[동] 양육하다, 양성하다			
72	adore	[동] 숭배하다, 아주 좋아하다			
73	arbitrary	[형] 임의의, 멋대로인			
74	barometer	[명] 기압계, 지표			
75	chuckle	[명] 킬킬 웃음 [동] 킬킬 웃다			
76	constitute	[동] 구성하다, 구성 요소가 되다			
77	deteriorate	[명] 나쁘게 하다, 나빠지다			
78	entangle	[동] 얽히게 하다			
79	flaw	[명] 흠, 결점			
80	imminent	[형] 절박한, 일촉즉발의			
81	integrate	[동] 통합하다			
82	lure	[명] 매혹물, 덫 [동] 유혹하다			
83	mortgage	[명] 저당, [동] 저당 잡히다			
84	perpetual	[형] 영속하는, 끊임없는			
85	radiation	[명] 방사, 방사물			
86	rectangular	[형] 직사각형의			
87	sarcastic	[형] 빈정대는, 풍자적인			
88	stale	[형] 싱싱하지 못한, 시시한			
89	toxic	[형] 유독한, 치명적인			
90	versatile	[형] 다재다능한, 용도가 다양한			

설명하고 있는 알맞은 의미의 단어를 퍼즐안에 넣어 봅시다.

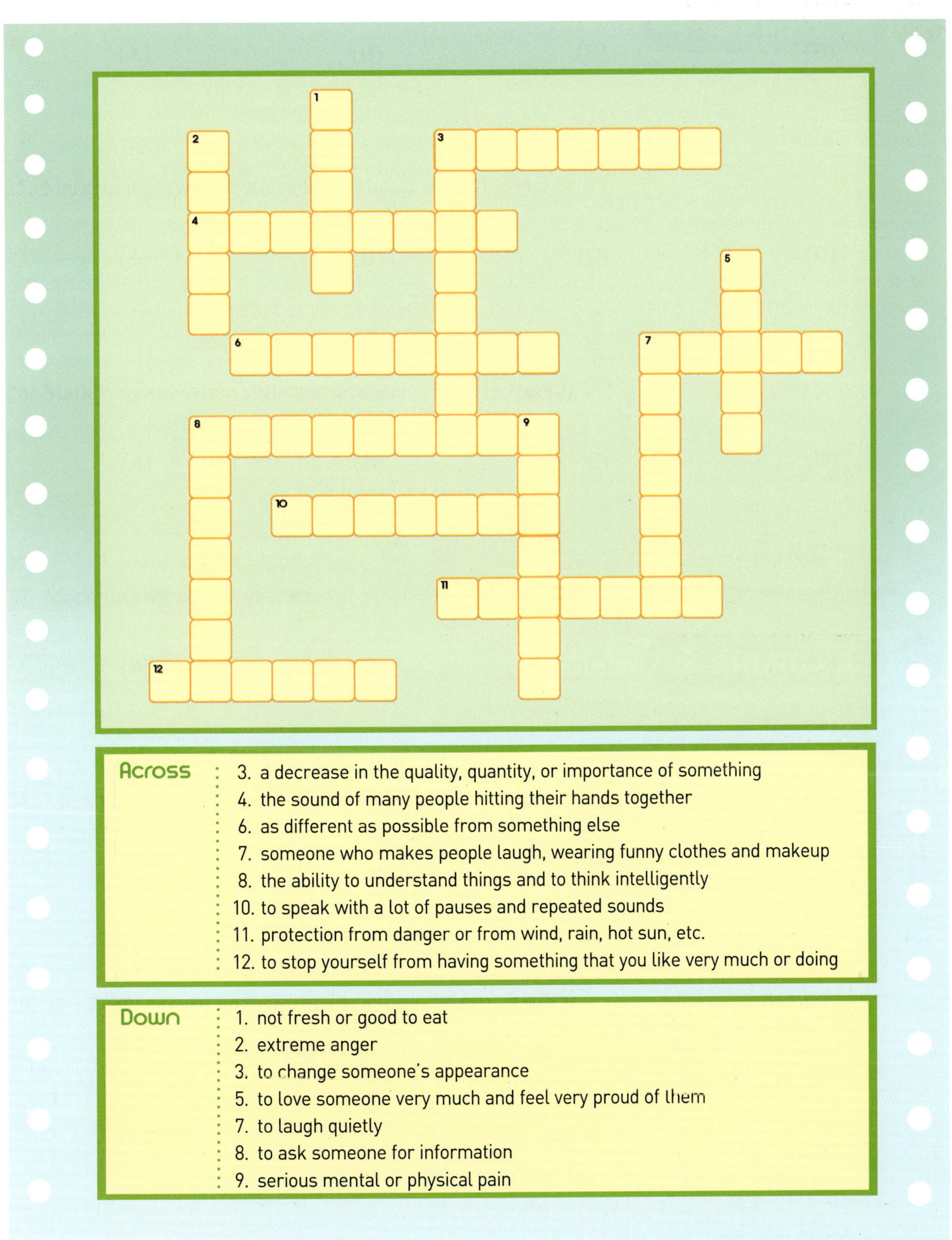

Across

3. a decrease in the quality, quantity, or importance of something
4. the sound of many people hitting their hands together
6. as different as possible from something else
7. someone who makes people laugh, wearing funny clothes and makeup
8. the ability to understand things and to think intelligently
10. to speak with a lot of pauses and repeated sounds
11. protection from danger or from wind, rain, hot sun, etc.
12. to stop yourself from having something that you like very much or doing

Down

1. not fresh or good to eat
2. extreme anger
3. to change someone's appearance
5. to love someone very much and feel very proud of them
7. to laugh quietly
8. to ask someone for information
9. serious mental or physical pain

예제를 통해 Part C의 유형을 연습해 봅시다.

 ## Example 1

 CD2 - Track 2

David is very upset about the woman next door because she plays her stereo so loudly. She plays it all day long, so the sound often makes it impossible for him to focus on something. She also plays it late at night when he is trying to sleep. Now the stereo is becoming a big trouble to David. He has to study for his final exam but he can no longer stand the constant noise from the next door. So David goes straight up to the door of her house and knocks. After a moment, she opens the door and comes out.

David는 옆집 여자 때문에 매우 화가 납니다. 그녀가 스테레오를 너무 크게 틀어놓기 때문입니다. 그녀는 하루 종일 스테레오를 켜두어서 그 소리 때문에 그는 종종 어떤 일에 집중하는 것이 불가능합니다. 그녀는 또한 그가 잠들려고 하는 늦은 밤에도 스테레오를 틀어놓습니다. 지금 스테레오가 David에게 큰 골칫거리가 되고 있습니다. 그는 기말고사 때문에 공부해야 하지만 옆집에서 나는 끊임없는 소음을 더 이상 참을 수 없습니다. 그래서 David는 그녀의 집 문 앞으로 곧장 가서 노크를 합니다. 잠시 후, 그녀가 문을 열고 나옵니다.

Q : What will David say to the woman next door?
    (A) Welcome to my house.
    (B) I am so sorry for the noise.
    (C) Could you please turn down the volume?
    (D) Take care of yourself.

Q : David는 옆집 여자에게 무엇이라고 말하겠습니까?
    (A) 우리 집에 오신 걸 환영합니다.
    (B) 소음에 대해 너무 죄송합니다.
    (C) 음향 소리 좀 낮춰 주시겠어요?
    (D) 잘 지내세요.

정답 : (C)　선택지의 (B)는 David의 반응이 아닌, 옆집 여자가 소음에 대해 사과를 할 때의 표현이므로 정답이 아닙니다.

*　**upset** 화가 난 / **stereo** 전축 등의 음향기구 / **bother** 괴롭히다 / **constant** 지속적인 / **stand** 참다, 견디다 / **knock** 두드리다

 ## Example 2

 CD2 - Track 3

Billy is in the bookstore near his house. He is looking for a book, titled "How to Step Up Your Writing Skills." He needs this book for doing his writing homework. He is searching the education section in the bookstore, but he cannot find the book. At just the right time he sees a clerk come near to him. So he asks if she can help him with the book.

Billy는 집 근처의 서점에 있습니다. 그는 "쓰기 능력을 높이는 방법"이라는 제목의 책을 찾고 있습니다. 작문숙제를 하기 위해 이 책이 필요합니다. 서점의 교육 코너에서 찾아보고 있지만 그 책을 찾을 수가 없습니다. 마침 그는 점원 한 사람이 가까이 다가오는 것을 봅니다. 그래서 그녀에게 책을 찾는 것을 도와줄 수 있는지 물어봅니다.

Q : How will the clerk most likely respond?
    (A) It's your job to look for the book, isn't it?
    (B) I need that book, too. Will you help me to find it?
    (C) You should go to the education section.
    (D) Sorry, but the book is currently out of stock.

Q : 점원이 무엇이라고 대답을 할까요?
    (A) 책을 찾는 것은 당신의 일입니다. 그렇지 않습니까?
    (B) 저도 그 책이 필요합니다. 찾는 것을 좀 도와 주시겠습니까?
    (C) 교육 코너로 가셔야 합니다.
    (D) 죄송하지만, 책은 현재 품절되었습니다.

정답 : (D)　서점의 점원이 손님의 부탁에 대하여 (A)처럼 말한다면 대단히 무례한 일이겠죠? (B)는 점원이 손님에게 할 수 있는 말로 적절하지 않습니다. (C)가 정답이 될 수 없는 것은 현재 Billy가 이미 교육 코너에 와서 책을 찾고 있는 중이기 때문입니다. 손님이 책을 찾고 있으나 책이 이미 품절된 상태라면 점원이 (D)와 같이 말하는 것이 자연스럽습니다.

*　**education** 교육 / **section** 구역 / **currently** 현재 / **out of stock** 품절되어, 매진되어 / **title** 제목(을 붙이다) / **search** 탐색하다, 찾다 / **at just the right time** 마침

PART C. Listen and Predict CD2 - Track 4

Directions *: In this part of the test, you will hear short talks. The talks are not in print and will only be played one time. Listen carefully to each talk and answer the following questions in your test booklet. Then fill in the corresponding space on your answer sheet.*

1. What is Linda likely to ask? CD2 - Track 5

   (A) Is my computer working?
   (B) Can I get some help for the Internet?
   (C) Are the room services available?
   (D) Can you give me a wake-up call?

2. How will Helen likely respond? CD2 - Track 6

   (A) My father misses me very much.
   (B) Can you cover up for me tomorrow?
   (C) They are living in the downtown.
   (D) No problem. I'll make up for you.

3. What is Kate likely to say? CD2 - Track 7

   (A) No problem. I will surely join the party.
   (B) I'd love to, but I have another appointment.
   (C) What a coincidence! We have the same birthday.
   (D) Don't worry. I can cancel my birthday party.

4. What is Tom likely to say? CD2 - Track 8

   (A) Don't worry. Everything will be fine.
   (B) I think you should stop now.
   (C) Go home and get some rest.
   (D) That's perfect. Now you are OK.

5. What will Steven most likely say?　CD2 - Track 9

   (A) My mistake. Let's find another place.

   (B) My treat. Help yourself.

   (C) You shouldn't have.

   (D) Thanks for reserving seats for us.

6. How will Mark most likely respond?　CD2 - Track 10

   (A) Just skip several meals and you will know.

   (B) Quick diet works fine in some time.

   (C) Eating habits and regular exercises are most important.

   (D) Sometimes you need to relax yourself.

7. What is Ruth likely to say?　CD2 - Track 11

   (A) This is so called a surprise party.

   (B) I don't like a party, so it is not worthy.

   (C) I already know what you are planning.

   (D) What a nice surprise! Thanks a lot.

8. What is Mike likely to ask?　CD2 - Track 12

   (A) When did the exam start today?

   (B) Can I borrow a pen to write with?

   (C) Did you wake up too late?

   (D) Can you find my pens for me?

9. What will Sam probably say?　CD2 - Track 13

   (A) Action speaks louder than the words.

   (B) There is no place like home.

   (C) In any situation, eating comes first.

   (D) To see is to believe.

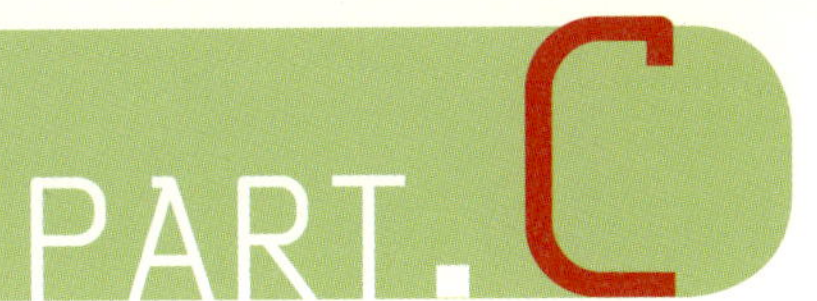

10. How will Linda likely respond? CD2 - Track 14

   (A) Let's record this program for us.
   (B) Nothing more, nothing less.
   (C) Recycling is quite important.
   (D) Documentary is always serious.

11. What will Daniel likely say? CD2 - Track 15

   (A) I prefer Korean-style food.
   (B) Let's have a cup of coffee.
   (C) It's on me. Let's go to a pizza parlor.
   (D) Baseball is my favorite sport.

12. What will Terry probably say? CD2 - Track 16

   (A) I enjoyed soccer practice a lot.
   (B) It is between you and me.
   (C) I need to report this to the teacher.
   (D) My teacher will scold us if he knows this.

13. What is Jack likely to say? CD2 - Track 17

   (A) I don't like traveling abroad.
   (B) Cultural differences are important.
   (C) Culture shock is hard to overcome.
   (D) Experience is better than understanding.

14. What will Paul probably ask? CD2 - Track 18

   (A) Can you wait in line?
   (B) Can you hold on?
   (C) Here or to go?
   (D) Can I get free refills?

15. What will Marie probably ask? CD2 - Track 19

    (A) Can I meet Dr. Brown?
    (B) How much is the book?
    (C) Where can I find the book here?
    (D) Can I place an order of that book?

16. What will Carol probably say? CD2 - Track 20

    (A) Can you help me?
    (B) What is the address of that Internet site?
    (C) Anyway, thanks.
    (D) I will let you know my address.

17. What is Alice likely to ask? CD2 - Track 21

    (A) Did you save the file?
    (B) What happened to your computer?
    (C) Can you help me to finish my report?
    (D) What am I supposed to do?

18. How will Eric most likely respond? CD2 - Track 22

    (A) I appreciate for your kindness.
    (B) No problem. Just tell me which button to press.
    (C) I don't like to take a picture alone.
    (D) I like this picture the most.

19. What is Ann likely to say? CD2 - Track 23

    (A) The waitress is the best I've ever seen.
    (B) I apolpgize. I forgot to leave a tip.
    (C) I'm sorry but you overcharged me.
    (D) This restaurant makes me feel cosy.

20. How will Ryan probably respond? CD2 - Track 24

    (A) It doesn't hurt to try.

    (B) Look who is talking.

    (C) I wasn't born yesterday.

    (D) I can learn and play by ear.

다음의 어휘들을 익히고 Checkups에 기록해 보세요.

489 Intensive Words			Checkups		
			1st	2nd	3rd
91	supervise	[동] 감독하다			
92	prospect	[명] 전망, 예상, 기대, 가망성			
93	revolve	[동] 회전(공전)하다			
94	induce	[동] 유도, 권유하다			
95	interaction	[명] 상호작용			
96	register	[동] 등록하다, 등기하다			
97	range	[명] 줄, 열, 산맥, 범위			
98	inherit	[동] 상속받다, 물려받다			
99	struggle	[동] 몸부림치다, 싸우다			
100	privilege	[명] 특권			
101	humiliate	[동] ~에게 창피를 주다			
102	cognitive	[형] 인지적인			
103	interfere	[동] 끼어들다			
104	carnivore	[명] 육식 동물			
105	odd	[형] 이상한, 홀수의			
106	pedestrian	[명] 보행자			
107	identical	[형] 동일한			
108	preserve	[동] 보호, 보존하다			
109	deposit	[동] 적립하다, 침전시키다			
110	exhibit	[동] 보이다, 전시하다			
111	altar	[명] 제단			
112	synthesize	[동] 종합하다			
113	sneak	[동] 살금살금 들어오다(나가다)			

489 Intensive Words		Checkups		
		1st	2nd	3rd
114	council	[명] 회의, 협의회, 평의회			
115	shorthand	[명] 속기			
116	nutrition	[명] 영양			
117	advent	[명] 출현, 도래			
118	archaeology	[명] 고고학			
119	barter	[동] 물물 교환하다 [명] 물물 교환			
120	cluster	[명] 무리 (과일) 송이			
121	contempt	[명] 경멸, 업신여김			
122	diagnosis	[명] 진단			
123	entitle	[동] …의 칭호를 주다, 권리(자격)를 주다			
124	foe	[명] 적, 원수			
125	implement	[동] 이행하다 [명] 도구			
126	intestine	[명] (보통 pl.) 창자, 장			
127	magnificent	[형] 장려한, 훌륭한			
128	mummy	[명] 미라, 바짝 마른 것			
129	persecute	[동] 박해하다, 괴롭히다			
130	radical	[형] 근본적인, 급진적인			
131	refrain	[동] 그만두다, 삼가다			
132	scorch	[동] 태우다, 그슬리다.			
133	stereotype	[명] (인쇄) 연판, 고정관념			
134	tranquil	[형] 조용한			
135	viable	[형] 생존가능한, 실행가능한, 실용적인			

예제를 통해 Part D의 유형을 연습해 봅시다.

 Example 1

🔵 CD2 - Track 26

M : I bought a bike yesterday. I will ride it to school.

W : But don't you usually drive?

M : Yes, I do. But from now on I'm going to ride my bike.

W : What for?

Q : What will the man say next?
  (A) Please don't feel jealous.
  (B) I'm tired of sitting in heavy traffic every morning.
  (C) No way. I actually prefer driving.
  (D) I hope you ride a bike with me.

M : 나 어제 자전거를 샀어. 학교에 타고 다닐 거야.

W : 너 보통 운전하지 않니?

M : 응, 그래. 하지만 지금부턴 자전거를 타고 다닐 거야.

W : 무엇 때문이지?

Q : 남자는 다음에 무엇이라고 말할까요?
  (A) 질투하지 마.
  (B) 아침마다 교통 체증에 걸린 채 차 안에 앉아 있는데 질렸어.
  (C) 절대 안 돼. 난 사실 운전이 더 좋아.
  (D) 네가 나와 함께 자전거를 탔으면 좋겠어.

정답 : (B) 여자의 마지막 말 'What for(무엇 때문이지)?'는 이유를 묻는 표현입니다. 보통 운전을 했음에도 불구하고, 이제부터 남자가 자전거를 타겠다는 말에 대하여 여자가 'What for?'라고 물었으므로 남자는 자전거를 타는 이유를 말해야 합니다.

* **jealous** 질투하는, 시기하는 / **heavy traffic** 심하게 막히는 교통 / **No way!** 절대 안 돼, 절대 아니야 / **from now on** 지금부터 계속

Example 2

🔵 CD2 - Track 27

W : Welcome home! I missed you so much.

M : So did I. Thank you for picking me up.

W : Don't mention it. That's what friends are for.

M : I'm afraid I can't overcome the jet lag soon.

Q : What will the woman say next?
  (A) It feels like I'm still flying.
  (B) I cannot thank you enough.
  (C) Don't worry. You will be okay before long.
  (D) Don't try to take an airplane again.

W : 고국에 돌아온 것을 환영해! 너를 정말 보고 싶었어.

M : 나도 그랬어. 마중 나와줘서 고마워.

W : 천만에. 친구 좋다는 게 다 이런 거지 뭐.

M : 시차를 금방 극복하지 못할까봐 걱정이야.

Q : 여자는 다음에 무엇이라고 말할까요?
  (A) 아직도 비행을 하고 있는 느낌이야.
  (B) 어떻게 감사해야 할지 모르겠어.
  (C) 걱정 마. 곧 괜찮아질 거야.
  (D) 다시는 비행기를 타려고 하지 마.

정답 : (D) 해외에서 귀국하는 친구를 공항에서 맞이하는 장면입니다. 남자가 마지막 말에서 시차를 극복하지 못할까봐 걱정된다고 말했으므로 여자는 격려하는 말로 받아주는 것이 자연스럽습니다.

* **I cannot thank you enough.** 아무리 감사해도 부족하군요. 어떻게 감사해야할지 모르겠습니다. / **before long** 머지않아, 곧 / **pick up** 마중 나가다, (차로) 태우러 가다 / **That's what friends are for.** 친구 좋다는 게 다 그런 거지요. / **overcome** 극복하다 / **jet lag** (장거리 비행기 여행 후에 발생하는) 시차

PART D. Listen and Speak CD2 - Track 28

Directions *: In this part of the test, you will hear a series of short conversations. The conversations are not in print and will only be played one time. Listen carefully to each conversation. After you hear each conversation, read the four choices in your test booklet and choose the best response to follow the last statement or question in the conversation. Then fill in the corresponding space on your answer sheet.*

1. What will the woman say next? CD2 - Track 29
   (A) Look on the sunny side of things.
   (B) All right. It will be ready within 10 minutes.
   (C) The sun is going to rise soon.
   (D) It depends on you.

2. What will the woman say next? CD2 - Track 30
   (A) Oh, are you? I'm here on holiday.
   (B) I will stay at the Renaissance Hotel in New York.
   (C) How long will you stay in the United States?
   (D) Do you want me to give you my business card?

3. What will the man say next? CD2 - Track 31
   (A) I didn't have to do my best for the exam.
   (B) I hurt my chin, so I can barely open my mouth.
   (C) Thanks. It's a comfort talking with you.
   (D) What have I done to deserve this?

4. What will the man say next? CD2 - Track 32
   (A) What's your ideal type like?
   (B) Good to hear that you met your dream guy.
   (C) I'm still looking for Mr. Right.
   (D) I don't want to have another blind date.

5. What will the woman say next? CD2 - Track 33
   (A) It's the body temperature in the spring.
   (B) It's unusual tiredness in the spring.
   (C) It's the name of an epidemic disease.
   (D) It's the festival for welcoming the upcoming spring.

6. What will the man say next? CD2 - Track 34

    (A) I am ready to give you knee boots.

    (B) Knee boots are all in size seven.

    (C) I'm sorry but they are out of stock.

    (D) We don't sell hair ribbons.

7. What will the woman say next? CD2 - Track 35

    (A) It's been two years.

    (B) I really enjoyed Thanksgiving day.

    (C) It takes about five hours to get there.

    (D) I will stay for five days.

8. What will the man say next? CD2 - Track 36

    (A) Please let me leave my message to him.

    (B) Mr. Evans will be very upset about this.

    (C) Oh, that's a relief!

    (D) I know. Please tell him. I'm sorry for the late notice.

9. What will the woman say next? CD2 - Track 37

    (A) It is too expensive for an hour.

    (B) Two hours is enough to look around this park.

    (C) Let's find out a rental shop first.

    (D) I am so tired that I can't walk.

10. What will the man say next? CD2 - Track 38

    (A) Please be honest.

    (B) Take some sleeping pills before you go to bed.

    (C) I know you like my apartment.

    (D) I would like to, but the rent for your apartment is too high.

11. What will the man say next? CD2 - Track 39

    (A) That is not a good idea.

    (B) I don't want to bother them.

    (C) Yes, I did. But I couldn't find it.

    (D) Yes, and they said they have.

12. What will the woman say next? CD2 - Track 40

    (A) I didn't break it at all.

    (B) Hiking is not easy for me.

    (C) I would rather stay at home.

    (D) We made up, thanks to Kate.

13. What will the man say next? CD2 - Track 41

    (A) Never mind. It's nothing.

    (B) You mean you went for business?

    (C) Ok, tell me what happened.

    (D) What a coincidence! It is good for you, though.

14. What will the woman say next? CD2 - Track 42

    (A) I was born and raised in New York.

    (B) I traveled around France when I was 20.

    (C) I already made a reservation at the hotel nearby.

    (D) I heard there is a beautiful bridge in San Francisco.

15. What will the man say next? CD2 - Track 43

    (A) I wanted to see that kind of fashion show.

    (B) Sounds interesting. Where and when will it be?

    (C) I'm up for it. Let's find out where we can buy clothes.

    (D) The stores will be closed because of heavy rain.

16. What will the woman say next?　CD2 - Track 44

    (A) Would you like to pay in cash or credit card?

    (B) Sorry about that. May I have a receipt?

    (C) It shouldn't be. It worked well until yesterday.

    (D) It is against the policy. It passed 90 days.

17. What will the man say next?　CD2 - Track 45

    (A) I will show you. Follow me, please .

    (B) It is easy. You can't miss it.

    (C) Thanks. You've been a great help.

    (D) Then there must be a bus stop.

18. What will the woman say next?　CD2 - Track 46

    (A) Too much coke is not good for your health.

    (B) Ok, I'll get some coke as soon as possible.

    (C) Trust me. You will regret your choice.

    (D) Then how about fruit juice like oranges or grapes?

19. What will the man say next?　CD2 - Track 47

    (A) Korea is the better place for you to live.

    (B) That's why you are bilingual.

    (C) You can take Korean language lessons.

    (D) It would be better for you to speak Korean.

20. What will the woman say next?　CD2 - Track 48

    (A) I have to prepare my report.

    (B) There is no time for you to take a rest.

    (C) Then how about going to a movie for a change?

    (D) Let's drop by the next rest area.

다음의 어휘들을 익히고 Checkups에 기록해 보세요.

	489 Intensive Words		Checkups		
			1st	2nd	3rd
136	grant	[동] 승인하다, 인정하다, 수여하다			
137	raft	[명] 뗏목			
138	crash	[동] ~와 충돌하다			
139	extravagant	[형] 사치스러운, 과도한			
140	conflict	[명] 충돌, 갈등 [동] 대립하다, 충돌하다			
141	reside	[동] 거주하다			
142	investigate	[동] 조사하다			
143	confess	[동] 자백하다			
144	chore	[명] 허드렛일, 잡일			
145	administer	[동] 관리하다, 경영하다			
146	humid	[형] 습기 찬, 축축한			
147	esteem	[명] 존경 [동] 존경하다			
148	former	[형] 이전의			
149	shatter	[동] 산산조각내다(되다)			
150	inspire	[동] 숨을 들이쉬다, 영감을 주다			
151	peddler	[명] 행상인			
152	identify	[동] 확인하다, 동일시하다			
153	deserve	[동] 받을 만한 자격이 있다			
154	withdraw	[동] ~에서 돈을 인출하다, 철수하다			
155	prohibit	[동] 금히다, 금지하다			
156	alter	[동] 변경하다, 바꾸다			
157	concentrate	[동] 집중하다(on)			
158	poach	[동] 밀렵하다			

489 Intensive Words		Checkups		
		1st	2nd	3rd
159	pile	[명] 무더기, 더미 [동] 쌓아 올리다			
160	grasp	[동] 잡다, 이해하다			
161	sustain	[동] 떠받치다, ~를 부양하다			
162	adverse	[형] 거스르는, 반대하는, 불리한			
163	artery	[명] 동맥			
164	bewilder	[동] 당황하게 하다			
165	commodity	[명] 상품			
166	converse	[동] 이야기하다, 담화하다			
167	dilute	[동] 묽게 하다, 묽어지다 [형] 묽게 한			
168	epidemic	[명] 유행병			
169	fraud	[명] 사기, 기만			
170	improvise	[동] (시, 곡 등을) 즉석에서 하다			
171	intricate	[형] 얽힌, 복잡한			
172	magnify	[동] 확대하다, 과장하다			
173	municipal	[형] 도시의, 시의			
174	perspire	[동] 땀을 흘리다			
175	rally	[동] 불러 모으다 [명] 대회, 집회			
176	rejoice	[동] 기뻐하다			
177	segregation	[명] 분리, 차별			
178	tentative	[형] 시험적인, 임시의			
179	transition	[명] 변천, 과도기			
180	vice versa	[형] 거꾸로, 반대로			

설명하고 있는 알맞은 의미의 단어를 퍼즐안에 넣어 봅시다.

Across

3. to have an accident in a car, plane, etc. by violently hitting something else
6. exactly the same, or very similar
8. happening or existing before, but not now
10. a small job that you have to do regularly, especially work that you do to keep a house clean
11. large numbers of cases of a disease that happen at the same time
13. an enemy
15. uncomfortable because the air is very wet and usually hot

Down

1. pleasantly calm, quiet, and peaceful
2. a special advantage that is given only to one person or group of people
4. a flat floating structure, usually made of pieces of wood tied together
5. to move around like a wheel, or to make something move around like a wheel
7. a state of disagreement or argument between people, groups, countries, etc.
9. to feel or show that you are very happy
12. a dead body that has been preserved by wrapping it in cloth
14. strange or unusual

SECTION II

TOSEL
HIGH JUNIOR

READING AND WRITING

PART A. Error Recognition

PART B. Sentence Completion

PART C. Reading and Logical Thinking

PART D. Reading and Retelling

PART E. Read and Write

예제를 통해 Part A의 유형을 연습해 봅시다.

 **Example 1**

U.S. economic growth (A)<u>accelerated</u> at a faster pace than the (B)<u>previously</u> estimates, (C)<u>according</u> to the (D)<u>recent</u> report about the gross domestic product of the third quarter of the year.

삼사분기의 국내총생산에 대한 최근의 보고에 따르면, 미국의 경제가 이전의 추정치보다 더 빠른 속도로 성장하고 있습니다.

정답 : (B) … previous

하나의 문장은 단어들의 모임인데 단어가 문장 속에서 하는 역할과 단어의 품사 사이에는 일정한 함수관계가 있습니다. 예를 들면, 문장의 주어는 항상 명사나 대명사이어야 합니다. 다른 단어를 꾸며주는 수식어도 마찬가지입니다. 형용사는 명사를 꾸며주고 부사는 동사를 꾸며줍니다. 주어진 문장은 '비교급 + than ~'을 사용하여 주어인 U.S. economic growth(미국의 경제성장)와 the previous estimates(이전의 추정치)를 비교하고 있습니다. 주어인 명사의 비교대상이 되기 위하여 than 뒤에 오는 비교대상도 반드시 주어로 사용할 수 있는 명사이어야 합니다. 원래 estimate는 동사와 명사 두 가지 품사의 단어로 사용되지만 문제 속에서 (B)가 꾸며주는 estimates는 주어진 문장의 구조상 반드시 명사이어야 하고, 따라서 부사 (B)previously(이전에)는 명사 estimates를 꾸며 줄 수 없으므로 형용사 previous(이전의)로 바뀌어야 합니다.

* **accelerate** 가속하다, 촉진시키다, 빨라지다, 촉진되다 / **previous** 이전의 / **previously** 이전에, 미리 / **estimates** 평가, 견적, 추정하다, 어림잡다 / **gross domestic product(GDP)** 국내총생산 / **quarter** 분기

 **Example 2**

(A)<u>As</u> the Ice Age ended, some animals were able to (B)<u>adopting</u> to the new climate, but others (C)<u>that</u> could not adjust (D)<u>failed</u> to survive.

빙하기가 끝나자, 어떤 동물들은 새로운 기후에 적응할 수 있었지만, 적응할 수 없었던 동물들은 살아남지 못하게 되었습니다.

정답 : (B) … adopt

(B)가 틀렸습니다. 'be able to' 다음에는 동사의 원형이 이어져야 하므로 (B)를 'adopt'로 바꾸어 주어야 합니다. (C)의 관계대명사 that이 이끄는 문장은 동사 adjust까지이고 이것이 앞의 선행사 others를 꾸며주기 때문에 (D)는 서술어 자리가 되어 동사가 나와야 합니다. 따라서 과거형 동사 failed를 사용한 것은 맞는 표현입니다.

* **the Ice Age** 빙하시대 / **adopt to** ~에 적응하다 / **survive** 생존하다

PART A. Error Recognition

Directions : *In this part of the test, you will read short selections with four underlined segments. Choose the segment that contains a word or phrase that is INCORRECT. Fill in the corresponding space on your answer sheet.*

1. One of the purposes of Authors' writing is to persuade people. For example, newspaper editorial
       (A)   (B)
   writers trying to persuade readers to accept their opinions.
       (C)   (D)

2. Multiple choice questions contain more than three possible answer. If you fail to find out the correct
                          (A)   (B)
   answer, remove the choices which are wrong until you have only one left.
                          (C)   (D)

3. Much photographers argue that dawn is the best time for taking pictures, regardless of the subject.
   (A)   (B)   (C)   (D)

4. Flying kites depend on the principle of aerodynamics, which simply means the study of forces that are
                (A)   (B)   (C)
   put into action through moving air.
                      (D)

5. There are three basic labor right; the right to organize, the right to collective bargaining, and the right
                          (A)   (B)   (C)   (D)
   to collective action.

6. Australia is the <u>only</u> continent <u>where</u> Kangaroos and Koalas are found <u>because</u> the island continent
             (A)   (B)   (C)

was <u>isolate</u> from the rest of the world for a long time.
   (D)

7. Dinosaur fossils are buried so <u>deeply</u> in solid rocks that scientists must first get the bones <u>out of the</u>
                   (A)   (B)

rocks without <u>damaging</u> them. Enormous patience <u>are</u> required for this task.
        (C)   (D)

8. The reason <u>why</u> life can exist <u>on</u> Earth is that it <u>has</u> air. Plants and animals on Earth cannot <u>lived</u>
       (A)   (B)   (C)   (D)

without the air.

9. A <u>proverb</u> is a <u>shortly and wisely</u> saying in simple language. <u>One</u> of the examples is "Honesty <u>is the</u>
 (A)   (B)   (C)   (D)

best policy."

10. <u>Most</u> children in the world feel <u>delighting</u> to visit the zoo. Many zoos have a section especially <u>for</u>
  (A)   (B)   (C)

children where they can pat rabbits, ducks, and other gentle <u>animals.</u>
       (D)

11. It is a lot of <u>fun</u> to eat out, but for some people, <u>cooking</u> for <u>them</u> family <u>at home</u> is an enjoyable way
    (A)   (B) (C)   (D)

to spend leisure time.

12. <u>An</u> acute illness <u>lasts</u> a short period of time and usually <u>have</u> severe symptoms. A chronic illness,
 (A)   (B)   (C)

however, <u>lasts</u> a long period of time.
     (D)

13. Modern inventions and new machines <u>have released</u> us <u>from</u> many household chores. For example,
    (A)   (B)
    the dryer <u>sets</u> us free from <u>hang</u> laundry on a clothes line.
    (C)   (D)

14. Asian people <u>are</u> inclined to <u>respecting</u> the elderly, but <u>in</u> America, age does not necessarily <u>bring</u>
    (A)   (B)   (C)   (D)
    respect.

15. Sedentary lifestyles <u>indicate</u> sitting down a lot of time and not <u>moving</u> or exercising very much.
    (A)   (B)
    People in sedentary occupations, such as taxi drivers and writers, need to <u>make</u> a special <u>efforts</u> to
    (C)   (D)
    exercise.

16. Antonyms <u>are</u> words with <u>oppositely</u> meanings. For <u>instance</u>, right and wrong are antonyms, and so
    (A)   (B)   (C)
    <u>are</u> long and short.
    (D)

17. Skyscrapers in metropolitan areas <u>speeds</u> up <u>the</u> increase of overcrowded <u>cities</u>. For example, some
    (A)   (B)   (C)
    16,000 people work in the Sears Tower <u>in Chicago</u>.
    (D)

18. Computers make it <u>convenient</u> <u>to delete</u> unwanted information from a report without having to <u>typing</u>
    (A)   (B)   (C)
    <u>the report</u> all over again.
    (D)

19. On 1888, Edward Bellamy wrote about a utopia, an ideal world where everyone would have an enough
    (A)   (B)   (C)
    income, work only until the age of 45, and then enjoy leisure.
              (D)

20. When you write a letter of complaint to a company, state what you want the company to do about
    (A)   (B)   (C)
    your demand in the begin and repeat this request at the end.
                          (D)

21. Joseph Haydn was a very productive composer in the Classical Period. He wrote, among many other
                              (A)   (B)
    musical works, 104 symphony.
              (C)   (D)

22. People have considering dogs as trusty companions. This is well reflected in the traditional name for a
                    (A)   (B)   (C)
    dog, "Fido," which means "faithful one."
                    (D)

다음의 어휘들을 익히고 Checkups에 기록해 보세요.

	489 Intensive Words		Checkups		
			1st	2nd	3rd
181	tendency	[명] 경향			
182	victim	[명] 제물, 희생자			
183	share	[명] 몫, 배당분 [동] 나누다, 분배하다			
184	apparatus	[명] 기계, 기구, 장치			
185	multiple	[형] 다양한, 다수의 [명] 배수			
186	appreciate	[동] 감상하다, 감사하다, 진가를 인정하다			
187	testify	[동] 증명하다, 증언하다			
188	recommend	[동] 추천하다			
189	illiterate	[형] 글을 읽고 쓸 줄 모르는			
190	submerge	[동] 가라앉히다, 잠기게 하다			
191	humble	[형] 겸손한, 겸허한, (신분이) 천한			
192	paradox	[명] 역설			
193	immortal	[형] 죽지 않는, 불후의			
194	scatter	[동] 흩뿌리다			
195	expire	[동] 만기되다, 숨을 내쉬다			
196	debate	[명] 토론 [동] 토론하다			
197	stir	[동] 휘젓다, ～을 흔들다, ～을 움직이다			
198	waterproof	[형] 방수의 [명] 방수복			
199	bother	[동] 괴롭히다, 폐를 끼치다			
200	forbid	[동] 금하다, 금지하다			
201	alternate	[동] 번갈아 하다 [형] 번갈아 하는			
202	accompany	[동] 동반, 동행하다, 반주하다			
203	bump	[동] 꽝당 부딪히다			

489 Intensive Words		Checkups		
		1st	2nd	3rd
204	furious	[형] 격노한, 사나운		
205	flatter	[동] 아첨하다		
206	furnance	[명] 화덕, 용광로		
207	arthritis	[명] 관절염		
208	afflict	[동] 괴롭히다, 시달리게 하다		
209	bleak	[형] 황량한		
210	compassion	[명] 측은히 여김, 동정		
211	counterfeit	[형] 위조의, 가짜의 [동] 위조하다		
212	discern	[동] 식별하다, 분별하다		
213	eradication	[명] 근절, 박멸		
214	frigid	[형] 몹시 추운, 써늘한		
215	impudent	[형] 뻔뻔스러운, 염치없는		
216	jeopardize	[동] 위험에 빠뜨리다		
217	malicious	[형] 악의 있는, 고의의		
218	nasty	[형] 더러운, 불쾌한		
219	pious	[형] 경건한, 독실한		
220	random	[형] 임의의, 닥치는 대로의		
221	remit	[동] 보내다, 용서하다 [명] 송부, 사면		
222	shabby	[형] 초라한, 낡아빠진		
223	testament	[명] 유서, 유언		
224	tread	[동] 걷다, 밟다		
225	wag	[동] 흔든다, 흔들리다		

PART.B

예제를 통해 Part B의 유형을 연습해 봅시다.

Example 1

A new research suggests that even mild stress can cause long-term disability _______________.

(A) that prevents people from working
(B) which prevents people to work
(C) preventing people work
(D) prevents the work of people

한 새로운 연구는 약한 스트레스라 할지라도 _____________ 장기적인 무기력 상태를 유발할 수 있다는 것을 보여줍니다.

(A) that prevents people from working
　　(사람들이 일에서 손을 놓게 만드는)
(B) which prevents people to work
(C) preventing people work
(D) prevents the work of people

정답 : (A)

문장의 내용을 살펴보면 빈칸에 disability(무기력 상태)를 수식하는 구절이 이어져야 합니다. 이 문제를 풀기 위하여 수식어구의 서술어 역할을 하는 동사 prevent가 어떤 형태의 동사구를 이끄는지 알아둘 필요가 있습니다. → prevent ~ from … ~가 …하는 것을 막다, 방해하다

(A)에서 주격관계대명사 that이 이끄는 관계사절 안의 동사구가 올바른 형태입니다. (B)는 to work을 from working으로 바꾸어야 맞습니다. (C)에서 현재분사 preventing이 disability를 수식하는 것은 가능하지만, 역시 work을 from working으로 바꾸어야 맞습니다. (D)에서는 동사 prevents가 앞에 있는 명사 disability를 꾸며줄 수 없으므로 관계대명사 which 또는 that을 동사 앞에 놓아 관계사절로 만들거나, 동사 prevent가 접속사 없이도 앞에 놓인 명사를 직접 꾸며줄 수 있도록 이를 preventing으로 고쳐주어야 합니다.

＊ **long-term** 장기적인 / **disability** 장애, 무기력, 무능력 상태

Example 2

Tedious chores, like washing disges, are less boring if you do them ______ talking with a friend.
(A) while listening or to the radio
(B) while listening to the radio or
(C) listening to the radio or while
(D) listening to the radio while or

설거지와 같이 싫증나는 집안일은 _____________ 친구와 이야기를 하면서 하면 덜 지루합니다.

(A) while listening or to the radio
(B) while listening to the radio or (라디오를 듣거나)
(C) listening to the radio or while
(D) listening to the radio while or

정답 : (B)

while(~하는 동안에)이 이끄는 시간부사절의 어순에 대한 문제입니다. while이나 when이 이끄는 시간부사절에서는 부사절의 주어가 주절의 주어와 일치하고 동사가 be동사이면 이를 생략할 수 있습니다. 즉, 위 문장에서 if가 이끄는 절은 원래 다음 문장에서 괄호 안의 부분이 생략됨으로써 while이 분사구문을 이끄는 형태로 만들어진 것입니다. → ~ if you do them while (you are) listening to the radio or talking with a friend.

if절 안의 어순을 생각해 보면, 우선 you do them이라는 절과 시간부사절을 연결하는 접속사 while이 앞서야 합니다. 그 뒤에 listening to the radio(라디오 듣기)라는 분사구문과 talking with a friend(친구와 이야기하기)라는 분사구문이 이어지는데, 그 사이에 등위접속사 or를 두어 '병렬구조'를 이루도록 해야 합니다.

＊ **tedious** 지루한, 싫증나는 / **chore** (집안의) 잡일, 지루한 허드렛일

PART B. Sentence Completion

Directions *: In this part of the test, each question consists of a sentence which contains one blank space and four choices marked (A), (B), (C), and (D). Each of the choices consists of words that can be used to fill in the blank in the sentence. Choose the one that best fits the intended meaning of the sentence. Then, on your answer sheet, find the number of the question and fill in the space that corresponds to the letter of the answer you have chosen.*

1. Advertisements are an important part of the promotion used by companies to persuade us _______________.

    (A) their products to buy many
    (B) their many products to buy
    (C) to buy their products many
    (D) to buy their many products

2. People lost in the desert _______________ that there is a lake right in front of them.
    (A) sometimes experience the illusion
    (B) experience the illusion sometimes
    (C) sometimes experiences the illusion
    (D) experiences the illusion sometimes

3. Ballet dancers sometimes _____________ when they land with too great of an impact after a leap.
    (A) break their toes severe
    (B) break their toes severely
    (C) break severe their toes
    (D) break their severely toes

4. The legendary unicorn, which is _________________, is often shown as having a lion's tail and a goat's beard.
   (A) a one horn animal with horselike
   (B) a horselike with one horn animal
   (C) a horselike animal with one horn
   (D) one horn animal with a horselike

5. There's a great diversity of breakfast cereals at the supermarket. There are _________________ that they occupy half an aisle.
   (A) so many different kinds
   (B) many so different kinds
   (C) so different many kinds
   (D) many different so kinds

6. The Mississippi River derives its name from Indian words _________ "big river."
   (A) meant
   (B) meaning
   (C) means
   (D) is meaning

7. _____________ when you bake a cake, so that there will be enough room for it to rise.
   (A) Use a deep pan
   (B) Use a deeply pan
   (C) Use a pan deep
   (D) Use a pan deeply

8. Meryl Streep ______ the winner of an Academy Award for her role in 'Sophie's Choice' in 1982, only three years after her first Academy Award.
   (A) is
   (B) was
   (C) has been
   (D) had been

9. Dr. Martin Luther King, Jr. followed the principle of fighting for social change ______________.
   (A) without using any violence
   (B) without use any violence
   (C) without to use any violence
   (D) without used any violence

10. A certain substance in a spider's thread makes the bugs it catches ______________.
    (A) adheres to the web
    (B) adhere to the web
    (C) to adhere to the web
    (D) and adhere to the web

11. Alexander Graham Bell invented not only the telephone ________ that could carry people.
    (A) and a kite
    (B) so a kite
    (C) or a kite
    (D) but also a kite

12. In her autobiography, 'The Story of My Life', Helen Keller tells how she ______________ despite her blindness and deafness.
   (A) is able to learn
   (B) was able to learn
   (C) is able learning
   (D) was able learning

13. Think about the fact that books, some furniture, and wooden houses ____________ trees.
   (A) are made from
   (B) have made from
   (C) make from
   (D) made from

14. Some pizza clerks now call back to make sure that ____________ since kids sometimes call out for a pizza as a joke.
   (A) each order
   (B) each order real
   (C) real each order
   (D) each order is real

15. Any subway system ________________ deserves to receive praise.
   (A) that is clean and safe
   (B) that is cleanly and safely
   (C) which are clean and safe
   (D) which are cleanly and safely

16. When the clock's hands moved slowly toward 2:30, the students ____________ their limits waiting for the bell to finish the last class.
    (A) seemed reach
    (B) seemed to reach
    (C) seemed reaching
    (D) seemed to be reached

17. A wedding ring is worn to show a couple's commitment ____________.
    (A) to each other
    (B) to each others
    (C) to one other
    (D) to one others

18. There are thick pine forests at the foot of the mountain, but higher up, the trees ____________.
    (A) become rare
    (B) become rarely
    (C) became rare
    (D) became rarely

19. ____________ are harmless, but if they come with a fever and a stiff neck, they can be a sign of a serious illness.
    (A) Most headache
    (B) Almost headache
    (C) Most headaches
    (D) Almost headaches

20. One cannot easily drown in Utah's Great Salt Lake ________________.
    (A) because the lake's high percentage of salt
    (B) because of the lake's high percentage of salt
    (C) since the lake's high percentage of salt
    (D) since of the lake's high percentage of salt

21. One ________________ to ride is also one of the simplest. That is a unicycle, a vehicle with only one wheel.
    (A) of the most difficult vehicles
    (B) of the more difficult vehicles
    (C) most difficult than vehicles
    (D) more difficult than vehicles

22. Being night creatures, owls are ________________ during the day.
    (A) likely to see
    (B) unlikely to see
    (C) likely to be seen
    (D) unlikely to be seen

23. Science does not provide ________________ to answer the question of whether aliens exist in the universe or not.
    (A) enough evidence
    (B) evidence enough
    (C) many evidence
    (D) evidence many

다음의 어휘들을 익히고 Checkups에 기록해 보세요.

	489 Intensive Words		Checkups		
			1st	2nd	3rd
226	trait	[명] 특징, 특성			
227	separate	[동] 분리하다 [형] 분리된, 떨어진			
228	contrast	[명] 대조 [동] 대조시키다			
229	accommodation	[명] 편의, 숙박시설			
230	deliver	[동] 전달하다, 말하다, 분만하다			
231	moody	[형] 변덕스러운			
232	cavity	[명] 움푹 패인 곳, 충치			
233	skyscraper	[명] 고층빌딩, 마천루			
234	plight	[명] 처지, 나쁜 상태, 곤경			
235	obstacle	[명] 장애물, 방해(물)			
236	progress	[명] 진보, 향상 [동] 전진하다			
237	affection	[명] 애정, 사랑			
238	brisk	[형] 활발한, 원기 있는			
239	satellite	[명] 위성			
240	respire	[동] 호흡하다			
241	controvert	[동] 논쟁하다, 논박하다			
242	adhesive	[형] 접착성의, 고집하는			
243	ethics	[명] 윤리, 윤리학, 도덕			
244	trial	[명] 시도, 재판			
245	embargo	[명] 억류, 통상금지, 봉쇄조치			
246	offspring	[명] 자손			
247	attach	[동] 붙이다			

489 Intensive Words		Checkups		
		1st	2nd	3rd
248	dump	[동] 털썩 내버리다, 투매하다		
249	property	[명] 재산, 소유, 특징		
250	considerate	[형] 사려 깊은, 남을 배려하는		
251	vulnerable	[형] 상처받기 쉬운, 취약한		
252	affluent	[형] 풍부한, 부유한		
253	ascent	[명] 상승, 오름		
254	blunder	[명] 큰 실수 [동] 큰 실수를 하다		
255	comply	[동] 따르다, 응하다		
256	cramp	[명] 꺾쇠, (근육의) 경련, 쥐		
257	disposition	[명] 배열, 처분, 성향		
258	evacuate	[동] 비우다, 철수시키다		
259	futile	[형] 헛된, 하찮은, 무능한		
260	inflict	[동] (벌 등을) 주다, 과하다		
261	juvenile	[형] 소년[소녀]의 [명] 청소년		
262	manifest	[형] 명백한 [동] 명백하게 하다		
263	notify	[동] 알리다, 통지하다		
264	poke	[동] 찌르다, 구멍내다		
265	rational	[형] 이성적인, 합리적인		
266	reproach	[동] 비난하다, 질책하다 [명] 비난, 질책		
267	sinister	[형] 불길한, 사악한		
268	thrive	[동] 번영하다, 무성해지다		
269	treaty	[동] 조약, 협정		

설명하고 있는 알맞은 의미의 단어를 퍼즐안에 넣어 봅시다.

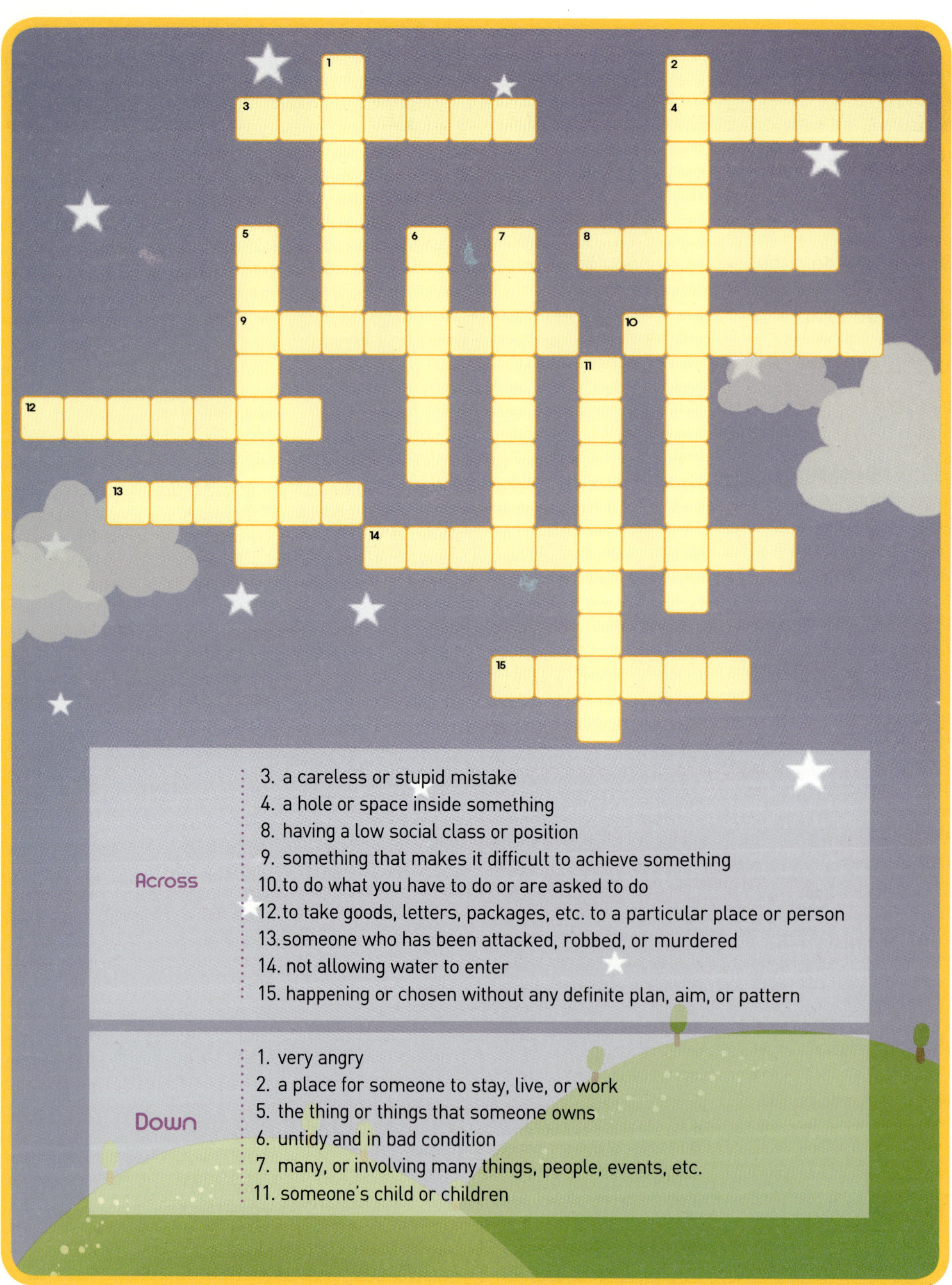

Across

3. a careless or stupid mistake
4. a hole or space inside something
8. having a low social class or position
9. something that makes it difficult to achieve something
10. to do what you have to do or are asked to do
12. to take goods, letters, packages, etc. to a particular place or person
13. someone who has been attacked, robbed, or murdered
14. not allowing water to enter
15. happening or chosen without any definite plan, aim, or pattern

Down

1. very angry
2. a place for someone to stay, live, or work
5. the thing or things that someone owns
6. untidy and in bad condition
7. many, or involving many things, people, events, etc.
11. someone's child or children

예제를 통해 Part C의 유형을 연습해 봅시다.

Example 1

Because of the high __________ rate, we have a lot more people to be homeless and bankrupt.

(A) birth
(B) possibility
(C) stock market
(D) unemployment

높은 ____률 때문에 훨씬 더 많은 사람들이 집을 잃거나 파산하고 있습니다.

(A) 출생
(B) 가능성
(C) 주식시장
(D) 실업

정답 : (D)

Because of가 이끄는 이유부사절 안에 빈칸이 있으므로 사람들이 집을 잃거나 파산하도록 내모는 원인이 빈칸에 와야 글의 내용이 성립합니다.

＊ **stock market** 주식시장 / **unemployment** 실업 / **rate** 비율 / **homeless** 집 없는 / **bankrupt** 파산한

Example 2

There was no langer any __________ : everyone agreed that the all-male dining club should now accept female members.

(A) agreement
(B) consent
(C) controversy
(D) accord

더 이상의 어떠한 __________도 없었습니다. 즉, 남성 회원만으로 이루어졌던 정찬 모임이 이제 여성 회원도 받아들여야 한다는 것에 모두가 동의했습니다.

(A) 합의
(B) 동의
(C) 논쟁
(D) 의견일치

정답 : (C)

문장부호 콜론(:)은 '즉(that is)'이라는 의미로서 콜론 뒤에 오는 말은 앞 문장의 내용을 부연하여 설명하는 것이므로 콜론을 사이에 둔 앞뒤의 문장은 서로 모순이 있어서는 안 됩니다. 콜론 뒤에 오는 말이 남성 전용 정찬 모임이 여성회원을 받는 데 '모두 동의했다'고 말했으므로 '더 이상 어떠한 논쟁도 없다'는 것을 알 수 있습니다.

＊ **no longer** 더 이상 ～ 아니다 / **agree** 동의하다 / **accept** 받아들이다, 수용하다

PART C. Reading and Logical Thinking

Directions *: In this part of the test, you will read short selections. Each selection contains an underlined segment indicating missing word(s). Choose the word(s) that most logically fit(s) the selection from the answer choices. Fill in the corresponding space on your answer sheet.*

1.

Except for a very small amount of registration fee, the camp for needy children is entirely _________ , which means they don't have to pay for the camp.

(A) free
(B) chargeable
(C) reasonable
(D) moderate

2.

To teach young children _________ , many parents tend to ask them what to do in imaginary situations. For example, the parents ask the children what they would do if a stranger offered them a ride.

(A) rules
(B) safety
(C) honesty
(D) patriotism

3.

> *War and Peace*, written by Tolstoy, is a long and __________ novel that weaves the detailed life stories of various characters together in a very complicated way.

(A) simple
(B) true
(C) complex
(D) realistic

4.

> People who live in big cities are more vulnerable to _______ problems than residents of small town are because big cities are likely to have more air pollution.

(A) traffic
(B) economic
(C) environmental
(D) population

5.

> Mark Twain believed that charges of copying others' ideas were absurd because no one can be original. He wrote, "We cannot _______ ; we can only copy."

(A) create
(B) write
(C) prove
(D) think

6.

One of the teacher's jobs is to __________ students to learn eagerly, but it is not easy to encourage the students, who have no energy to learn, to study harder.

(A) prove
(B) disprove
(C) discourage
(D) motivate

7.

When the teacher asks students to write a(an) __________ , he or she means it is to write the life story of a human not an animal.

(A) biography
(B) novel
(C) essay
(D) history

8.

Learning that a painting had been displayed upside down for weeks in New York's Museum of Modern Art in 1961, people made fun of its administrators, who felt ______________ .

(A) ashamed
(B) delighted
(C) proud
(D) confident

9.

The Peace Corps, the volunteer aid organization for poor countries, keeps sending many volunteers to work in the nations suffering from __________ .

(A) pollution
(B) poverty
(C) an earthquake
(D) a disease

10.

Striking an iceberg, the ship Titanic sank to the bottom of the sea and caused a(an) __________ in which nearly 1,600 people died.

(A) disaster
(B) breakthrough
(C) battle
(D) inflation

11.

Children are fond of doing __________ activities when they prepare a surprise party for celebrating the birth of their parents.

(A) public
(B) secret
(C) popular
(D) careful

12.

> All the residents in the town are not allowed to _________ their lawns for a while because a shortage of rain has seriously reduced the water supply.

(A) water
(B) cut
(C) grow
(D) treat

13.

> Great Britain's Princess Diana was obviously very _________. In spite of her personal weak points, she drew people's attention and affection from all over the world.

(A) mysterious
(B) attractive
(C) luxurious
(D) selfish

14.

> Mahatma Gandhi inspired millions of fellow Indians to join him enthusiastically in searching for _________ solutions to national problems, without using violent ways.

(A) honest
(B) simple
(C) beautiful
(D) peaceful

15.

Most of the actors cannot achieve __________ overnight, but the road for them to become a star is long and difficult.

(A) fame
(B) friendship
(C) relationship
(D) freedom

16.

The fact that only one hundred dolls are produced every year leads these life-size dolls to be sold so ______________.

(A) cheaply
(B) expensively
(C) greatly
(D) frequently

17.

It's lucky Santa Claus doesn't have a fear of being in a very limited space. Otherwise, he would be too __________ of small spaces to come down the chimney.

(A) fond
(B) frightened
(C) favored
(D) favorite

18.

> On Halloween children often dress up as ghosts and witches and ask their neighbors for candies. Therefore, the holiday is ________ for candy manufacturers.

(A) harmful
(B) damaging
(C) profitable
(D) reasonable

19.

> In some fairy tales, the hero, who is usually a prince, explores the dangerous world, searching for a missing princess who was ________ by a monster.

(A) kidnapped
(B) produced
(C) amazed
(D) purified

20.

> The author Stephen King doesn't use his ________ name on some of his books so readers cannot recognize that some of his novels on the market are written by him.

(A) real
(B) fake
(C) false
(D) pen

21.

All of the litter dropped by people in the park certainly __________ the beauty of the trees and flowers.

(A) improves
(B) damages
(C) increases
(D) upgrades

22.

Many people fail to brush their teeth properly. However, you must make an effort to brush __________ not to have cavities.

(A) vaguely
(B) vainly
(C) casually
(D) carefully

23.

Some mentally ill people may have __________ ideas. For instance, they may think that the TV is talking to them or that others can steal their thoughts.

(A) weird
(B) moderate
(C) ideal
(D) vivid

다음의 어휘들을 익히고 Checkups에 기록해 보세요.

	489 Intensive Words		Checkups		
			1st	2nd	3rd
270	hypnosis	[명] 최면			
271	gravity	[명] 중력, 인력			
272	infrastructure	[명] 하부구조, 사회간접시설			
273	exceed	[동] 넘다, 초과하다			
274	satisfy	[동] 만족시키다			
275	scar	[명] 흉터, 상처			
276	estimate	[동] 추정하다, 견적을 내다 [명] 견적			
277	rigid	[형] 엄격한, 경직된, 뻣뻣한			
278	donate	[동] 기부하다, 기증하다			
279	convince	[동] 설득시키다, 확신시키다			
280	procedure	[명] 수속, 절차			
281	segment	[명] 구분, 단편 [동] 분열하다(시키다)			
282	urge	[동] 재촉하다, 촉구하다			
283	scarce	[형] 모자라는, 드문			
284	conspire	[동] 공모하다, 음모를 꾸미다			
285	dispute	[명] 논쟁, 토론 [동] 논쟁하다			
286	represent	[동] 나타내다, 대표하다			
287	ethnic	[형] 인종적인, 민족적인			
288	ashamed	[형] (잘못하여) 부끄러운			
289	plain	[명] 평야 [형] 평평한, 명백한, 검소한			
290	antique	[형] 고대의, 고풍스러운 [명] 골동품			
291	instruct	[동] 가르치다, 명령하다			

489 Intensive Words		Checkups		
		1st	2nd	3rd
292	bunch	[명] 송이, 다발		
293	splash	[동] 물 튀기다, 첨벙거리다		
294	arithmetic	[명] 산수		
295	manipulate	[동] 조작하다, 조종하다		
296	ailment	[명] 병, 불쾌		
297	ascribe	[동] ~의 탓으로 돌리다		
298	breakthrough	[명] 돌파구, 비약적 발전		
299	concede	[동] 양보하다		
300	creed	[명] 교의, 신념		
301	divert	[동] ~으로 전환하다, 기분전환을 시키다		
302	evade	[동] 회피하다		
303	gigantic	[형] 거대한, 막대한		
304	inhale	[동] 흡입하다		
305	kidnap	[동] (아이를) 유괴하다		
306	manual	[형] 손의 [명] 소책자, 안내서		
307	notorious	[형] 악명 높은		
308	pollen	[명] 꽃가루, 화분		
309	realm	[명] 왕국, 범위, 영역		
310	resolute	[형] 굳게 결심한, 단호한		
311	skull	[명] 두개골, 해골		
312	throb	[동] 고동치다, 감동하다		
313	tyrant	[명] 폭군		

예제를 통해 Part D의 유형을 연습해 봅시다. (지문 1개 + 문제 1개 유형)

 Example 1

Asian people cook ramen very often for a snack or a daily meal. They have their own recipe when they cook ramen. There are a variety of ingredients for people to put into ramen. They usually put an egg into the pot with ramen noodles and paste. Some people put Kimchi or seaweed to make more flavor and taste. People who love richness of the soup boil ramen in chicken stock or beef stock instead of tap water. If you put carrots and bean sprouts in ramen, it will make the soup clean and light. Kids love ramen with a slice of cheddar cheese or bacon on. You can make a bowl of tasty ramen only for you with your own ingredients.

What is the main idea of the passage?

(A) Ramen is popular with people from all different ages.
(B) The taste of ramen can vary with different ingredients.
(C) It is a good idea to put healthy ingredients in ramen.
(D) Ramen is a part of our daily diet.

윗글의 주제는 무엇입니까?

(A) 라면은 모든 연령의 사람들에게 인기가 있다.
(B) 라면의 맛은 재료에 따라 다양할 수 있다.
(C) 라면에 몸에 좋은 재료들을 넣는 것은 좋은 생각이다.
(D) 라면은 우리의 하루 식단의 일부이다.

아시아 사람들은 간식이나 한 끼 식사로 라면을 매우 즐겨 요리합니다. 사람들은 라면을 끓일 때, 그들만의 요리법을 가지고 있습니다. 사람들이 라면에 넣는 다양한 재료들이 있습니다. 그들은 주로 라면의 면과 스프와 더불어 계란을 넣습니다. 어떤 사람들은 더 많은 풍미와 맛을 위해 김치나 미역을 넣습니다. 진한 국물을 좋아하는 사람들은 물 대신에 닭이나 소고기 육수에 라면을 끓입니다. 만약 라면에 당근이나 콩나물을 넣는다면, 국물이 맑고 담백해질 것입니다. 아이들은 체다 치즈나 베이컨 한 장을 곁들인 라면을 좋아합니다. 당신도 당신만의 재료를 이용하여 당신만을 위한 맛있는 라면 한 그릇을 만들 수 있습니다.

정답 : (B)
윗글은 라면에 다양한 재료를 첨가함으로써 여러 가지 풍미와 맛을 즐길 수 있다는 것을 열거하고 있습니다.

* **snack** 샌드위치처럼 가볍게 먹는 식사, 간식 / **recipe** 요리법 / **ingredient** (요리의) 재료 / **flavor** 맛, 풍미 / **seaweed** 해초, 미역 / **richness** 부유함, 풍부함, 농후함 / **stock** 육수 / **bean** 콩 / **sprout** 싹, 발아, 싹처럼 자라난 것 / **bean sprout** 콩나물 / **slice** 얇은 조각 / **bowl** 사발, 공기 / **tasty** 맛있는

 **Example 2**

Many people think that a game developer is one of the top careers in the future because the game industry is on a rise. There are more jobs that can be categorized into the promising careers in the future. One of them is a technical writer, whose job is to help people understand how to use software and equipment. Another is a nutritionist, who can guide people to a healthy life as health issues are becoming a major concern. A nurse is a profession that will never go out of demand. Due to the decent income and job satisfaction, the number of people working in this sector is expected to rise over time.

What is NOT true about the promising careers?

(A) A game developer gets popular as the game industry develops.
(B) A technical writer is writing a novel about modern technology.
(C) A nutritionist helps people lead a healthy life.
(D) A nurse is always in demand.

유망한 직업에 관하여 사실이 아닌 것은 무엇입니까?

(A) 게임 산업이 발전함에 따라 게임 개발자가 인기를 얻고 있다.
(B) 기술 분야 작가는 현대의 기술에 관한 소설을 쓴다.
(C) 영양사는 사람들이 건강한 삶을 영위하도록 돕는다.
(D) 간호사는 항상 수요가 있다.

게임 산업이 상승 추세이다 보니 많은 사람들이 게임 개발자가 미래에 최고 직업 중의 하나가 되리라고 생각합니다. 미래의 유망한 직업으로 분류해볼 수 있는 더 많은 직업들이 있습니다. 그 중의 하나는 기술 분야 작가인데 그들이 하는 일은 사람들이 소프트웨어와 장비의 사용법을 이해하도록 도와주는 것입니다. 또 하나는 영양사로서 건강문제가 주된 관심사가 되어감에 따라 사람들이 건강한 삶을 살 수 있도록 안내하는 역할을 합니다. 간호사는 틀림없이 수요가 끊이지 않을 직종입니다. 남부럽지 않은 임금과 직업에 대한 만족 때문에 이 분야에서 종사하는 사람들의 수는 시간이 지날수록 증가하리라고 예상됩니다.

정답 : (B)
미래에 유망하리라 기대되는 여러 가지 직업에 대한 소개의 글입니다. 그 중 기술 분야 작가는 사람들에게 소프트웨어나 장비의 사용법을 알려주기 위하여 글을 쓰는 사람입니다. 이런 종류의 글은 소설이 아닙니다.

* **career** 직업 / **on a rise** 상승하는, 등귀하는 / **categorize** 분류하다 / **promising** 유망한 / **equipment** 장비 / **nutritionist** 영양사 / **demand** 수요 / **due to** ~ 때문에 / **decent** 남부럽지 않은, 버젓한 / **satisfaction** 만족발, 공기 / **tasty** 맛있는

예제를 통해 Part D의 유형을 연습해 봅시다. (지문 1개 + 문제 2개 유형)

 **Example 1**

Dracula was first introduced in a novel in the late 19th century. This novel was written by Bram Stoker from Dublin, Ireland. The main character of the novel was the vampire, Count Dracula. The first publication of the book was in 1897. At first, it was not a bestseller, but the critics liked the novel. People at that time enjoyed the novel just for fun and adventure, but the story has more than that. Many contemporary writers such as Arthur C. Doyle praised the depth of this powerful and horrible story. Similarly, good reviews also appeared when the book was published in the U. S. in 1899. Dracula has been used for many literary genres including vampire literature and horror fiction. The popularity of the vampire stories is increasing recently once more and the stories have been made into movies. People are still allured by the attraction of Dracula into the appalling story.

1. What is the passage about?
   (A) novels in the Victorian period
   (B) the importance of contemporary works
   (C) the attraction of the Dracula novel
   (D) how to choose a good novel

2. What is NOT true about this novel?
   (A) It has been made into movies.
   (B) It was criticized severely by the critics.
   (C) Many writers appreciated its true value.
   (D) It was published in the U.S. 2 years after the first publication.

1. 윗글은 무엇에 대한 것입니까?
   (A) 빅토리아 시대의 소설들
   (B) 현대 작품들의 중요성
   (C) 드라큘라 소설의 매력
   (D) 좋은 소설을 고르는 법

2. 이 소설에 대해 사실이 아닌 것은 무엇입니까?
   (A) 영화로 만들어져왔다.
   (B) 비평가들에 의해 혹독하게 비판받았다.
   (C) 많은 작가들이 진정한 가치를 인정했었다.
   (D) 첫 출판 후 2년이 지나 미국에서 출판되었다.

드라큘라는 19세기 말에 최초로 한 소설에 등장하였습니다. 이 소설은 아일랜드 더블린 출신의 Bram Stoker에 의해 쓰여졌습니다. 소설의 주인공은 뱀파이어 백작 드라큘라였습니다. 최초의 출판은 1897년이었습니다. 처음에는 베스트셀러가 아니었지만 비평가들은 그 소설을 좋아했습니다. 당시 사람들은 이 소설을 재미와 모험 때문에 읽었지만, 이 소설은 그것 이상을 가지고 있습니다. Arthur C. Doyle과 같은 많은 동시대의 작가들은 이 강렬하고 섬뜩한 이야기의 깊이를 칭찬했습니다. 이와 비슷하게 1899년 미국에서 이 책이 출판되었을 때도 좋은 비평들이 나왔습니다. 드라큘라는 뱀파이어 문학이나 공포영화와 같은 다양한 문학 장르에 사용되어 왔습니다. 뱀파이어 이야기의 인기는 최근에 다시 한 번 증가하고 있고, 그 스토리는 영화로도 제작되어 오고 있습니다. 사람들은 여전히 드라큘라의 매력 때문에 섬뜩한 이야기에 이끌리고 있습니다.

정답 1 : (C)   윗글은 드라큘라를 등장시킨 소설이 많은 이들에 의해 끊임없는 인기를 얻고 있다고 말합니다.
정답 2 : (B)   드라큘라 소설은 출판되었을 때, 베스트셀러는 아니었지만 비평가들은 그 작품을 좋아했다고 말합니다.

* **vampire** 흡혈귀 / **publication** 발행, 간행 / **critic** 비평가 / **contemporary** 동시대의, 현대의 / **literature** 문학 / **review** 비평, 논평 / **literary** 문학의 / **genre** 장르, 유형 / **fiction** 소설, 허구의 이야기 / **allure** 꾀다, 유혹하다 / **appalling** 섬뜩한

PART D. Reading and Retelling

Directions : *In this part of the test, you will read longer passages. Choose the best answer from four choices to answer the questions following each passage. Then fill in the corresponding space on your answer sheet.*

In 1174, the residents of Pisa, Italy, determined to build a bell tower for the cathedral. They found two renowned architects and asked them to design the tower. Workers began to construct the tower in accordance with the design. Before long, they discovered a critical mistake was made in constructing it. They overlooked the fact the ground under the tower was too soft to support it. At last the tower began to sink to one side. The construction stopped and the structure remained unfinished for more than 150 years. The Leaning Tower of Pisa still stands, but continues to lean a little more each year.

1. Why is the Tower of Pisa leaning to one side?
   (A) The ground is too soft.
   (B) It is not finished yet.
   (C) It was built a long time ago.
   (D) It was not built according to the design.

Salt is essential to the human body, but too much salt can cause health problems. Most Americans eat 20 times more than salt they really need. Where do they get salt? For one thing, processed foods are the main source to get more salt because food companies use excessive salt in producing the foods. People are also likely to add more salt to their foods. In fact, most foods already have lots of salt before cooked. These eating habits are unhealthy, so they should be changed. We should choose processed foods with a low salt content and try not to add extra salt to foods.

2. What do we have to do to take in less salt?
   (A) to buy more processed foods
   (B) to buy processed foods with less salt
   (C) to add more salt to the foods
   (D) to avoid taking in any salt in the foods

There is not enough water for drinking or for raising crops in dry regions such as Saudi Arabia. For years, scientists have studied how to provide water for this dry region. The solution they suggest is to ship icebergs from the Antarctic Ocean to the Saudi Arabian desert. How could such a huge chunk of ice be carried to the desert across the ocean? Some researchers argue it is possible to move the iceberg by using large ships and helicopters. Other scientists, however, are skeptical about the chances for success. They say much of the iceberg would melt in the warm ocean water.

3. What can supply water to Saudi Arabia according to the passage?
   (A) a ship and a helicopter
   (B) an iceberg
   (C) an ocean
   (D) a desert

We celebrate Mother's Day to show love to our mothers every year. The origin of this holiday dates back to May 10th, 1908. On that day, Anna Javis had a special church service to pay respect to her own mother, who had died two years earlier. From then, Anna started to spread this idea nationwide. She suggested that one day be set aside each year for people to honor their mothers. Anna's proposal gained public interest. In 1910, Mother's Day holiday was proclaimed officially by three states in the U.S. Now it is one of the important holidays in America.

4. What was Anna's proposal about Mother's Day?
   (A) to pay respect to her mother
   (B) to have a special church service for mothers
   (C) to gain public interest
   (D) to have an official day for honoring mothers

The electric car, an automobile run on battery power, is not a new idea. Actually, an electric automobile was first invented in 1899. Electric cars, however, have never caught on because they have several limitations. One disadvantage is that the autos are very expensive, which are more than $15,000. Also, they are relatively slow compared to gasoline cars. Besides, they need to be recharged every 60 miles. Yet, many people still regard electric cars as a workable and practical way to reduce air pollution and to overcome the increasing cost and declining supply of gasoline.

5. Which is not a reason for the electric car's unpopularity?
    (A) the high price
    (B) the slow speed
    (C) frequent recharges
    (D) reducing air pollution

The United States Olympic Committee decided to hire a new coach for training athletes. It is a computer. The committee is using computers to improve the technical abilities of American athletes who will participate in Olympic competition. It has been discovered that computers are very effective in testing how well athletes perform. The tests are used in sports in which proper technique is very important such as volleyball, weight lifting, fencing, track, and bicycling. By using computers, scientists have discovered that a slight shift in an athlete's arm or leg can have very positive results.

6. Why are computers useful for training athletes?
    (A) They can discover athletes' physical problems.
    (B) They can test athletes' technical performance.
    (C) They are effective in checking athletes' physical condition.
    (D) They can reduce the cost for training athletes.

A waiter named Ernest had a very unusual collection as a hobby. He liked to collect photographs and autographs from well known people. Ernest made contact with celebrities by mail for more than 40 years. People searching his apartment discovered thousands of mementos of famous people from all over the world after he died. People found out that many of Ernest's souvenirs were valuable. Some were sold at an auction for no less than $200 each. But we should keep in mind that Ernest did not collect autographs to earn money. It was just fun for him to exchange correspondence with strangers who were famous and popular.

7. Why did Ernest collect celebrities' autographs?
   (A) to make money
   (B) to enjoy contacting with them
   (C) to collect valuable souvenirs
   (D) to be famous and popular

Two words with the same meaning are synonyms. The easiest way to explain the meaning of a new word is to use its synonym. Let's look at the words, congregate and gather. One way to define congregate is to say it means "gather." Most questions on vocabulary tests are about the best synonym for a difficult word. Therefore, if you learn synonyms for new words, you can get good scores on vocabulary tests. Knowing synonyms can be helpful in enhancing reading comprehension of what you read. If you encounter a difficult word in your reading, you can replace it with a synonym, which results in much easier understanding of the ideas in reading.

8. Why should we learn synonyms?
   (A) to understand difficult words easily
   (B) to read long books
   (C) to summarize ideas in reading
   (D) to explain simple words in reading

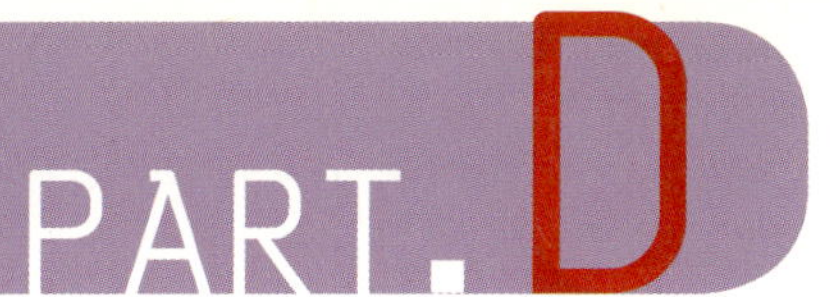

[9-10]

In a supermarket, you often find two categories of products; name brands and store brands. Name brands are items manufactured by a famous company, whereas store brands are products made by the order of the supermarket where you are shopping. Store brand products are usually less expensive than their name brand competitors. However, shoppers often choose name brand products instead of cheaper store brands. They believe that the quality of name brand products is much higher than that of store brands. They assume the ingredients in the name brands are different from those in the store brands. In fact, many store brand products are manufactured by the same companies that produce name brands, which means the contents inside the packages are exactly the same. Only the labels are different. Still, many consumers hesitate to buy store brands. They feel more comfortable with a name brand they know. The name brand has been imprinted deeply in their minds through advertisements.

9. What is the difference between store brands and name brands?
   (A) ingredient
   (B) price
   (C) quality
   (D) store

10. Why do consumers prefer to buy name brand products?
   (A) Brand name products are more familiar.
   (B) Brand name products are cheaper.
   (C) Brand name products are of better quality.
   (D) Brand name products contain better ingredients.

[11-12]

Do you know who invented the telephone? The answer is Alexander Graham Bell. Do you also know the fact that the telephone was his greatest failure? Bell never intended to create an instrument for people who could hear. All his life and career were committed to supporting deaf people. Bell's compassion for the deaf was related with his family. His mother was deaf, which encouraged him to study how people learn to speak. Then he began to specialize in offering speech therapy to young deaf children. Later, he fell in love with a deaf woman and married her. Bell determined to change the silent world of the deaf. He believed if he could improve a machine that would make sound waves visible, the deaf would be able to perceive speech as easily as others hear it. Unfortunately, Bell was unable to complete his mechanism for the deaf. He fell into despair. Eventually, he nearly threw away his designs. However, the concepts of Bell's machine were used to develop the telephone. The telephone never gave Bell true happiness though, because the invention gave sound only to those who could already hear it.

11. What did Bell focus on all his life?
    (A) helping the deaf
    (B) changing the world
    (C) inventing the telephone
    (D) inventing instruments for non-deaf people

12. Why was Bell not happy with the telephone?
    (A) He couldn't use the telephone.
    (B) His mother died before using it.
    (C) It was not for the deaf.
    (D) It was not paid enough.

[13-14]

In June 1752, Benjamin Franklin performed a special experiment for proving that lightning is a type of electricity. In the experiment, he flew a kite with a key tied to the bottom of the line during a thunderstorm. Before his experiment, many people believed that lightning was a supernatural power. After the success of his experiment, Franklin inferred that lightning could be led into the ground through a metal rod attached to a house if it could be drawn to a kite in a storm. His idea was confronted with much doubt, but he was confident that it would work. Before long, lightning rods could be seen on houses or buildings in America and later in Europe. The success of Franklin's kite experiment gained him international fame and respect. He was elected to the Royal Society of London and the French Academy of Sciences, among other honors

13. What did Franklin prove with the kite experiment?
    (A) Kites can fly during a thunderstorm.
    (B) Lightning is electric energy.
    (C) Lightning is dangerous.
    (D) Lightning is supernatural.

14. What did Franklin get from the success of his experiment?
    (A) confidence and economical supports
    (B) success and wealth
    (C) doubt and distrust
    (D) reputation and social positions

[15-16]

Many people think that Abraham Lincoln publicly objected to slavery from the beginning as president. This is not the case. Whatever his personal opinions were, he did not criticize slavery publicly. He pledged to respect the South's rights to own slaves for fear of losing the southern states from the Union. He also pledged that the government would respect the South's runaway slave laws. According to the laws, all American citizens were required to send slaves back to their masters. It was clear that Lincoln did not want the country separated. On September 22, 1862, however, President Lincoln delivered the Emancipation Proclamation, which stated that all slaves in the South should be set free. Since the southern states had already withdrawn from the Union, they ignored the proclamation. However, the proclamation did enhance the North's military strength. About 200,000 black men, mostly former slaves, enlisted in the Union Army. Two years later, the 13th Amendment to the Constitution ended slavery in all parts of the United States.

15. What was Lincoln's early official attitude about the slavery?
    (A) He was strongly opposed to it.
    (B) He did not mention it publicly at all.
    (C) He agreed to it.
    (D) He blamed it.

16. Why did Lincoln not criticize the slavery system?
    (A) He didn't want the country divided.
    (B) He supported the slavery system personally.
    (C) He wanted to strengthen the North's army.
    (D) He had prejudice against black slaves.

[17-18]

When it comes to dinosaurs, most people think of enormous ones, but there existed many kinds of small dinosaurs. They also have the Latin names describing what they are like as the larger dinosaurs. A small, but fast species of dinosaur was Saltopus, which means "leaping foot." Saltopus weighed only about 2 pounds and grew to be 2 feet long even when they were grown up. Scotland is the only place where its fossils have been found. Another small dinosaur has an interesting name, Compsognathus, meaning "pretty jaw." About the same length as the Saltopus, Compsognathus weighed about three times more. Chances that they knew each other are almost zero since Compsognathus remains have been found only in France and Germany. Lesothosaurus was another small dinosaur, which means "Lesotho lizard." Its name was originated from its appearance which was like a lizard, but the first half of its name is based on the place its remains were found, Lesotho, in southern Africa.

17. What do the names of larger dinosaurs describe?
    (A) appearance
    (B) habitat
    (C) preference
    (D) lifestyle

18. Why is it not possible Saltopus and Compsognathus knew one another?
    (A) Their weights were different.
    (B) They lived in different places.
    (C) They lived in different times.
    (D) They were small dinosaurs.

[19-20]

> Meteorology, the scientific study of weather conditions, was not born until the development of accurate measuring instruments such as a barometer for measuring atmospheric pressure, a thermometer, a hygrometer for measuring the amount of moisture in the air, and a weather map. Scientists began to study the relationships between the measurements of these basic elements and other atmospheric conditions such as wind, clouds, and rainfall. Still it was not enough for complete weather reporting. The invention of the telegraph later made the weather forecast perfect by ensuring the rapid transfer of information all over the world. Today, the forecasts of meteorologists are an international effort. There are thousands of weather stations around the world, which send the weather information. This information is relayed to national weather bureaus, where meteorologists analyze it. The information is then provided to the public by newspapers, television, and radio stations.

19. What made the weather forecast scientific?
    (A) the observation of atmospheric conditions
    (B) the invention of measuring instruments
    (C) the weather stations around the world
    (D) the invention of the telegraph

20. How can people get the weather information?
    (A) through mass media
    (B) through weather stations
    (C) by studying the weather conditions
    (D) by checking the atmospheric conditions

[21-22]

If you encountered words you don't know the meaning of, while reading, what would you do? Looking up the words in the dictionary would be the best way. Dictionaries are books that give definitions of words in alphabetical order. Guide words are at the top of each page, showing the first and last words listed on the page. All other words between the two guide words are listed on the page in alphabetical order. They should be arranged in alphabetical order, which will help you locate the target words quickly and easily. There are more things contained in the dictionary such as pronunciation, the individual syllables, the part of speech, and the plural form or verb forms if the base word changes. Some dictionaries provide considerably more information. For example, The Tormont Webster's Illustrated Encyclopedic Dictionary includes many color illustrations of terms, a pronunciation key on every other page, and introductory information on how to use the dictionary effectively.

21. What are the guide words for?
    (A) for showing the range of the words on the page
    (B) for explaining how to use the dictionary effectively
    (C) for showing how to pronounce each word
    (D) for providing clear definitions of each word

22. Why are the words listed in alphabetical order?
    (A) to guide the users to better understanding of each word
    (B) to help the users look up the words fast
    (C) to make the word arrangement look better
    (D) to contain as more words as possible

[23-24]

It is believed that the earliest music had a strong connection with religion. Ancient people believed the world was under the power of various gods. Singing was one of the best ways for them to show respect to the gods. Singing is still an important part of most religions. If you have ever sung a song, religious or otherwise, you know that singing is fun. The feeling of joy or delight from singing must also have made ancient people feel blissful. Singing at work was also a typical type of songs in ancient times. Egyptian slaves sang as they carried the heavy stones to build the pyramids. Soldiers sang as they marched into battle. Farmers sang when they planted or when they harvested. Singing must have made the workers feel less burdened. They could escape from the pain of hard work while singing. Sometimes songs had instructions they should follow. Following the instructions in the songs, people felt it easier to do the task.

23. What was the religious purpose of singing?
    (A) to enjoy fun
    (B) to make religious ceremonies sacred
    (C) to bless religious leaders
    (D) to honor gods

24. How did the ancient people feel when they sang songs at work?
    (A) They could forget the pain for a while.
    (B) They felt more painful.
    (C) They felt burdensome because of the songs.
    (D) They felt tougher to do the task.

[25-26]

If you know anything about violin music, you have probably heard the word Stradivarius. Stradivarius is the name of the world's greatest violins. It is named after their creator, Antonio Stradivari. Stradivari was born in northern Italy in 1644. Cremona, the town where he lived, was a famous place for manufacturing violins. Stradivari started to learn how to play the violin when he was very young. As he grew, he got more interested in making violins than playing them. Since violins were new instruments during Stradivari's time, they had no standard size or shape. Therefore, people made them in different sizes and shapes and of different types of wood. Stradivari was said to have had a superior ability to select the best wood for violins. He also knew how to polish the wood. These special talents contributed to producing the most magnificent instruments in the world.

25. Why did people make violins of different size during Stradivari's time?
    (A) Violin music was not popular.
    (B) Violins were hard to be shaped equally.
    (C) Violin-making was in the beginning stage.
    (D) Stradivari wanted a variety of violins.

26. What was the most helpful for Stradivari to be a violin maker?
    (A) He knew how to deal with the wood.
    (B) He was born in northen Italy.
    (C) He learned how to play the violin.
    (D) Violins were new those days.

[27-28]

Dairy cows are raised for producing milk. It is not until after its first calf is born that a dairy cow can produce milk. A cow usually gives birth to only one calf and then produces a lot of milk to feed it. When the calf is 2 days old, it is taken away from its mother. After that, the cow is milked twice a day. A dairy cow's milk production is not at the same level all the time. When the cow is pregnant, milk production gradually decreases. For 2 months before her calf is born, a cow is said to be "dry"and is not milked. This happens because, like humans, much of the cow's food is actually being used to nourish the unborn calf. Farmers give the cow extra food at this time to make sure the mother and unborn calf are well-nourished. Again, like humans, well-nourished mother cows are more likely to produce healthy babies.

27. What happens when a cow is "dry"?
    (A) It cannot produce milk at the same level.
    (B) It cannot give birth to a calf.
    (C) It cannot produce any milk.
    (D) It cannot be pregnant.

28. Why does a cow become "dry"?
    (A) to nourish her unborn baby
    (B) to be pregnant again
    (C) to produce better milk
    (D) to have extra food

[29-30]

People heard important news from town criers, walking through cities and reading news reports before newspapers were born. The earliest newspapers were probably handwritten notices posted in towns for the public to read. The first true newspaper was a weekly paper started in Germany in 1609. It was possible because Johann Gutenberg developed movable type. One of the first English-language newspapers, The London Gazette, was first printed in England in 1665. Gazette is an old English word that means "official publication", so many newspapers still use the word, gazette, in their names. In America, the first successful newspaper, The Boston News Letter, began printing in 1704. The first penny newspaper, The New York Sun, was published in 1833. The paper actually costed only a penny. The penny newspapers were very similar to today's papers: they printed news while it was still new, they were the first to print advertisements and to sell papers in newsstands, and they were the first to be delivered homes.

29. Why is the word gazette still used in newspapers' names?
    (A) It is an old English word.
    (B) People like the word gazette.
    (C) It means newspaper.
    (D) Its meaning is related to publication.

30. In what point was the first penny newspaper important?
    (A) It costed a penny.
    (B) It was a birth of modern newspapers.
    (C) It was published in New York.
    (D) It was printed once a week.

[31-32]

Snow leopards are in danger of extinction. The land where they live is being settled by more and more people. People kill snow leopards to extend the land for feeding their sheep or goats. Another reason people hunt snow leopards is their fur. Hunters can earn a lot of money by selling the fur. It is important to encourage people not to buy the fur. If people don't buy the fur, hunters couldn't help stopping hunting snow leopards. Happily many organizations are trying to help snow leopards. A group called the International Snow Leopard Trust (ISLT) has come up with many different ideas for saving this animal. Groups like the ISLT raise money from people who care about endangered animals, then they use the money in ways they think it will be helpful. For example, the ISLT gives money to help people track snow leopards. Money is also given to local farmers for any livestock killed by snow leopards so the farmers will not go out and kill snow leopards.

31. How can we make hunters stop killing snow leopards for the fur?
    (A) by selling the fur instead of them
    (B) by giving them much money
    (C) by telling people not to buy the fur
    (D) by punishing them for hunting snow leopards

32. Why is the money given to local farmers?
    (A) to make up for the loss of their sheep or goats
    (B) to raise money from people
    (C) to kill snow leopards
    (D) to make them rich

[33-34]

Hundreds of years ago, it was dangerous to travel to sea. There was a danger of being attacked and even killed by pirates, privateers, or buccaneers. Pirates were the robbers of the sea. They attacked ships at sea, stealing the goods. Sometimes they attacked people living on the coast. The pirates kept everything they stole for themselves. Privateers were hired by the government of a country to attack the ships of another country when they were at war. They shared the goods they stole with the government that had hired them. Privateers often became pirates to make more money. When peace agreements were made between countries, the privateers claimed that the agreements were not for them. Then, they became buccaneers, privateers who were no longer paid by their government. Buccaneers then began attacking ships on their own. They thought that they were better than pirates. But really, there was little difference among pirates, privateers, and buccaneers. It was difficult to tell one from the other.

33. Why did privateers become pirates?
    (A) They wanted to end the war.
    (B) They could give money to another country.
    (C) They could be hired by another country.
    (D) They didn't have to share the stolen things with the government.

34. What did Buccaneers think about Pirates?
    (A) They thought pirates were worse than themselves.
    (B) They thought pirates were worse than privateers.
    (C) They thought privateers were worse than pirates.
    (D) They thought pirates were better than privateers.

[35-36]

Caves are dark and damp, however, they can be a good shelter as the temperature is consistent. For thousands of years, caves have provided a shelter for people and animals. Even today, in some parts of the world, people live in caves. In the past, people used caves as tombs for the dead. To protect the dead body from wild animals, the cave was blocked with a large stone or fires. People still build their houses inside caves. During World War Ⅱ, the people of the island of Malta lived in caves to protect themselves from the bombs exploded around them. In some areas of France, caves at the bottom of cliffs have been changed to permanent houses. In South Australia, a town called Coober Pedy is constructed entirely under the ground in man-made caves. The people in Coober Pedy live and work under the ground to protect themselves from the hot and dry climate.

35. What makes caves be a good shelter?
    (A) The temperature in caves doesn't change depending on the season.
    (B) Caves are dark and damp.
    (C) Caves are hot in the summer and cold in the winter.
    (D) Caves are close to people's houses.

36. Why were stones or fires put in front of the caves?
    (A) to make the dead body dry and steady
    (B) to stop wild animals from damaging the dead body
    (C) to make the caves look more beautiful
    (D) to protect the caves from other people

[37-38]

Earth is always changing because of forces working beneath its surface. Scientists believe that the hard upper layer of Earth, known as the crust, is made of nine major plates. These plates are moving on a solid layer of hot rock called the mantle which slowly rotates deep in the Earth. The movement of the mantle makes the plates move. They move apart and bump against each other. These movements cause huge layers of rock to be pushed up. They are exposed to wind, water, and changing temperature, uncovering fossils buried within the rock. Many fossils have been found in these rocks. A rocky area is not the only place where fossils are found. Often they can be found in non-rocky areas, too. For example, amber has fossil insects inside it. Sometimes we can discover fossilized animals in caves, as well.

37. What makes the Earth change all the time?
    (A) the solid layer of hot rock
    (B) energy working under its surface
    (C) the hard upper layer
    (D) the surface of the Earth

38. What is the direct reason for making fossils in the rocks come out?
    (A) the animals in caves
    (B) wind, water, and changing temperature
    (C) non-rocky areas
    (D) the mantle

[39-40]

The first wigs were worn thousands of years ago by ancient Egyptians. A wig had two purposes. It gave the wearer a high social status and it provided protection from the hot sun. Wigs became popular in the 1600s and 1700s when English and French royalty began wearing wigs. In the case of Queen Elizabeth I of England, wearing a wig was essential because her hair began to fall out from using chemical shampoos and makeup. Everyone thought he or she should wear a wig, too if the queen wore one. King Louis XIV of France had a similar problem to that of Queen Elizabeth. King Louis had always been admired for his curly hair. When it began to fall out, he began wearing a wig. This started a new fashion for men. The size of a wig seemed to show a social status. A bigger wig symbolized a nobler status. For some, like Queen Marie Antoinette of France, it was important to look tall. Marie Antoinette had wigs made with metal supports to make her look taller. Today many people still wear wigs to hide baldness or to alter the style of their hair.

39. Why did ancient people wear wigs?
    (A) to hide their bald hair
    (B) to show their social status
    (C) to protect their hair from rain
    (D) to protect their hair from falling out

40. What made King Louis XIV of France wear a wig?
    (A) to be like Queen Elizabeth
    (B) to cover his bald hair
    (C) to use chemical shampoos
    (D) to look taller

[41-42]

An airplane is a great work of engineering. One question that is always asked about the airplane is "How can something that weighs hundreds of tons stay in the air?" Probably the most important part of an airplane is its wings. The top part of each wing is curved and the bottom is flat. To stay in the air, "lift" must be generated. Air travels a longer distance and faster over the curved top of an airplane's wings than it does under the bottom, flat part. The fast air going over the top of the wing causes air pressure to drop. So, the air pressure above the wings is lower than the pressure under the wings. It is this difference in air pressure that causes an airplane to have lift. It then becomes up in the air. An airplane has to create a lot of speed for this to happen. Flight has made the world be a smaller place. Instead of taking weeks or months to reach somewhere, it now takes only hours or days. It took Columbus ten weeks to sail from the Canary Islands to the Bahamas. Today, that trip would only take hours, thanks to the invention of the airplane.

41. What makes the airplane have lift?
    (A) the difference in air pressure
    (B) the high air pressure
    (C) the low air pressure
    (D) the high speed

42. Why did Columbus spend ten weeks traveling from the Canary Islands to the Bahamas?
    (A) He had enough time to travel.
    (B) The airplane was not invented yet.
    (C) He could not buy airplane tickets.
    (D) He got lost during the trip.

[43-44]

Gorillas and chimpanzees are closely related to humans. Both of these great apes look and behave much like human beings. Both are highly intelligent and are family animals that like the company of others. Humans share about 98 percent of the same genetic materials as gorillas and almost 99 percent with chimpanzees. For many years, chimpanzees were made to perform in zoos and the circus. But as people gained more understanding of these apes, they saw how important it is to keep them in a natural environment. All over the world, animal-rescue organizations are working to return the circus and pet chimpanzees to protection areas. Gorillas are huge gentle creatures, but they are very strong. For this reason they have not been made to perform in the same way as chimpanzees. However, the treatment they have received has been just as cruel. Illegal hunters kill gorillas and chimpanzees and sell their body parts against the law.

43. What are animal-rescue organizations doing for chimpanzees?
    (A) making them perform in zoos
    (B) getting them out of a natural environment
    (C) returning them to the circus
    (D) bringing them to protected areas

44. Why have gorillas not been made to perform in the circus?
    (A) They are gentle creatures.
    (B) They are like chimpanzees.
    (C) They are huge and strong.
    (D) They are similar to humans.

[45-46]

To graffiti is to write or draw on a surface in a public place, which is usually done without permission. Young people paint their names or messages on other people's property. Adults consider this as an act of crime. In fact, it's illegal to paint on people's property without asking them. These days, however, graffiti is being seen by many people as a form of art. Words and pictures painted on city walls and buildings are valued as a form of self-expression. Now graffiti artists are asked to decorate the outsides of buildings as a part of graffiti-art projects. Graffiti-art projects help make cities into places full of energy. It puts the work of young artists in the place where people can see it. In some places, classes and materials are offered to young graffiti artists. Many of the graffiti artists have had troubled lives, but now have new hopeful lives because of graffiti-art projects. Some have found work painting shop signs and wall paintings. Others have studied art professionally.

45. What is graffiti?
    (A) offering classes to young artists
    (B) erasing writings and drawings on city walls
    (C) expressing one's ideas in a public place by painting
    (D) asking others to paint something on their property

46. What benefit is given to cities thanks to graffiti-art projects?
    (A) It makes the cities more lively.
    (B) It makes the people in the cities look good.
    (C) It makes criminals decrease.
    (D) It makes cities more bigger.

[47-48]

Children learn to speak from what they hear. If children cannot hear, it affects their development seriously. So it is important to test a baby's hearing. Any possible hearing loss can be detected early that way. Children with a hearing problem may fall behind in school if they are neglected without getting any help. However, aided with proper measures, deaf children will do fine in school. There are many things that can be done to assist hearing-impaired children in the classroom. Most of these are very simple. The teacher can write instructions on the board as well as tell children what to do. Having a hearing-impaired child sit in the front row can help cut out background noise. Making sure that people look at the child as they speak can help them lip-read. Teachers and other classmates can learn sign language. Sometimes tutors or interpreters can help.

47. Why is it important to test a baby's hearing?
(A) to affect their development seriously
(B) to detect their hearing problem early
(C) to make them fall behind in school
(D) to make them do fine in school

48. Why do people have to look at the child with hearing problems when they speak?
(A) to assist them to read their lips
(B) to get rid of background noise
(C) to learn sign language
(D) to tell them what to do

다음의 어휘들을 익히고 Checkups에 기록해 보세요.

	489 Intensive Words		1st	2nd	3rd
		Checkups			
314	astrology	[명] 점성술			
315	promote	[동] 촉진시키다, 승진시키다			
316	convenience	[명] 편의, 편리			
317	condense	[동] 응집하다, 응축시키다			
318	rack	[명] 선반(=shelf)			
319	slaughter	[동] 도살하다, 대량학살하다			
320	gasp	[동] 헐떡거리다 [명] 헐떡거림, 숨참			
321	secondhand	[형] 중고의			
322	correspond	[동] 상응하다, 서신교환(통신)하다			
323	survey	[동] 조사하다, 측량하다			
324	procession	[명] 행렬, 행진			
325	segregate	[동] 분리하다			
326	territory	[명] 영토			
327	prejudice	[명] 선입견			
328	perspire	[동] 땀 흘리다			
329	pros and cons	[명] 찬반양론			
330	spank	[명] 매질 [동] 매질하다			
331	tremble	[동] 부들부들 떨다, 전율하다			
332	reap	[동] 기둬들이다, 수확하다			
333	suspicious	[형] 의심스러운			
334	observe	[동] 관찰하다, 준수하다			
335	execute	[동] 실행하다, 처형하다			

489 Intensive Words		Checkups		
		1st	2nd	3rd
336	wreath	[명] 꽃다발, 화환		
337	whirl	[동] 빙빙 소용돌이치다		
338	equate	[동] 등식화하다, 균등하게 하다		
339	sanitation	[명] 공중위생		
340	alleviate	[동] 덜다, 완화하다		
341	assassinate	[동] 암살하다		
342	brink	[명] 가장자리, 직전		
343	stimulant	[명] 자극, 격려		
344	curb	[명] 재갈, 속박 [동] 억제하다		
345	dreary	[형] 황량한, 따분한		
346	excavate	[동] 파다, 발굴하다		
347	growl	[동] (개 등이) 으르렁거리다		
348	inquisitive	[형] 질문을 좋아하는, 탐구적인		
349	lament	[동] 슬퍼하다 [명] 비탄		
350	mediate	[동] 조정하다, 중재하다		
351	nurture	[명] 양육 [동] 양육하다, 기르다		
352	portray	[동] 그리다, 묘사하다		
353	recession	[명] 후퇴, 퇴각		
354	retort	[동] 반박[항변]하다, 말대꾸하다 [명] 말대답		
355	sober	[형] 술 취하지 않은, 냉정한 [동] 냉정하게 하다		
356	throne	[명] 왕좌, 왕위		
357	ulcer	[명] 궤양, 폐해		

설명하고 있는 알맞은 의미의 단어를 퍼즐안에 넣어 봅시다.

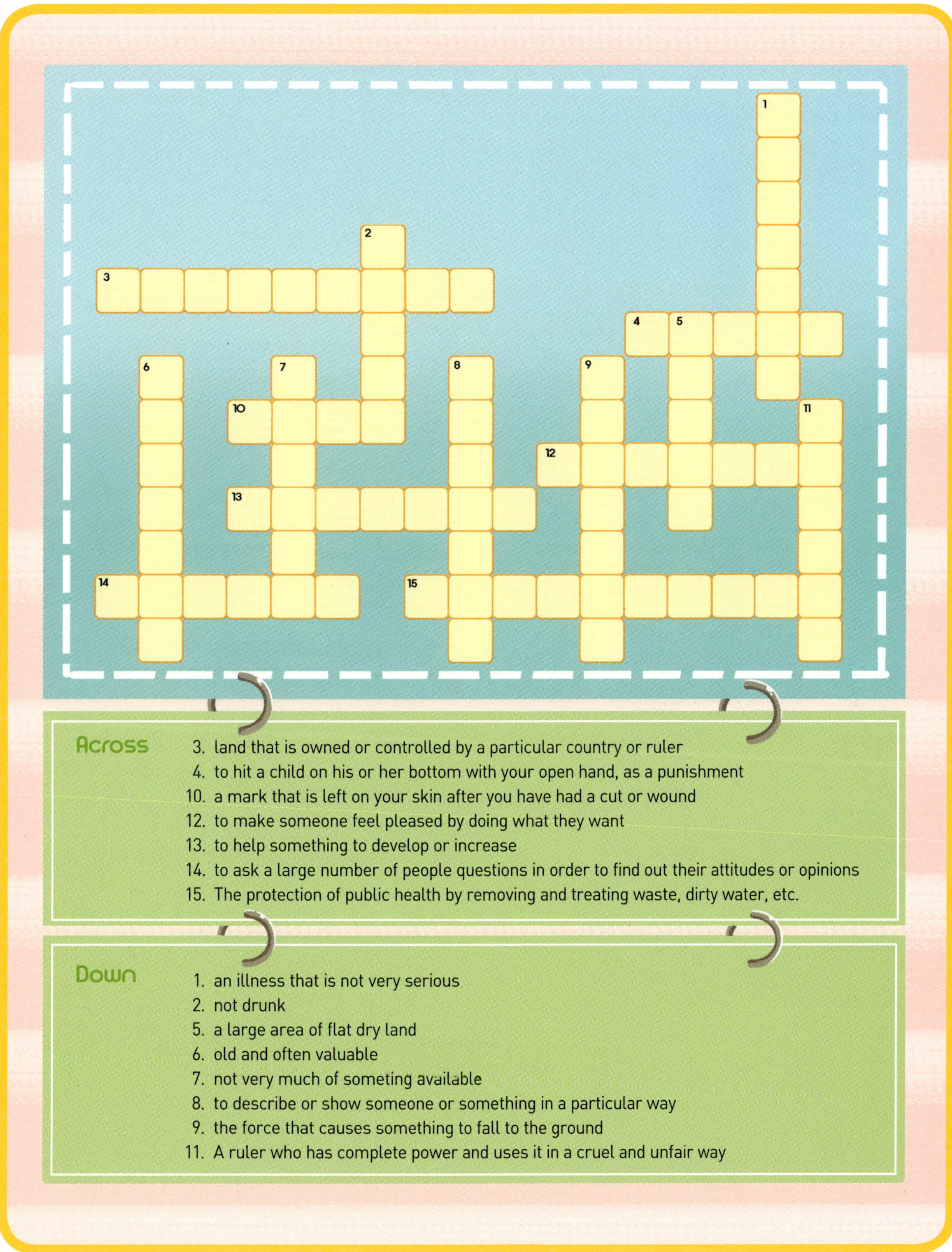

Across

3. land that is owned or controlled by a particular country or ruler
4. to hit a child on his or her bottom with your open hand, as a punishment
10. a mark that is left on your skin after you have had a cut or wound
12. to make someone feel pleased by doing what they want
13. to help something to develop or increase
14. to ask a large number of people questions in order to find out their attitudes or opinions
15. The protection of public health by removing and treating waste, dirty water, etc.

Down

1. an illness that is not very serious
2. not drunk
5. a large area of flat dry land
6. old and often valuable
7. not very much of someting available
8. to describe or show someone or something in a particular way
9. the force that causes something to fall to the ground
11. A ruler who has complete power and uses it in a cruel and unfair way

예제를 통해 Part D의 유형을 연습해 봅시다.

Example 1

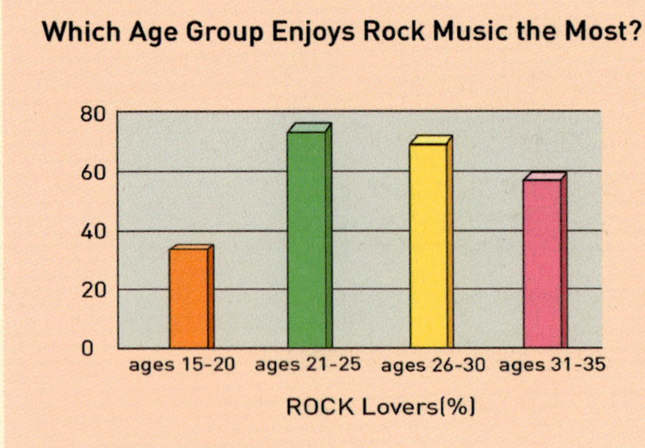

What is NOT true about the graph?

(A) 3 out of 10 people in ages 15 to 20 enjoy rock music.
(B) People in 21 to 25 enjoy rock music the most.
(C) As people get older, their preference to rock music decreases.
(D) Over half of people in 31 to 35 are Rock lovers.

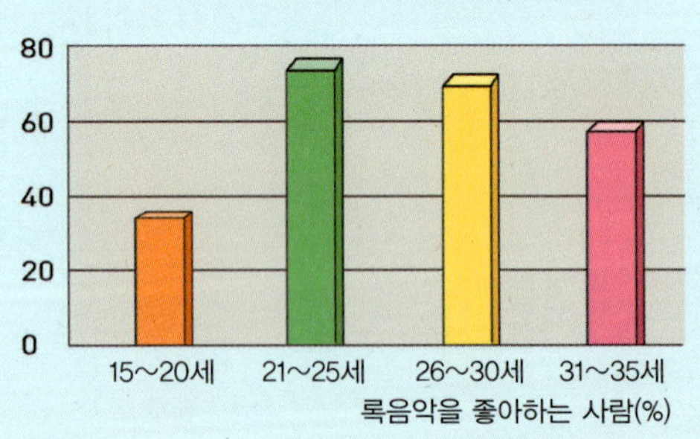

다음 그래프에 대해 사실이 아닌 것은 무엇입니까?

(A) 15에서 20세에 해당하는 10명의 사람 중 3명이 록음악을 즐긴다.
(B) 21에서 25세에 해당하는 사람들이 록음악을 가장 많이 즐긴다.
(C) 나이가 들수록 록음악에 대한 선호도가 줄어든다.
(D) 31세에서 35세에 해당하는 사람들의 절반이상이 록 애호가 이다.

정답 : (C)

위 그래프에 따르면 15세에서 20세에 해당하는 사람들보다 21세에서 25세에 해당하는 사람들이 훨씬 더 록음악을 즐기므로, 나이가 들수록 록음악에 대한 사랑이 줄어든다고 말할 수 없습니다.

* **preference** 선호도

Example 2

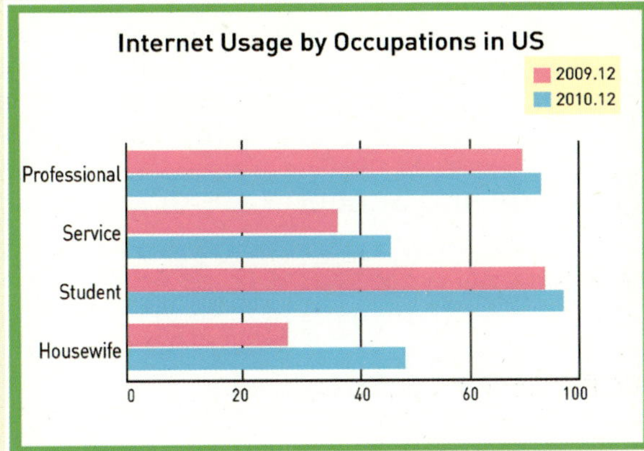

What is true about the graph?

(A) Students in December 2010 showed a less Internet usage rate than professionals in December 2010.
(B) The Internet usage rate for professionals was the highest in December 2009.
(C) The increase in the Internet usage rate for housewives was less than that for people in the service industry.
(D) By December 2010, all four occupations showed an increase in the Internet usage rate from a year earlier.

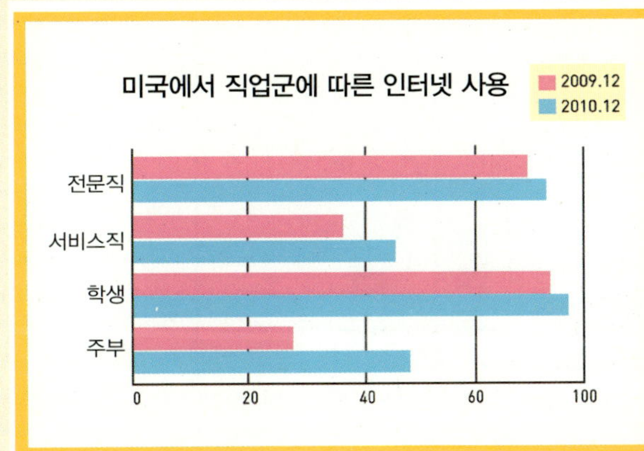

그래프에 대해 사실인 것은 무엇입니까?

(A) 2010년 12월에 학생들은 전문직 종사사보다 더 적은 인터넷 이용비율을 나타냈다.
(B) 전문직 종사자의 인터넷 이용비율은 2009년 12월에 가장 높았다.
(C) 전업주부의 인터넷 이용비율 증가가 서비스업 종사자의 이용비율보다 더 적었다.
(D) 2010년 12월 무렵, 4개 직업군은 1년 전에 비해 인터넷 사용비율이 증가했다.

정답 : (D)

그래프에 따르면 (A) 2010년 12월에 학생들은 전문직 종사자보다 더 많은 인터넷 이용비율을 나타내고, (B) 전문직 종사자의 인터넷 이용비율은 2010년 12월에 가장 높았습니다. (C) 전업주부의 인터넷 이용비율은 서비스산업 종사자의 비율보다 더 크게 증가하였습니다.

* **professional** 전문직 종사자 / **industry** 산업 / **occupation** 직업

PART D. Reading and Retelling

Directions : *In this part of the test, you will read longer passages. Choose the best answer from four choices to answer the questions following each passage. Then fill in the corresponding space on your answer sheet.*

Average Weekly Hours of Using Internet by Age and Gender

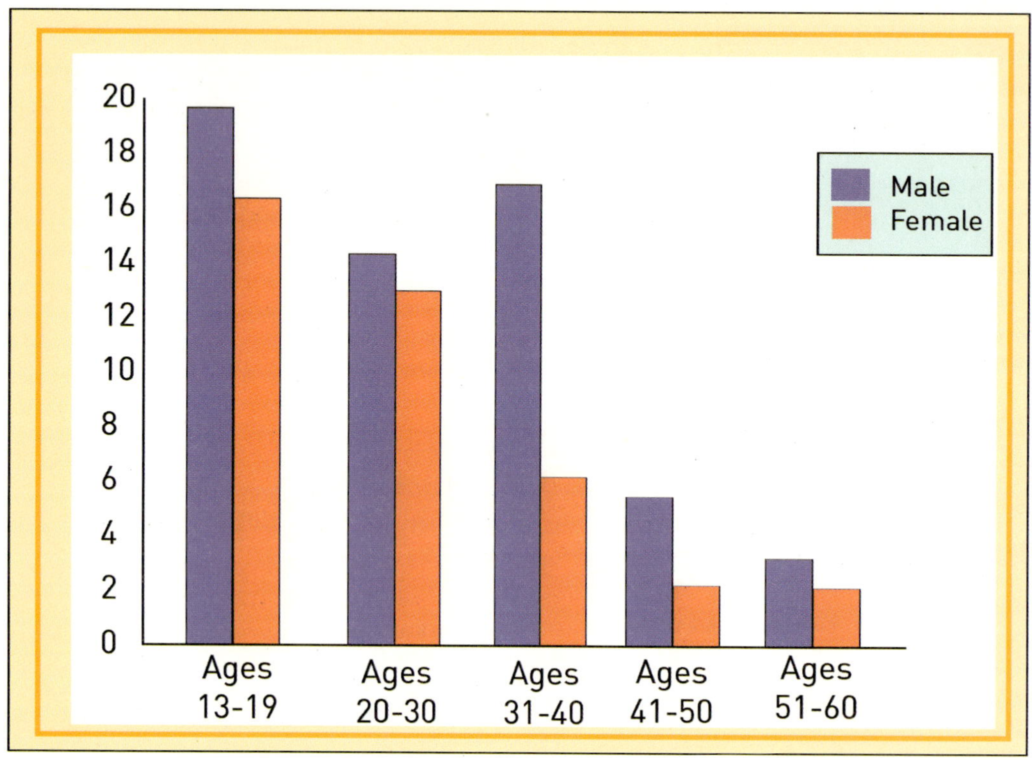

1. According to the chart, which of the following can be inferred?
   (A) Women use Internet less than men.
   (B) Men over 51 are the least frequent users.
   (C) Men spend less time doing Internet as they get older.
   (D) The group of ages 31-40 shows the least difference by gender.

The Correlation between Weekly Reading Hours and Reading Test Scores of the Fifth Graders by Gender

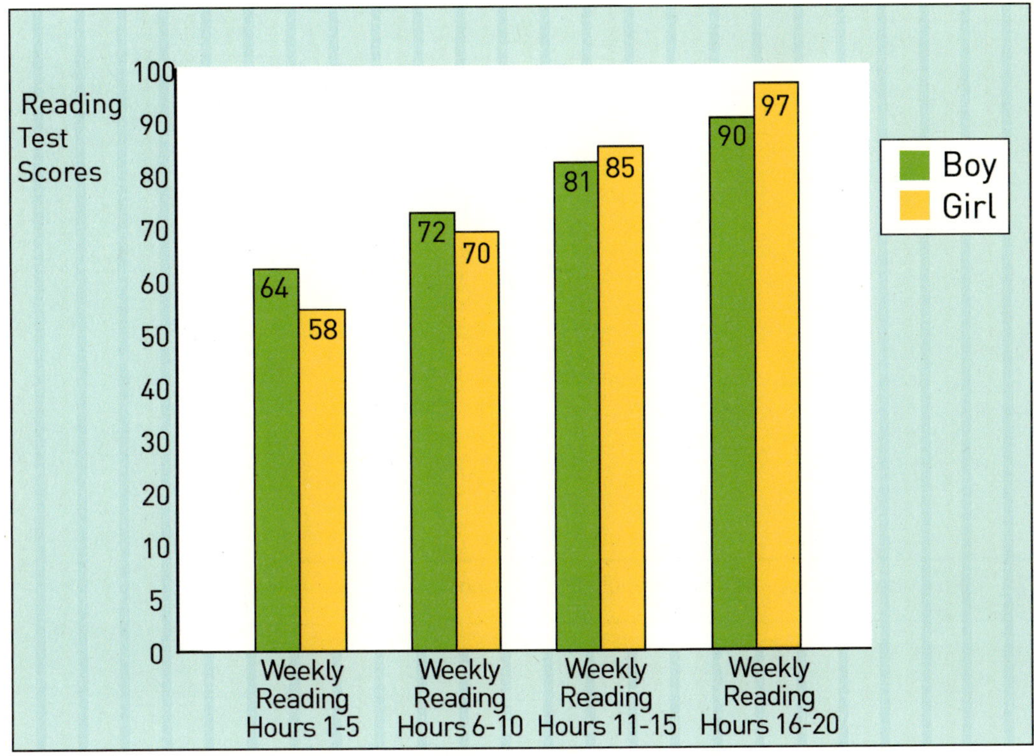

2. In the case of girls, which group shows the highest test scores?

(A) girls reading books for 1-5 hours weekly

(B) girls reading books for 6-10 hours weekly

(C) girls reading books for 11-15 hours weekly

(D) girls reading books for 16-20 hours weekly

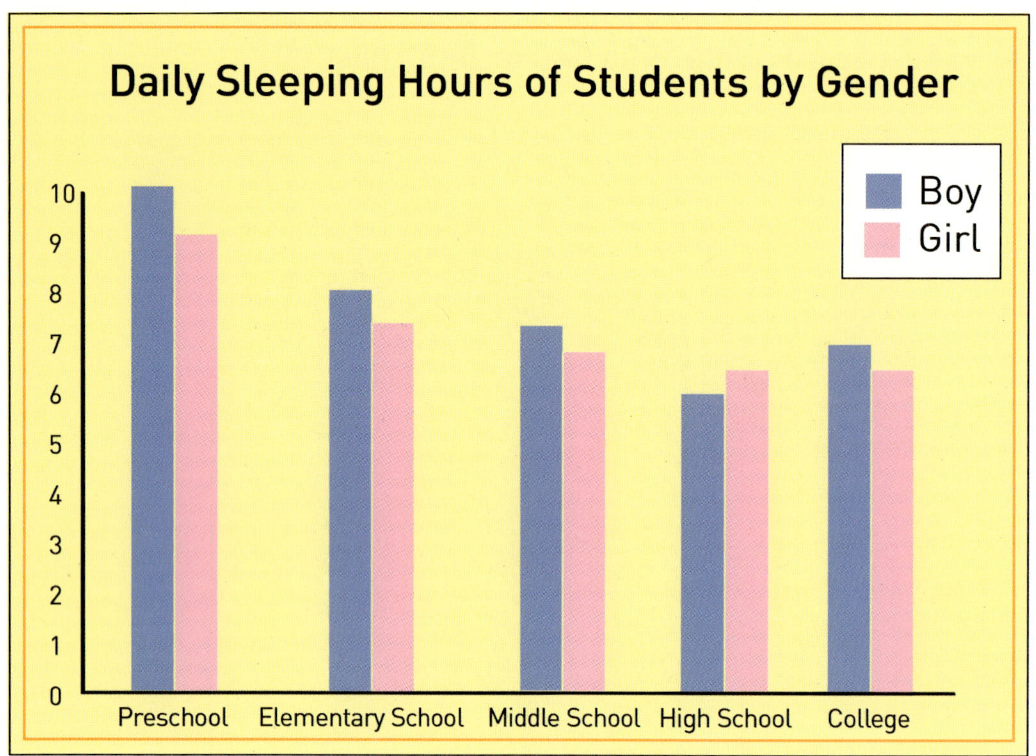

3. Which school students do NOT follow the general trend of the others?

(A) Preschool students

(B) Elementary School students

(C) Middle School students

(D) High School students

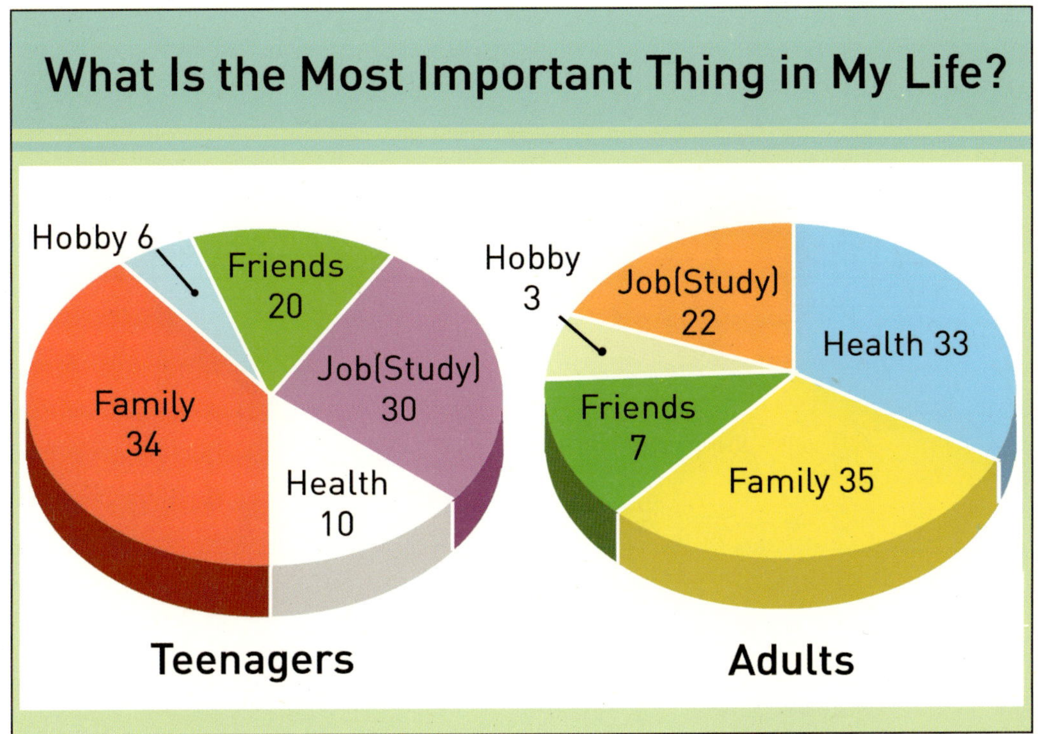

4. Which category shows the biggest gap between adults and teenagers?

(A) Family

(B) Health

(C) Job(Study)

(D) Friends

다음의 어휘들을 익히고 Checkups에 기록해 보세요.

	489 Intensive Words		Checkups		
			1st	2nd	3rd
358	astronomy	[명] 천문학			
359	extend	[동] 늘이다, 연장하다			
360	explore	[동] 탐험하다, 탐색하다			
361	expose	[동] 드러내다, 노출시키다			
362	replace	[동] 제자리에 돌려놓다, 대체하다			
363	sprain	[동] (발목, 손목을) 삐다			
364	banner	[명] 깃발			
365	institution	[명] 기관, 단체			
366	perceive	[동] 지각하다, 인지하다			
367	poll	[명] 여론조사, 투표			
368	proceed	[동] 나아가다			
369	fuse	[명] 퓨즈, 도화선 [동] 융합하다			
370	alien	[형] 외국의, 성질이 다른 [명] 외국인, 외계인			
371	inclusive	[형] 포함하여, 포괄적인			
372	aspire	[동] 야망을 품다			
373	blame	[동] 비난하다, 탓하다			
374	mischief	[명] 손해, 장난, 장난기			
375	shiver	[동] 떨다, 전율하다 [명] 떨림			
376	agitate	[동] 흔들다, 선동하다			
377	reveal	[동] 드러내다, 폭로하다			
378	axis	[명] 굴대, 축			
379	sane	[형] 제정신의, 온전한			

489 Intensive Words		Checkups		
		1st	2nd	3rd
380	aisle	[명] 통로, 복도		
381	bankrupt	[형] 파산한		
382	stroll	[동] 거닐다		
383	acute	[형] (아픔) 격렬한, (감각) 예리한		
384	anatomy	[명] 해부, 해부학		
385	assault	[명] 습격, 급습 [동] 급습하다		
386	bruise	[명] 타박상, 멍 [동] 멍들게 하다		
387	conform	[동] 따르다, 순응하다		
388	curtail	[동] 단축하다, (비용 등을) 삭감하다		
389	dwindle	[동] 차츰 작아지다		
390	extravagant	[형] 낭비하는, 사치스러운		
391	harass	[동] 괴롭히다, 귀찮게 굴다		
392	inscription	[명] 비명, 새긴 글씨		
393	lavish	[형] 헤픈, 사치스런 [동] 낭비하다		
394	meditate	[동] 명상하다, 숙고하다		
395	oar	[명] 노 [동] 노를 젓다		
396	predator	[명] 약탈자, 포식동물		
397	wane	[동] 작아지다, 약해지다, 감퇴하다 [명] 감퇴		
398	rhetoric	[명] 수사법, 수사학, 설득력		
399	speculate	[동] 사색하다, 투기하다		
400	throng	[명] 군중, 다수 [동] 떼를 지어 모이다		
401	velocity	[명] 속력, 속도		

예제를 통해 Part E의 유형을 연습해 봅시다. (지문 1개 + 요약 1개 유형)

Example 1

One of the characteristics in today's society is to put people under too much pressure and make them suffer from it constantly. Therefore, it is very important to find your own ways to relieve the stress you face. One of the ways is to engage actively in their hobbies. People are likely to feel comfortable and relieved when they enjoy their leisure activities. Another is to spend time with their family or friends. You can just play basketball or chat over coffee with them. Such a happy time lets you go out of the daily routines and gives you enough strength to fight against stress. If you cannot leave right now from the complicated urban lives, you should learn how to deal with stress.

Summary: People in [1.] ____________ society seem to be burdened with much stress. Two or more ways can be used to [2.] _________ it. The first recommendation is to [3.] _________ in leisure activities. Another is to get together with your family or friends and have fun with them. You are able to get rid of stress [4.] _________ in these ways.

① considerably   ② modern   ③ ancient   ④ participate
⑤ increase   ⑥ reduce   ⑦ revive   ⑧ poorly

오늘날 사회의 한 가지 특징은 사람들에게 너무나 많은 스트레스를 가하고 그로 인해 끊임없이 고통을 겪도록 한다는 것입니다. 따라서 당신이 직면하는 스트레스를 완화하기 위한 당신 나름의 방법을 터득하는 것이 매우 중요합니다. 그 중의 한 방법은 취미생활에 적극 참여하는 것입니다. 사람들은 여가 활동을 즐길 때 편안함을 느끼는 경향이 있습니다. 또 다른 방법은 가족이나 친구들과 시간을 보내는 것입니다. 당신은 단지 그들과 농구를 하거나 커피를 마시며 잡담을 할 수도 있습니다. 그러한 즐거운 시간이 당신을 지루한 일상으로부터 벗어나도록 하고 스트레스와 맞서 싸울 충분한 힘을 줍니다. 지금 당장 복잡한 도시 생활로부터 벗어날 수 없다면 당신은 어떻게 스트레스를 다루어야 할지 배워야 합니다.

요약 : [1.] ② 사회의 사람들은 많은 스트레스를 받고 있는 것으로 보입니다. 스트레스를 [2.] ⑥ 위해 두 가지 이상의 방법을 사용해볼 수 있습니다. 첫 번째 추천 방법은 여가 활동에 [3.] ④ 것입니다. 또 하나의 방법은 가족이나 친구들과 모여 그들과 흥겨운 시간을 갖는 것입니다. 이러한 방법을 통하여 당신은 스트레스를 [4.] ① 제거할 수 있을 것입니다.

① 꽤 많이, 상당히   ② 현대의   ③ 고대의   ④ 참여하다
⑤ 증가시키다   ⑥ 감소시키다   ⑦ 소생시키다   ⑧ 빈약하게

정답 : 1. ② 2. ⑥ 3. ④ 4. ①
이 글은 현대인은 많은 스트레스에 시달린다고 말하며 스트레스를 해소할 수 있는 두 가지 방법을 제안하고 있습니다.

* **characteristic** 특징 / **put ~ under pressure** ~에게 스트레스를 주다 / **relieve** 완화시키다, 경감시키다 / **face** 직면하다 / **engage in** ~에 종사하다, 참여하다 / **comfortable** 편안한 / **leisure** 여가 / **chat** 잡담하다 / **routine** 판에 박힌 일 / **complicated** 복잡한 / **urban** 도시의 / **deal with** ~을 다루다 / **be burdened with** ~의 부담을 지다 / **recommendation** 추천(하는 것) / **get together with** ~와 함께 모이다 / **get rid of** ~을 제거하다, 없애다

Example 2

A research suggests that teenage kids showed a very low ability in reading comprehension. Reading ability is fundamental in every learning process. Students who struggle in reading need to be taught specific reading strategies in order to catch up. All children can learn to read, and it may simply take extra patience and teaching with care. First of all, keep the children with reading problem from being afraid of reading. Let them read books for fun. When they start to enjoy reading books, teachers can ask them to answer the short and clear questions about facts in the book. By answering the questions, children try to think continuously about the story. Sooner or later, they can evaluate the book using higher reading skills.

Summary: Kids with reading [1.]____________ need to learn how to read with some strategies. First of all, teachers let the children to read books just for [2.]__________. Later, teachers can ask [3.]__________ questions to lead them to think deeply about the flow of the story. In the process, children soon get to know how to make [4.]____________ on what they read.

① fear	② complex	③ assessment	④ amusement
⑤ disability	⑥ plain	⑦ strategies	⑧ patience

한 연구 결과를 통하여 10대 아이들이 읽기 이해도에 있어서 매우 낮은 능력을 보이는 것을 알 수 있습니다. 읽기 능력은 모든 학습 과정의 기초가 됩니다. 읽기 때문에 고생하는 학생들은 따라 잡기 위하여 구체적인 읽기 전략을 배울 필요가 있습니다. 모든 아이들은 읽기를 배울 수 있고, 그것은 단지 더 큰 인내심과 주의 깊은 가르침만 있으면 될 일인지도 모릅니다. 무엇보다 읽기에 문제를 가진 아이들이 읽기를 두려워하지 않도록 하십시오. 아이들이 재미로 책을 읽을 수 있게 하십시오. 아이들이 책을 즐기기 시작하면 교사들은 아이들로 하여금 책에 나오는 사실에 관한 짧고 분명한 질문에 대답해보도록 할 수 있습니다. 질문에 대답하면서 아이들은 책에 나오는 이야기에 대해 계속 생각하려고 애쓰게 됩니다. 머지않아 그들은 보다 높은 차원의 읽기 기술을 이용하여 책을 평가할 수 있습니다.

요약 : 읽기 [1.] ⑤ 를 가진 아이들은 몇 가지 전략을 이용하여 읽는 방법을 배워야 합니다. 우선 교사는 아이들이 단지 [2.] ④ 을 목적으로 책을 읽도록 허용합니다. 나중에 교사는 [3.] ⑥ 질문을 통해 아이들이 이야기의 흐름에 대해 깊이 생각하도록 이끕니다. 그 과정을 통해 아이들은 곧 그들이 읽은 것을 어떻게 [4.] ③ 해야 할지를 터득하게 됩니다.

① 두려움	② 복잡한	③ 평가	④ 즐거움
⑤ 장애	⑥ 알기 쉬운	⑦ 전략	⑧ 인내심

정답 : 1. ⑤ 2. ④ 3. ⑥ 4. ③

이 글은 읽기에 어려움을 보이는 아이들을 교사가 어떻게 지도하면 좋을지에 대하여 한 가지 방법을 제안하고 있습니다.

* **comprehension** 이해 / **fundamental** 기초적인, 근본적인 / **strategy** 전략 / **catch up** 따라잡다 / **evaluate** 평가하다 / **make assessment on** ~에 대해 평가를 내리다

예제를 통해 Part E의 유형을 연습해 봅시다.(지문 1개 + 요약 2개 유형)

Example 1

Some teachers argue that giving students daily homework is beneficial for them. First of all, it gives students an opportunity for reviewing the text books. It also helps to deepen their understanding of what they learned in classes. Others, however, have different ideas about that. They believe students need enough free time after school to play with friends and read books of their own choice. If given homework every day, they might have difficulty securing enough time for playing and reading books. And some of the students might think daily homework is enough, so that they might not spend more time reading or studying.

Student A's opinion : Concerning the paragraph above, I believe that students should be given daily homework. It helps the students to correct their [1]___________ and make up for what they lack at school. It also trains the students to [2]____________ their time to keep a balance between [3]__________ and playing. It should be taught as earlier as possible.

Student B's opinion : Concerning the paragraph above, I do not think that students need daily homework. Though studying is important for children, learning through everyday life should not be [4]__________, either. They should have enough time to play with their friends and [5]__________ with their family or community members. They learn a lot through these [6]__________ activities.

① organize	② interact	③ studying	④ social
⑤ ignored	⑥ considered	⑦ misunderstanding	⑧ individual

어떤 선생님들은 매일 숙제를 내주는 것이 학생들에게 도움이 된다고 주장합니다. 우선 숙제는 학생들이 교과서를 복습할 수 있는 기회를 제공합니다. 또한 수업시간에 배운 것을 깊이 이해하도록 합니다. 그러나 다른 선생님들은 이에 대하여 다른 생각을 가지고 있습니다. 그들은 학생들이 방과 후에 친구들과 놀거나 자신이 고른 책을 읽을 수 있는 충분한 시간이 필요하다고 믿습니다. 만약 매일 숙제가 주어진다면, 학생들은 놀거나 책을 읽는 데 필요한 충분한 시간을 확보하는 데 어려움을 겪을 수 있습니다. 그리고 어떤 학생들은 매일 숙제를 하는 것으로 충분하다고 생각하고 더 이상 책을 읽거나 공부하려고 하지 않을 수도 있습니다.

학생 A의 의견 : 윗 글과 관련하여 나는 학생들에게 매일의 숙제를 부과해야 한다고 생각합니다. 숙제는 학생들이 [1] ⑦ 를 수정하고 학교에서 부족한 부분을 보충할 수 있도록 도와줍니다. 또한 학생들로 하여금 [3] ③ 와 놀이 사이의 균형을 유지하기 위하여 주어진 시간을 [2] ① 훈련할 것입니다. 이것은 가능할수록 일찍 가르쳐야 합니다.

학생 B의 의견 : 윗 글과 관련하여 나는 학생들에게 매일의 숙제가 필요하다고 생각하지 않습니다. 아이들에게 공부가 중요하지만, 일상생활을 통한 학습 또한 [4] ⑤ 안 됩니다. 아이들은 친구들과 놀고 가족이나 이웃들과 [5] ② 충분한 시간을 가져야 합니다. 그들은 이러한 [6] ④ 활동을 통해서 많은 것을 배웁니다.

① 조직하다	② 상호작용하다	③ 공부	④ 사회적인
⑤ 무시된	⑥ 고려된	⑦ 오해	⑧ 개인적인

정답 : 1. ⑦ 2. ① 3. ③ 4. ⑤ 5. ② 6. ④
학생들에게 숙제를 부과하는 것에 대한 찬반양론입니다.

* argue 주장하다 / beneficial 유익한 / deepen 깊게 하다, 심화하다 / make up for ～을 보충하다 / lack 부족하다

Example 2

The popularity of reality shows is on the rise continuously. Not only small cable companies but also major TV networks produce many different types of reality shows recently. Reality shows videotape lives of common people as well as celebrities and show the views as they are taped. It attracts viewers' attention successfully and requires comparatively lower costs to produce than scripted TV shows. Some of the shows give viewers hope and confidence through the dramatic life of the participants. However, the behaviors of participants sometimes greatly influence the viewers negatively. It also violates the privacy of the participants so much that they become the victim of the reality show in the end.

Student A's opinion : Concerning the paragraph above, I think that reality shows can be a good opportunity for you to show off your talents or to get 5._______ information to make people aware of social causes. Reality shows can teach you that you can 2._______ tough obstacles with family's support, hard work, and confidence. For example, a reality show about the stories of people from different backgrounds who suffered from serious personal problems like drug addiction 3._______the danger of drug addiction and gives the viewers the precious lessons about that.

Student B's opinion : Concerning the paragraph above, I believe that some reality shows 4._______ poor behaviors. For example, some reality dating shows do not focus on 5._______ mature relationships, but just emphasize the sexual aspects of dating. This can let young people to distort the idea of love eventually. Reality shows sometimes violate on the participants 6._______ so much that some of the participants have hard time continuing their social life even after the show finally ends.

① developing   ② overcome   ③ privacy   ④ emphasizes
⑤ healthful   ⑥ discourage   ⑦ encourage   ⑧ destroying

리얼리티 쇼의 인기는 계속 상승하고 있습니다. 작은 케이블 회사뿐만 아니라 주요 공중파 방송국도 최근 다양한 종류의 리얼리티 쇼를 제작합니다. 리얼리티 쇼는 유명 인사뿐만 아니라 일반인들의 생활까지도 녹화하여 녹화된 그대로 시청자에게 보여줍니다. 그것은 성공적으로 시청자의 관심을 끌 뿐만 아니라, 제작하는 데 대본이 있는 쇼 프로그램보다 비교적 적은 돈이 듭니다. 어떤 리얼리티 쇼는 참가자의 극적인 삶을 통하여 시청자들에게 희망과 자신감을 줍니다. 하지만 참가자의 행동은 가끔 시청자들에게 부정적으로 영향을 미칩니다. 그것은 또한 참가자의 사생활을 지나치게 침해하여 쇼가 끝난후에도 사회생활에 어려움을 줍니다.

학생 A의 의견 : 윗글에 대하여, 나는 리얼리티 쇼가 당신이 가진 재능을 뽐낼 수 있는 좋은 기회, 또는 사람들에게 사회적인 문제를 인식하도록 돕는 1. ⑤ 정보를 얻을 수 있는 좋은 기회를 제공하리라고 생각합니다. 리얼리티 쇼는 당신도 가족의 도움과, 노력, 그리고 자신감으로 힘든 장애물을 2. ② 있다고 가르쳐 줄 수 있습니다. 예를 들면, 마약 중독과 같은 심각한 개인적 문제로 고통 받고 있는 다양한 상황을 지닌 사람들의 이야기를 다루는 한 리얼리티 쇼는 마약중독의 위험성을 3. ④ 시청자들에게 마약 중독에 대한 소중한 교훈을 전달합니다.

학생 B의 의견 : 윗글에 대하여, 나는 어떤 리얼리티 쇼는 적절치 않은 행동을 4. ⑦ 믿습니다. 예를 들면, 어떤 리얼리티 데이트 쇼는 성숙한 관계를 5. ① 집중하지 않고, 데이트의 성적인 면만을 강조합니다. 이것은 젊은이들의 장래의 사랑에 대한 생각을 왜곡시킬 수 있습니다. 리얼리티 쇼는 가끔 참가자의 6. ③ 지나치게 침해하여 결국 참가자 몇몇은 쇼가 끝난 후에도 사회생활을 지속하는 데 어려움을 겪게 됩니다.

① 발전시키는 것   ② 극복하다   ③ 사생활   ④ 강조하다
⑤ 유용한, 유익한   ⑥ 좌절시키다   ⑦ 조장하다   ⑧ 파괴하는 것

정답 : 1. ⑤ 2. ② 3. ④ 4. ⑦ 5. ① 6. ③

참가자들의 실제 생활상을 그대로 녹화하여 내보내는 리얼리티 쇼 프로그램에 대한 찬반양론입니다.

* **celebrity** 유명인사 / **comparatively** 비교적 / **scripted** 대본이 쓰인 / **confidence** 확신 / **participant** 참가자 / **influence** 영향을 주다 / **negatively** 부정적으로 / **violate** 침해하다 / **victim** 피해자 / **in the end** 결국에 / **aware of** ~을 인식하는 / **bstacle** 장애물 / **addiction** 중독 / **emphasize** 강조하다 / **precious** 소중한 / **mature** 성숙한 / **aspects** 측면 / **distort** 왜곡시키다 / **eventually** 결국

PART E. Read and Write

Directions *: In this part of the test, you will read two different passages. From Questions 1 to 16, read the passage and complete the following summarized sentences by choosing the most suitable words from the given box. From Questions 17 to 40, read the passage and complete the two opposite arguments on the passage by choosing the most suitable words from the given box. Then fill in the corresponding space on your answer sheet.*

[1-4]

> We are all different. Even identical twins have different nature and opinions. It's impossible to find anyone who is exactly the same as ourselves. We are better or worse than others in one way or another. With little effort, we can quickly compare ourselves into downright misery. My sister looks more beautiful than me. I envy my friend who is richer than me. We don't even need others for these self-destructive comparisons; comparing ourselves to our past or future can do the same thing. Happiness comes from seeing ourselves as being okay, just as we are, today.

Summary: No one has the same nature and opinions even identical twins. We tend to make
1. ____________ between others and ourselves in a 2. ____________ way. Our past and future can be
3. ____________ of our comparison. To escape from comparison we should 4. ____________ ourselves just the way we are.

① targets	② accept	③ compare	④ right
⑤ misery	⑥ destructive	⑦ positive	⑧ comparison

[5-8]

According to some researches, a physical activity should be added to weight control programs in the form of weight training. The experiment consisted of two groups of women. Both were on diet, but one group also lifted weights while the other did not. The women in both groups lost 13 pounds on average, but the women who did weight training lost only fat. However, the women who did not lift weights lost muscles as well as fat. Muscles are so important to maintain our health that weight control programs should include any type of weight training activities.

Summary: Weight control programs including any type of weight training activities are more 5. ______________ than those without weight training. The experiment was 6. ______________ with two groups of women. It 7. ______________ that the weight control program with weight training helped lose only 8. ______________ .

① effective   ② muscle   ③ health   ④ fat
⑤ proved   ⑥ performed   ⑦ dangerous   ⑧ disproved

[9 - 12]

People are likely to believe that news is always true. That's not the case. Although it seems that the news is based on facts, these facts can be reported in the way media wants to report them. For instance, some information that seems to be news is based on only opinions, instead of facts. Besides, many journalists and reporters twist a news event in order to make a story more interesting, which often bends the truth and causes anger to the people involved with it. As a consumer of news we must learn to think critically about the news, the media, and what the truth is.

Summary: News is not always 9.___________ . In fact, the news is sometimes based on media's point of 10.___________ . Some journalists may add a 11.___________ story or change a part of it. Therefore, it is strongly recommended to accept news in a 12.___________ way.

① negative   ② true   ③ twist   ④ view
⑤ false   ⑥ objective   ⑦ subjective   ⑧ opinion

[13 - 16]

Competition can be healthy. It drives us to improve ourselves and to reach the highest level. Without it, we would never know how far we could push ourselves. In the business world, it makes our economy grow greater. But we can see the other side of competition. If it is used as a means of creating a self-image compared to others, the worst in a person can come out. Competition becomes dark when we use it as a way only to defeat others. Children who have been taught to measure themselves in this way often grow up to be adults who believe only a winner deserves love and respect.

Summary: When competition is used in a ¹³·___________ way, it can help ¹⁴·___________ us. However, it has a ¹⁵·___________ side at the same time. When it is used competitively, we can be those who are only interested in beating off others. These people may think a ¹⁶·___________ does not deserve anything.

① bright   ② destroy   ③ dark   ④ loser
⑤ positively   ⑥ develope   ⑦ winner   ⑧ healthy

[17 - 22]

Some people argue that corporal punishment should be allowed for teachers to control the students in the classroom. They believe there are some ill-behaved students who do not care about others at all. If they are left to interrupt others without any effective, though violent, intervention in the classroom, the other students will be the victims. However, others believe any kind of corporal punishment should not be permitted in the classroom. Corporal punishment is against the educational philosophy in that it justifies violence. It also invades students' human rights seriously. If students are punished violently, it will affect their mental condition negatively for a long time.

Student A's opinion: Concerning the paragraph above, I think corporal punishment is not a bad idea. Teachers can [17]_____________ trouble students to behave [18]_____________, who can be controlled only by corporal punishment. Speaking of the human rights, I believe the human rights of other good students and teachers should be [19]___________ than those of bad students.

Student B's opinion: Concerning the paragraph above, I object to using corporal punishment in the classroom. Corporal punishment causes [20]___________ of mind as well as [21]___________ damage. Nobody is given a right to hurt others' body or mind. Students' behaviors cannot be corrected through violence. They just [22]___________ to be changed to avoid more punishment.

① illness	② respected	③ physical	④ well
⑤ bad	⑥ pretend	⑦ necessary	⑧ discipline

[23-28]

> One of the controversial issues is whether or not cell phones should be permitted at school. Many people claim that students can use cell phones at school for several reasons. First, parents feel comfortable since they can contact their children anytime in an emergency. For teenagers, a cell phone is the most important tool to interact with others. They can continue to enjoy their private life. Others have different ideas about using cell phones at school. They think it distracts students' interest and attention from studying in classes. Besides, their reliance on using cell phones will get more serious. They point out that more and more teenagers feel irritated without touching cell phones.

Student A's opinion: Concerning the paragraph above, I agree to the idea that cell phones can be used in school. I believe most students know how or when to use cell phones at school without harming others. It is not an item of personal 23. ___________ but one of 24. ___________ in modern society even for students. It is important not to 25. ___________ students' personal lives excessively.

Student B's opinion: Concerning the paragraph above, I am strongly 26. ___________ the use of cell phones at school. Teenagers are already spending too much of their time doing something with cell phones such as games, listening to music, or watching videos. Even though cell phones are tools for 27. ___________ with others, teenagers are, 28. ___________ , less likely to interact with others because of them.

① against   ② necessities   ③ communicating   ④ for

⑤ ironically   ⑥ preference   ⑦ isolating   ⑧ limit

[29 - 34]

> There are reserved seats for the aged and the sick in subway trains. Some people say they are necessary, but others say they are not. People who are for having reserved seats believe it is showing how much we respect elderly people and consider sick people. It will pass down our good traditional custom to future generations. In contrast, others think they are useless. Many young people already ignore the sign on the reserved seats. Yielding seats to others cannot be compelled. It should be a heartfelt behavior. Besides, even though it is for the sick as well as the aged, young sick people are excluded in real life.

Student A's opinion: Concerning the paragraph above, I think the seats should be reserved for the older and the sick. It is impossible for them to ask others for 29. ______________ their seats however sick they feel standing in a subway train. Reserved seats will be like an 30. ___________ in the desert. Having reserved seats is also a good life 31. ___________ to younger generations.

Student B's opinion: Concerning the paragraph above, I don't think it is a good practice to ensure reserved seats. I think it is 32. ___________ to keep the seats 33. ___________ and to force young people not to sit down there. In a 34. ___________ against it, young people often try not to yield their seats in the non-reserved seat areas. Respect should be shown to men of great characters not to just old people.

① reaction	② ridiculous	③ yielding	④ occupied
⑤ oasis	⑥ empty	⑦ action	⑧ lesson

[35 - 40]

> Should the capital punishment remain or not? This is an ethical hot potato. Some are voicing that it should be abolished right away. Even the governmental authority has no right to take someone's life. Besides nobody can judge what is right or wrong perfectly. More than half of people executed are turned out to be innocent after death. This is ridiculous situation. However, others argue it should not be abolished because it has played a critical part not expanding brutal criminals. Without capital punishment, the world we live in would be filled with cruel criminals. It is the only way to make up for the victims of cruel crimes.

Student A's opinion: Concerning the paragraph above, I believe the death penalty should be ended soon. This is the cruelest act to be 35. ____________ by the nation, which is the 36. ____________ of the governmental power. If people are killed by a wrong 37. ____________, who will compensate for their loss of life? Besides, if it has been useful reducing serious offenses, why do we still have so many criminals?

Student B's opinion: Concerning the paragraph above, I support the idea that the capital punishment is necessary. There surely exist 38. ____________ crimes in this world, 39. ____________ humanities. Think about the victims of those cruel crimes. The government should take 40. ____________ action for those brutal behaviors. That's the death penalty.

① committed	② judgement	③ improving	④ destroying
⑤ abuse	⑥ perfect	⑦ unforgivable	⑧ legal

다음의 어휘들을 익히고 Checkups에 기록해 보세요.

489 Intensive Words			Checkups		
			1st	2nd	3rd
402	harsh	[형] 거친, 껄껄한, 조잡한			
403	neglect	[명] 태만, 소홀 [동] 게을리하다, 태만하다			
404	converse	[형] 뒤집은 [명] 반대, 역(逆) [동] 대화하다			
405	deflect	[동] 빗나가게 하다, 굴절시키다			
406	misplace	[동] 잘못 두다			
407	scent	[명] 향기			
408	delicate	[형] 우아한, 고상한, 섬세한, 연약한, 정교한, 세밀한			
409	institute	[명] 연구소, 학원 [동] 설립하다			
410	conceive	[동] 상상하다, 임신하다			
411	bulk	[명] 크기, 용적, 부피			
412	precede	[동] ~ 보다 앞서다			
413	integrate	[동] 통합하다, 조정하다			
414	swallow	[동] 삼키다 [명] 제비			
415	exclusive	[형] 배타적인, 포함하지 않는			
416	pity	[명] 불쌍히 여김, 애석한 일			
417	inhabit	[동] 거주하다			
418	discipline	[명] 훈육, 규율 [동] 훈육하다, 징계하다			
419	supreme	[형] 지고의, 절대의			
420	drag	[동] 끌다, 질질 끌다			
421	conceal	[동] 숨기다, 비밀로 하다			
422	sympathy	[명] 동정심, 연민			
423	faint	[동] 졸도하다 [형] 어렴풋한 [명] 기절			
424	corridor	[명] 복도			
425	substitute	[동] ~를 대신 사용하다			
426	toddle	[동] 아장아장 걷다			
427	adhere	[동] 점착하다, 고수하다			
428	anecdote	[명] 일화, 기담			
429	attribute	[동] ~의 탓으로 하다 [명] 속성			
430	cactus	[명] 선인장			
431	console	[동] 위로하다, 위문하다			

489 Intensive Words		Checkups		
		1st	2nd	3rd
432	defy	[동] 무시하다, 도전하다			
433	eccentric	[형] 별난, 괴벽스러운 [명] 별난 사람			
434	fad	[명] 변덕, 일시적 유행			
435	hazard	[명] 위험, 모험			
436	insomnia	[명] 불면(증)			
437	lethal	[형] 죽음의[에 이르는], 치명적인			
438	mishap	[명] 재난, 사고			
439	oath	[명] 맹세, 서약			
440	prevalent	[형] 일반적으로 행해지는, 유행하는			
441	warrant	[명] 정당한 이유, 보증, 영장 [동] 정당화하다, 보증하다			
442	salute	[동] 경례하다, 인사하다 [명] 경례, 인사			
443	spontaneous	[형] 자발적인, 자연적인			
444	thrust	[동] 밀다, 떠밀다 [명] 밀침, 찌름			
445	ventilate	[동] 공기를 통하다, 환기하다			
446	merge	[동] 녹아들게 하다, 융합하다			
447	strip	[동] 벗기다, 벗다			
448	assert	[동] 단언하다, 주장하다			
449	inflect	[동] (안쪽으로) 구부리다			
450	optimistic	[형] 낙관적인			
451	eradicate	[동] 근절하다, 박멸하다			
452	fragile	[형] 부서지기 쉬운, 깨지기 쉬운, 가냘픈			
453	brilliant	[형] 번쩍이는, 영리한			
454	famine	[명] 기근			
455	adopt	[동] 채택하다, 양자로 삼다			
456	intelligence	[명] 지능			
457	commercial	[명] 광고방송 [형] 상업의, 통상의			
458	statistics	[명] 통계			
459	derive	[동] 파생하다, 비롯되다			
460	steep	[형] 험준한, 가파른			
461	prey	[명] 먹이			

	489 Intensive Words		Checkups		
			1st	2nd	3rd
462	disciple	[명] 제자			
463	miserable	[형] 비참한, 딱한			
464	brook	[명] 시내, 실개천			
465	torrent	[명] 급류, 억수(~s)			
466	antipathy	[명] 반감			
467	refund	[명] 반환(물) [동] 반환하다			
468	cemetery	[명] 공동묘지			
469	illuminate	[동] 조명하다, 비추다			
470	crawl	[동] 기다, 포복하다			
471	adjacent	[형] 접근한, 인접한			
472	apprehend	[동] 체포하다, 파악하다			
473	authentic	[형] 진짜의, 믿을만한			
474	celebrity	[명] 유명인, 명성			
475	conspicuous	[형] 눈에 띄는			
476	depict	[동] 그리다, 묘사하다			
477	elaborate	[형] 정교한, 공들인 [동] 애써 만들다			
478	feasible	[형] 실행할 수 있는, 알맞은			
479	hypothesis	[명] 가설, 가정			
480	insulate	[동] 절연하다, 단열하다			
481	lofty	[형] 우뚝[높이] 솟은, 당당한			
482	momentous	[형] 중요한, 중대한			
483	obscure	[형] 분명치 않은, 흐린, 무명의			
484	quench	[동] 불을 끄다, 소멸시키다			
485	weird	[형] 기묘한, 이상한, 불가사의한			
486	sanction	[명] 인가, 제재, 처벌 [동] 인가하다			
487	sprout	[명] 싹 [동] 싹트다			
488	tilt	[명] 경사, 기울기 [동] 기울이다			
489	verge	[명] 테두리, 가장자리			

설명하고 있는 알맞은 의미의 단어를 퍼즐안에 넣어 봅시다.

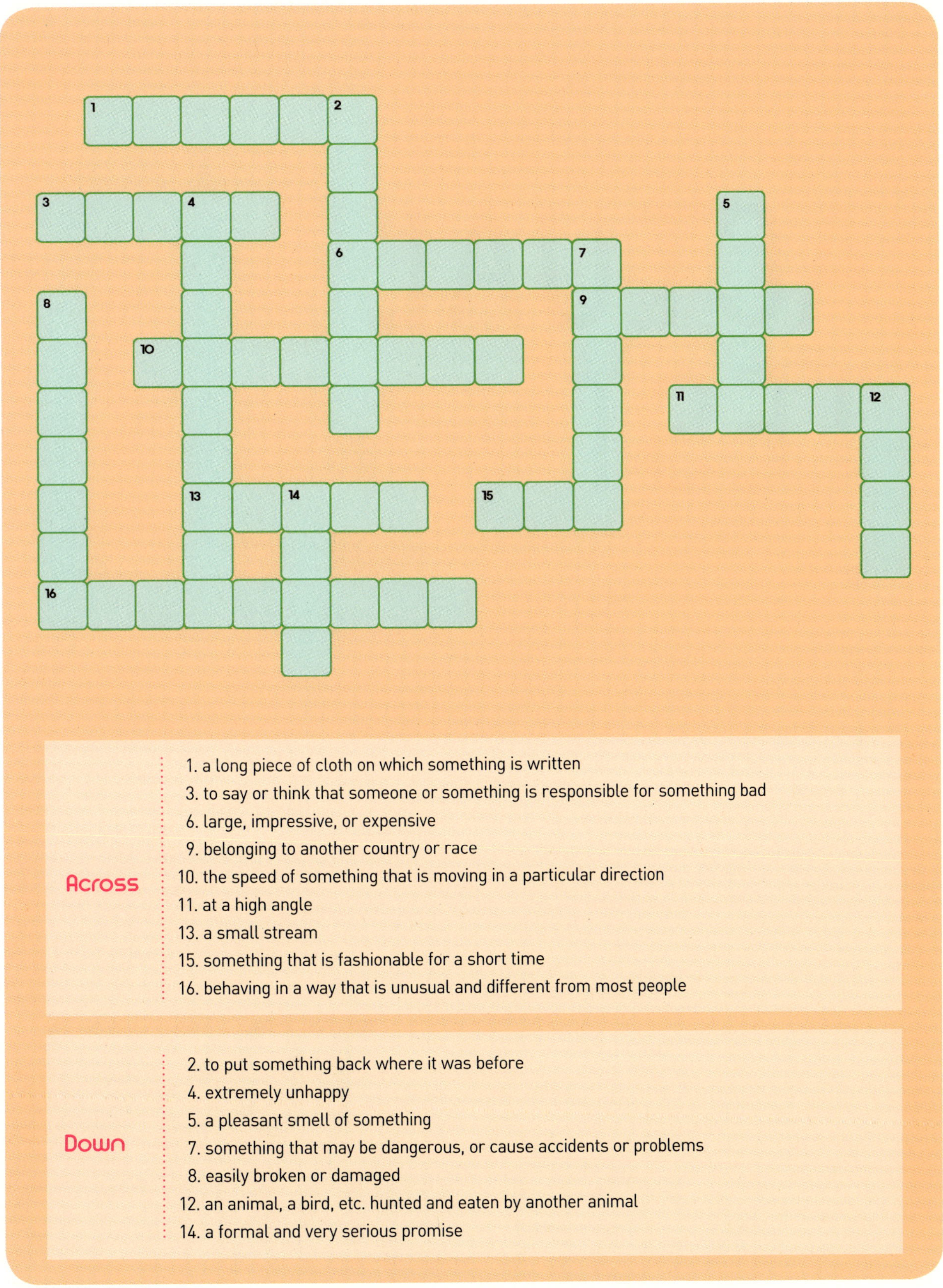

Across

1. a long piece of cloth on which something is written
3. to say or think that someone or something is responsible for something bad
6. large, impressive, or expensive
9. belonging to another country or race
10. the speed of something that is moving in a particular direction
11. at a high angle
13. a small stream
15. something that is fashionable for a short time
16. behaving in a way that is unusual and different from most people

Down

2. to put something back where it was before
4. extremely unhappy
5. a pleasant smell of something
7. something that may be dangerous, or cause accidents or problems
8. easily broken or damaged
12. an animal, a bird, etc. hunted and eaten by another animal
14. a formal and very serious promise

ACTUAL TEST

TOSEL
HIGH JUNIOR

SECTION I
LISTENING AND SPEAKING

PART A. [Listen and Respond : 10 Questions]
PART B. [Listen and Retell : 10 Questions]
PART C. [Listen and Predict : 5 Questions]
PART D. [Listen and Speak : 5 Questions]

SECTION II
READING AND WRITING

PART A. [Error Recognition : 5 Questions]
PART B. [Sentence Completion : 5 Questions]
PART C. [Reading and Logical Thinking : 5 Questions]
PART D. [Reading and Retelling : 15 Questions]
PART E. [Read and Write : 10 Questions]

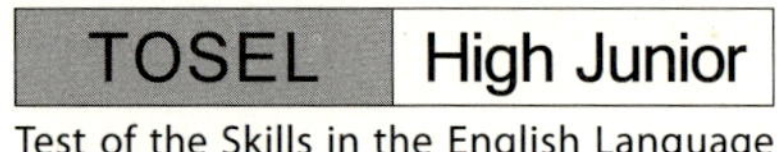

해설지 P.44

SECTION I

LISTENING AND SPEAKING

PART A. [Listen and Respond : 10 Questions]

PART B. [Listen and Retell : 10 Questions]

PART C. [Listen and Predict : 5 Questions]

PART D. [Listen and Speak : 5 Questions]

CD2 - Track 49

★ 161쪽에 있는 OMR 카드에 답을 쓰세요.

PART A. Listen and Respond

Directions: *In this part of the test, you will hear a short conversation. Then you will hear four possible answer choices. Each conversation and answer choices will only be played one time. Listen carefully and choose the most suitable response to the last statement. Then fill in the corresponding space on your answer sheet.*

1. Mark your answer on your answer sheet.

2. Mark your answer on your answer sheet.

3. Mark your answer on your answer sheet.

4. Mark your answer on your answer sheet.

5. Mark your answer on your answer sheet.

6. Mark your answer on your answer sheet.

7. Mark your answer on your answer sheet.

8. Mark your answer on your answer sheet.

9. Mark your answer on your answer sheet.

10. Mark your answer on your answer sheet.

PART B. Listen and Retell

Directions: *In this part of the test, you will hear a short conversation. Each conversation will be followed by a question. The conversations are not in print and will only be played one time. Listen carefully to each conversation and answer the questions in your test booklet. Then fill in the corresponding space on your answer sheet.*

11. What are they talking about?

    (A) a family tree

    (B) a future career

    (C) a favorite recipe

    (D) a current job

13. What is the boy doing?

    (A) watching TV

    (B) using his computer

    (C) sleeping in bed

    (D) making his bed

12. Why does the man call?

    (A) to change the appointment

    (B) to confirm the appointment

    (C) to make an appointment

    (D) to keep the appointment

14. What will the man use for his homework?

    (A) a laptop computer

    (B) fingers

    (C) a calculator

    (D) a cell phone

15. How is the weather now?

(A) sunny

(B) rainy

(C) hot

(D) cold

16. What is the man looking for?

(A) a DVD

(B) a book

(C) a CD

(D) a newspaper

17. Why does the woman give up the report?

(A) It was due two days ago.

(B) She doesn't have much time.

(C) She is busy this Friday.

(D) The report has a difficult topic.

18. What style does the woman want?

(A) straight hair

(B) curly hair

(C) short hair with bang

(D) ponny tail

19. What will the boy do next?

(A) go to school

(B) take a class

(C) go to the hospital

(D) help his mom

20. What will the woman do?

(A) take an exam

(B) go back home

(C) get her bag

(D) have lunch

PART C. Listen and Predict

Directions: *In this part of the test, you will hear short talks. The talks are not in print and will only be played one time. Listen carefully to each talk and answer the following questions in your test booklet. Then fill in the corresponding space on your answer sheet.*

21. What will Brian probably say to the team members?
    (A) You will get used to it.
    (B) You are in good hands.
    (C) Let's just call it a day.
    (D) Let's enjoy every minute of it.

22. What will Jamie probably say to Bill?
    (A) Break a leg!
    (B) I want you to write up the report for me.
    (C) Please wait. Let me give it some thoughts.
    (D) I am afraid I can't. I have so much work.

23. What will Julia probably say to Yuna?
    (A) That is so pathetic!
    (B) I will leave the rest up to your imagination.
    (C) I didn't expect to see you here. It's a small world.
    (D) Things are so expensive. Go to another shop.

24. What will Peter ask the girl?
    (A) Can you give me a call?
    (B) Is everybody here?
    (C) Is this seat taken?
    (D) Can you give me a ride?

25. What will Alice most likely say to Lisa?
    (A) That's just ridiculous.
    (B) I feel the same way.
    (C) I'd like to make a toast.
    (D) Please keep it to yourself.

PART D. Listen and Speak

Directions: *In this part of the test, you will hear a series of short conversations. The conversations are not in print and will only be played one time. Listen carefully to each conversation. After you hear each conversation, read the four choices in your test booklet and choose the best response to follow the last statement or question in the conversation. Then fill in the corresponding space on your answer sheet.*

26. What will the man say next?
    (A) My mouth is watering.
    (B) Japanese food is simple and clean.
    (C) You are to blame for it.
    (D) I am allergic to raw fish.

27. What will the man say next?
    (A) Don't rush me. I am not ready.
    (B) The price is out of our budget.
    (C) What a shame!
    (D) That's a good point.

28. What will the man say next?
    (A) She has gone too far.
    (B) I'd like give it a try.
    (C) It is cold this morning, isn't it?
    (D) It makes me feel better.

29. What will the man say next?
    (A) He has a baby face.
    (B) I'm worried for nothing.
    (C) It is three years since I came here.
    (D) Honestly, I taught myself.

30. What will the woman say next?
    (A) I guess it runs in your family.
    (B) What a wonderful world!
    (C) What do you have in mind?
    (D) We made it.

SECTION II

READING AND WRITING

PART A. [Error Recognition : 5 Questions]

PART B. [Sentence Completion : 5 Questions]

PART C. [Reading and Logical Thinking : 5 Questions]

PART D. [Reading and Retelling : 15 Questions]

PART E. [Read and Write : 10 Questions]

PART A. Error Recognition

Directions: *In this part of the test, you will read short selections with four underlined segments. Choose the segment that contains a word or phrase that is INCORRECT. Fill in the corresponding space on your answer sheet.*

1. In order to communicate <u>effective,</u> you must be <u>aware</u> of the forms <u>that</u> the academic audience
                (A)   (B)   (C)
<u>expects.</u>
(D)

2. <u>Almost</u> American Indians are <u>identical</u> in values, beliefs, and lifestyles to people <u>who</u> have come
  (A)   (B)   (C)
to North America <u>from</u> other countries.
       (D)

3. The <u>following</u> exercises <u>present</u> a summary of ways <u>which</u> the context of reading can <u>give</u> clues
   (A)   (B)   (C)   (D)
to the meanings of new vocabulary items.

4. <u>Experts</u> in psychology believe <u>that</u> for many people, wealth <u>symbolizing</u> their strength and their
  (A)   (B)   (C)
<u>influence</u> in the society.
   (D)

5. Some theories of ancient astronomy <u>seems</u> even more <u>fascinating</u> than <u>those</u> that have been
                (A)   (B)   (C)
<u>proven</u> about the Indians.
(D)

PART B. Sentence Completion

Directions: *In this part of the test, each question consists of a sentence which contains one blank space and four choices marked (A), (B), (C), and (D). Each of the choices consists of words that can be used to fill in the blank in the sentence. Choose the one that best fits the intended meaning of the sentence. Then, on your answer sheet, find the number of the question and fill in the space that corresponds to the letter of the answer you have chosen.*

6. Some celebrities donate money to Non-Governmental Organizations _______________ the world peace.

  (A) seek
  (B) seeking
  (C) sought
  (D) be sought

7. A system of checks and balances in the bank prevents one department of the government _______________ too powerful.

  (A) to become
  (B) becoming
  (C) become
  (D) from becoming

8. Psychologists examine the world of the unconscious, _______________ to be important symbols.

   (A) which language they believe
   (B) they believe its language
   (C) whose language they believe
   (D) they believe what language

9. Michael has _______________ to his father who has blue eyes and blond hair.

   (A) very stronger resemblance
   (B) a much stronger resemblance
   (C) strongly resembles
   (D) resemble much stronger

10. The United Nations has both an opportunity and an obligation _______________.
   (A) to help defeat deadly diseases
   (B) help defeating deadly diseases
   (C) helping to defeat diseases deadly
   (D) helped defeat diseases deadly

Part C. Reading and Logical Thinking

Directions: *In this part of the test, you will read short selections. Each selection contains an underlined segment indicating missing word(s). Choose the word(s) that most logically fit(s) the selection from the answer choices. Fill in the corresponding space on your answer sheet.*

11.

> Recent parents try to give more __________ to their children by touching and cuddling them sufficiently.

(A) tactile stimulus

(B) taste organs

(C) audible books

(D) visual configuration

12.

> Some of modern families are being transformed into __________ families by adopting children and moving in together with the parents.

(A) nuclear

(B) shortened

(C) extended

(D) single-parent

13.

> People living in North America are eager to move out of a __________ such as New York, Los Angeles, and Toronto.

(A) suburban life
(B) busy urban area
(C) relaxing atmosphere
(D) tranquility in the countryside

14.

> The result of the summit talk gives tremendously positive influence on the world economy, which will __________ help the recovery from the financial crisis.

(A) barely
(B) scarcely
(C) vastly
(D) merely

15.

> __________ , also referred to as periodic employment, means the state of unemployment dependent upon the weather and seasons.

(A) Recruitment strategy
(B) Unfair dismissal
(C) Seasonal unemployment
(D) Profession guide

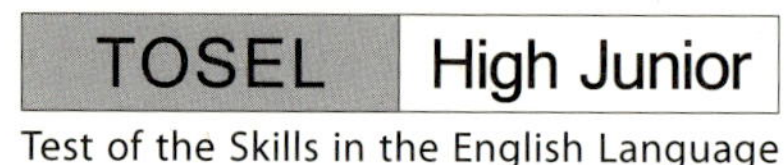

Part D. Reading and Retelling

Directions: *In this part of the test, you will read longer passages. Choose the best answer from four choices to answer the questions following each passage. Then fill in the corresponding space on your answer sheet.*

[16]

Mother Teresa was a catholic nun with the Indian citizenship. Her life was literally devoted to ministering to the poor and the sick as well as orphans for about 45 years until the moment of her death. She operated over 600 missions in more than 100 countries. They included hospitals, homes for AIDS patients, and orphan schools. She was awarded the Nobel Peace Prize in 1979. Despite her great accomplishments, some people give her some criticism about her philosophy about suffering. She thought that suffering was a way to get closer to her god, Jesus Christ. Her idea is still controversial, but it has no doubt that she was one of the greatest people helping the socially-disadvantaged.

16. What is NOT true about Mother Teresa?

  (A) She was an Indian woman.

  (B) She spent about 45 years in helping the disadvantaged.

  (C) Nobody has a doubt about her philosophy about suffering.

  (D) She operated hospitals, homes for AIDS patients, and schools for orphans.

[17]

A tsunami is a gigantic water wave with immense volume of water and the high energy. It can often result from an earthquake, volcanic eruptions, and underwater explosions. The wave is often higher than 100 meters. The speed of the wave ranges from 600 to 800 kilometers per hour. About 80% of tsunamis occur in the Pacific Ocean, which sometimes give devastating damage to areas such as the east coast of Japan and the west coast of North America. To keep the costal region from being destroyed by tsunamis, people put natural barriers such as mangroves, coral reefs, and forests along the coastline, which are proved to cause less damage in the areas.

17. What do people do to minimize the damage of tsunamis?

  (A) keep away from the coastline

  (B) build natural barriers

  (C) destroy the forest

  (D) leave the area

[18-19]

A doughnut is a typical American snack. It is a small round cake fried in oil, typically shaped into a ring. It is usually sweet and deep-fried from flour dough. It sometimes contains filling like cream cheese without a hole in the middle. In history, it is known to have been invented by the Dutch immigrants from the Netherlands in the United States. The name, doughnut is the Dutch name meaning "oily cake." The first doughnut machine was invented in 1920, in New York City, by a man named Adolph Levitt, a refugee from Russia. Levitt's doughnut machine was a big hit, which led to the increasing popularity of doughnuts. In 1934, at the World's Fair in Chicago, doughnut was chosen as "the food of the Century of Progress." Watching the machine automatically make doughnuts, people must have felt something futuristic. Doughnuts have become the American mainstream food as snacks. Today, in the United States alone, over 10 billion doughnuts are made every year.

18. What is the passage about?
    (A) nutrition facts of doughnuts
    (B) how doughnuts are made
    (C) life of Russian refugees in America
    (D) history of American doughnuts

19. Which is NOT inferred in the passage?
    (A) The doughnut machine was imported from the Netherlands.
    (B) Some doughnuts have filling inside the dough.
    (C) Adolph Levitt came from Russia.
    (D) Many American people enjoy doughnuts for snacks.

[20-21]

Oktoberfest, which means 'October Festival,' is one of the most famous events with more than 5 million people attending. Oktoberfest is held annually for more than two weeks in Munich, Germany. It runs from late September to the first weekend in October. The highlight of the Oktoberfest is the Costume and Riflemen's Parade. This colorful display of German culture takes place in the morning on the first Sunday of Oktoberfest. There are more than 30 beer tents at Oktoberfest, and you can make a reservation for a table in advance by phone, mail, or fax. Oktoberfest nowadays starts in September for practical reasons. The weather in Germany is better in September, and the nights are not so chilly. Historically, the last Oktoberfest weekend was always celebrated in October, and this tradition continues until today. Oktoberfest is more than drinking beer. It includes fun rides, ferris wheels, roller coasters, music, and parades to enjoy for the young as well as the old. People come here with their kids. Children are also welcome in the beer tents, although kids under the age of six must leave the tents by 8 p.m. The best time for children to visit Oktoberfest is on weekdays before 5 p.m.

20. What is the passage about?
    (A) the reasons kids are not allowed for Oktoberfest
    (B) the importance of reservation for Oktoberfest in advance
    (C) kinds of beers served in Oktoberfest
    (D) Oktoberfest, one of the most famous German festivals

21. What is NOT true about Oktoberfest?
    (A) The festival is held every two years.
    (B) You can reserve a table by fax.
    (C) Children can enjoy roller coasters.
    (D) Children are allowed to come in the beer tent.

[22-23]

A gesture is a typical component of spoken languages. However, you will have a tremendous problem if you have to communicate with people only by using gestures. A sign language is a language which uses visually transmitted sign patterns, instead of sound patterns, to convey meaning. It simultaneously combines hand shapes and movement of the hands or body and facial expressions to express a speaker's thoughts. Sign languages develop where a community of deaf people exists. Hundreds of sign languages are in use around the world. Sign languages have their own sign patterns to describe certain things, which means they are overall not dependent on written languages except for fingerspelling. Manual alphabets, also called fingerspelling, are used mostly for specialized vocabulary borrowed from written languages. For example, when a deaf person describes 'love' with sign language, he or she releases his or her thumb, index finger, and pinkie from a fist instead of using fingerspelling for L, O, V, and E.

22. What is fingerspelling used for?
   (A) sign patterns and sound patterns
   (B) specialized vocabulary from written languages
   (C) movements of the hands or body
   (D) facial expression to express thoughts

23. What is NOT true about sign language?
   (A) It uses sound patterns to convey meaning.
   (B) Fingerspelling is dependent on written languages.
   (C) It is usually for deaf people.
   (D) Fingerspelling means making the shape of each letter of the word.

[24-25]

Psychologists show that a person's birth order has a direct link with his or her personality. Parents understand their children by their birth order, and it can be helpful to design their children's future. According to the research, the first born child is more likely to lead the group and do things actively. Believe it or not, the first born children in the world share similar personality traits. The first born child is the child with the most attention directed at him or her. There are two typical types of the first born children, compliant and aggressive. The first born children who are compliant tend to please people, feel responsible for their siblings, and play a role as a favorable leader. The first born children who have aggressive traits are likely to make things perfect, have things under control, and dominate activities of a group. They usually want things their way. In spite of this, the first born children still have greater level of confidence, patience, and concentration. They are very well organized and focused. Therefore, they usually choose careers that require a high degree of precision such as law, medicine, computer programming, or architecture. They often manage and administer a company as a boss.

24. What is the passage about?
    (A) Personality traits of the first born children
    (B) The importance of choosing a future job
    (C) How birth order affects the patience of children
    (D) The role of parents for the first born children

25. What is NOT true about the first born children?
    (A) They tend to be a leader of a group.
    (B) Some of them have aggressive personality.
    (C) They suffer from the lack of confidence.
    (D) They have a good sense of patience.

[26-27]

Almost thirty years ago, researchers at Harvard University announced a connection between coffee consumption and cancer. Even though the result proved to be wrongly concluded, coffee has had an image of being unhealthy since then. However, coffee in fact is not to blame for cancer. Coffee contains no fat and tiny amount of carbohydrate and protein. Caffeine in coffee is a brain stimulant and can lead to temporary improvements in awareness. According to the facts that have turned out until recently, coffee can help prevent and treat certain illnesses and diseases such as Alzheimer's disease, diabetes, and skin cancer. Coffee may reduce the risk of developing gallstones, discourage the development of colon cancer, improve cognitive function, reduce the risk of liver damage in people at high risk for liver disease, and reduce the risk of Parkinson's disease. Coffee has also been shown to improve endurance in long-duration physical activities. Coffee is actually one of the healthiest beverages billions of people consume regularly.

26. What is the passage about?
    (A) the healthy benefits from drinking coffee
    (B) the negative influence of coffee on cancer
    (C) how caffeine is consumed inside the body
    (D) how to fight against fat-related diseases

27. How does caffeine work?
    (A) provides carbohydrate and protein
    (B) causes diabetes
    (C) stimulates the brain
    (D) relieves the muscles

[28-29]

Living green is a hot issue recently for many people, which makes them think about having a garden in their backyard. They believe they can easily grow vegetables for their daily diet and plants for decorating their house. However, gardening takes a lot of energy and effort. When people don't have enough information about the plants and farming, they experience severe difficulty in cultivating vegetables and taking care of plants. First of all, people need to get some information about what they want to grow, when to sow seeds, and when to harvest. With the information fully understood, people should get ready to give their labor to the garden. Watering the garden on a regular basis is the most important thing required for the growth of the vegetables and plants. Once in a while, people also need to sort out the rest to help promising ones grow well. Last but not least, you should take care of the plants and vegetables with affection and try to cultivate them with care.

28. What is the passage about?
    (A) how to keep the garden successfully
    (B) the benefits of living green
    (C) the mystery of having a garden
    (D) how to hire a good gardener

29. What is NOT required for having a good garden?
    (A) affection
    (B) labor
    (C) information
    (D) daily diet

[30]

The Population of Cities

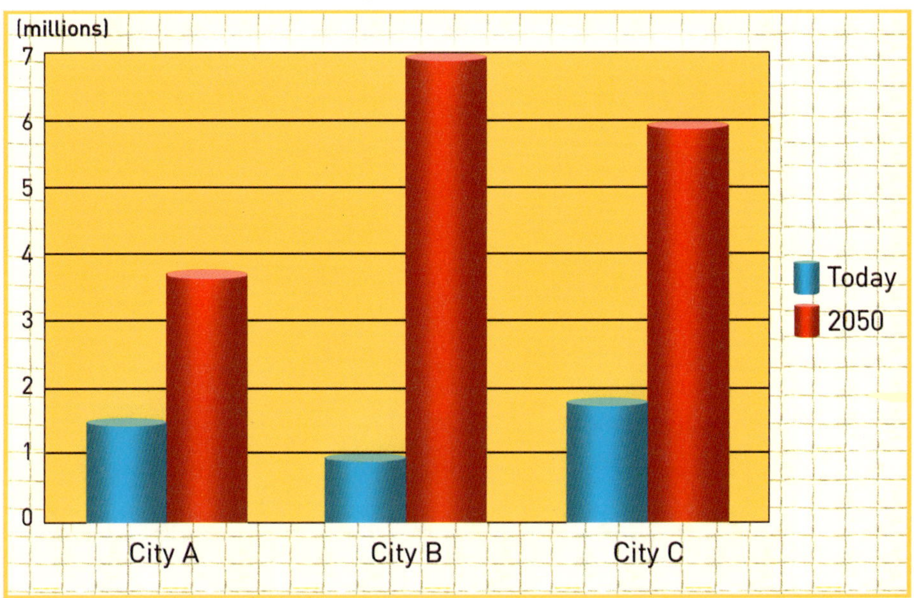

30. What can be inferred from the chart?

    (A) The population of City A will reach 5 million.

    (B) The population will increase until 2050 in three cities.

    (C) The population of City B will double by 2050.

    (D) City C will show the biggest increase between now and 2050.

Part E. Read and Write

Directions: *In this part of the test, you will read two different passages. From Questions 31 to 34, read the passage and complete the following summarized sentences by choosing the most suitable words from the given box. From Questions 35 to 40, read the passage and complete the two opposite arguments on the passage by choosing the most suitable words from the given box. Then fill in the corresponding space on your answer sheet.*

[31-34]

As the world is getting closer, the necessity of international language is rising recently. It helps people and nations understand each culture better and lets them communicate in an accurate way. When two countries make an agreement or a treaty about economy, the difference in each language may have misunderstandings about a certain word, which will lead to some conflicts between the two countries. In addition, wrongly-translated documents can also damage the financial status of trading companies from different countries.

Summary: The international language is 31._______ for the better understanding of each culture and the 32._______ of the communication. Language difference can cause 33._______ and conflicts between two countries. Similarly, trading companies can experience financial damage due to the documents translated in a 34._______ way.

① mistaken	② economy	③ misunderstandings	④ translation
⑤ financial	⑥ necessary	⑦ accuracy	⑧ documents

[35-40]

> Recently in the United States, tiger moms are controversial issue. Tiger moms are known to completely control the life of their children. They force their children to study very late for the exams. They strongly discourage their children from playing outside, having sleepovers, and taking part in school plays. They believe that they are obliged to guide their children. Many of these mothers in fact have made their children very successful in society. However, some of the people who are told about the way tiger moms treat their children think it is a kind of abuse and oppose the idea. They think moms should treat their children in a friendly way, which will affect the mental development of their children as an individual of society. They also think that tiger moms may suppress the natural needs of their children, ultimately damaging psychological process of thinking.

Student A's opinion: Concerning the paragraph above, I believe that mothers should be 35. __________ to help their children behave in an acceptable way. Children don't know exactly what to do now for their future. Mothers are 36. ____________ to guide them in the way, which will ensure their 37. ___________ life eventually.

Student B's opinion: Concerning the paragraph above, I don't think that mothers should hold all the 38. _____________ over their children. Children have their own rights to grow as a(an) 39. _____________ individual in the society. Despite the needs of parental 40. _____________ , parents ought not to be a coordinator but to be an assistant.

① guidance	② independent	③ authority	④ controversy
⑤ friendly	⑥ strict	⑦ successful	⑧ obliged

This is the end of the TOSEL High Junior ACTUAL TEST. Thank you.

국제영어능력인증시험 (TOSEL)

HIGH JUNIOR

한글이름

감독 확인란

수 험 번 호

(1)

(2)

응시생 유의사항

1. 수험번호 및 답안은 컴퓨터용 사인펜을 사용해야 하며, 〈보기〉와 같이 표기하세요.
   〈보기〉 바른 표기 : ● 틀린 표기 : ⊘ ⊗ ◑ ⊙
2. 수험번호(1)에는 아라비아 숫자로 쓰고, (2)에는 해당란에 ● 표기하세요.
3. 답안 수정은 수정 테이프로만 합니다.
4. 수험번호 및 답안 작성란 이외의 여백에 낙서를 하지 마시기 바랍니다.
   이로 인한 불이익은 수험자 본인 책임입니다.
5. 마킹오류로 채점 불가능한 답안은 0점 처리되오니, 이점 유의하시기 바랍니다.

SECTION I

문항	A B C D	문항	A B C D	문항	A B C D	문항	A B C D
1	A B C D	16	A B C D	1	A B C D	16	A B C D
2	A B C D	17	A B C D	2	A B C D	17	A B C D
3	A B C D	18	A B C D	3	A B C D	18	A B C D
4	A B C D	19	A B C D	4	A B C D	19	A B C D
5	A B C D	20	A B C D	5	A B C D	20	A B C D
6	A B C D	21	A B C D	6	A B C D	21	A B C D
7	A B C D	22	A B C D	7	A B C D	22	A B C D
8	A B C D	23	A B C D	8	A B C D	23	A B C D
9	A B C D	24	A B C D	9	A B C D	24	A B C D
10	A B C D	25	A B C D	10	A B C D	25	A B C D
11	A B C D	26	A B C D	11	A B C D	26	A B C D
12	A B C D	27	A B C D	12	A B C D	27	A B C D
13	A B C D	28	A B C D	13	A B C D	28	A B C D
14	A B C D	29	A B C D	14	A B C D	29	A B C D
15	A B C D	30	A B C D	15	A B C D	30	A B C D

SECTION II

문항	1 2 3 4 5 6 7 8
31	1 2 3 4 5 6 7 8
32	1 2 3 4 5 6 7 8
33	1 2 3 4 5 6 7 8
34	1 2 3 4 5 6 7 8
35	1 2 3 4 5 6 7 8
36	1 2 3 4 5 6 7 8
37	1 2 3 4 5 6 7 8
38	1 2 3 4 5 6 7 8
39	1 2 3 4 5 6 7 8
40	1 2 3 4 5 6 7 8

국제 토셀 위원회

Memo

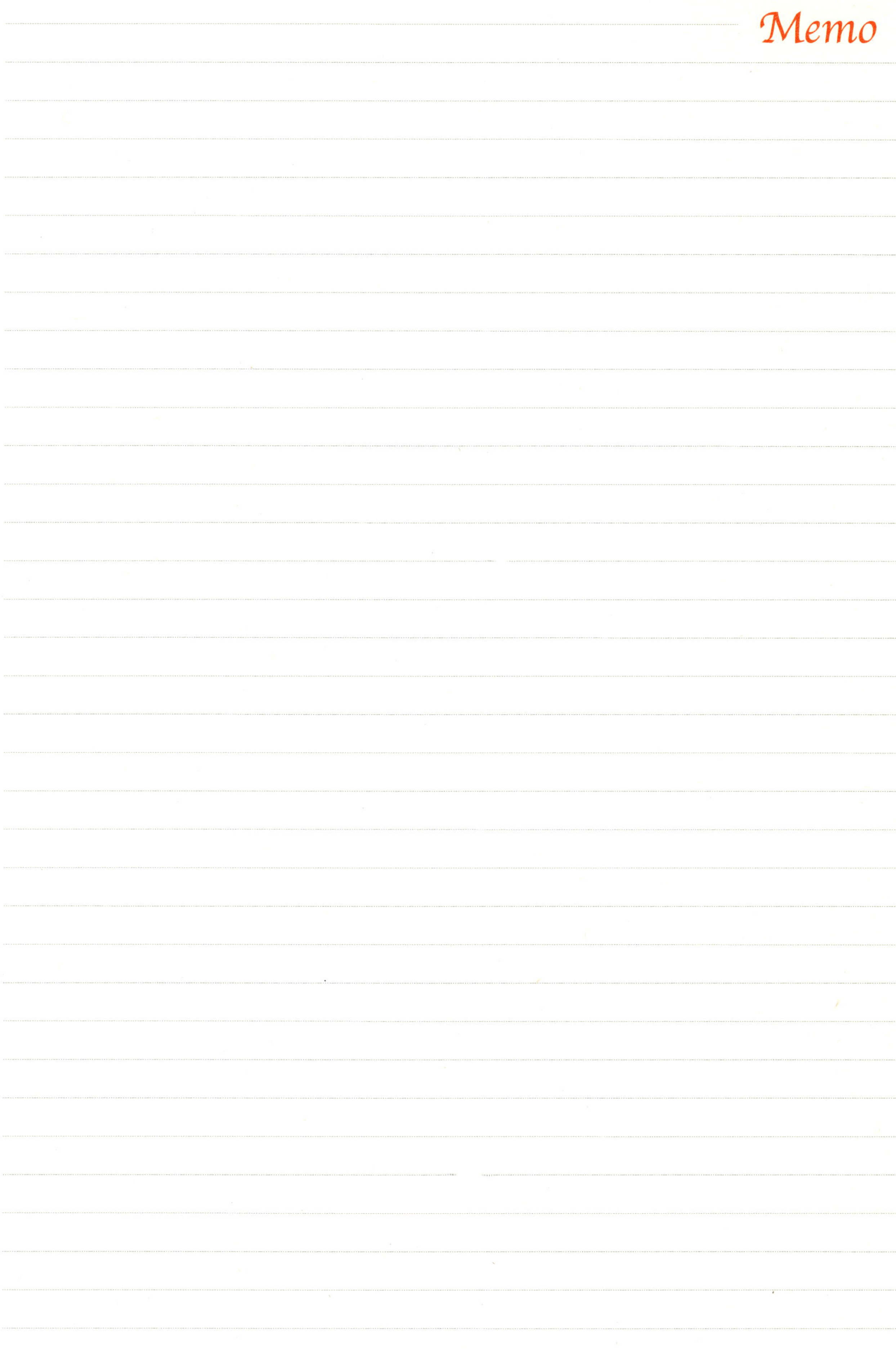

Memo

EBS가 주관하는 TOSEL®
국제토셀위원회 공식 추천 교재

TOSEL UP+
HIGH JUNIOR

심화편

Test of the Skills in the English Language

정답 및 해설

강남준 감수 / 김희영 이지혜 전민호 최부근 저

YEAMOONSA 예문사   BIEN HOUSE

TOSEL HIGH JUNIOR
>> SECTION I

SECTION I LISTENING AND SPEAKING

PART A. Listen and Respond

01. [B]	02. [A]	03. [D]	04. [D]	05. [D]
06. [A]	07. [B]	08. [B]	09. [A]	10. [B]
11. [A]	12. [C]	13. [A]	14. [B]	15. [B]
16. [D]	17. [A]	18. [C]	19. [A]	20. [A]
21. [B]	22. [A]	23. [C]	24. [C]	25. [B]
26. [D]	27. [A]	28. [B]	29. [A]	30. [D]
31. [C]	32. [A]	33. [B]	34. [C]	35. [C]
36. [B]	37. [C]	38. [D]	39. [A]	40. [B]

1 **W:** Look who's here! Isn't it you, Steve?
이게 누구야! 너 Steve 아니니?

M: Sarah. How have you been?
Sarah. 어떻게 지냈니?

W: _______________________

(A) Sure. I cannot forget it.
물론이야. 난 그것을 잊을 수 없어.

(B) Not too bad. I have so much to tell you.
그럭저럭 나쁘진 않았어. 네게 할 말이 많아.

(C) I feel better. Thanks for your concern.
몸이 나아졌어. 관심 가져줘서 고마워.

(D) Sorry. Have we met somewhere before?
미안합니다. 우리가 전에 어디선가 만난 적 있나요?

해설 오랜만에 우연히 친구를 만난 상황입니다. 남자가 안부를 묻고 있으므로 여자는 그 동안 어땠는지를 말해주어야 합니다.

★ **Not too bad.** : (안부를 묻는 말에 대한 대답으로) 나쁘진 않았어. 그저 견딜 만해. / **concern** 관심

2 **M:** What movie do you want to watch?
어떤 영화를 보고 싶으세요?

W: Anything but a horror movie.
공포 영화 말고 아무 거나요.

M: _______________________

(A) But horror is my favorite genre.
하지만 공포 영화는 내가 가장 좋아하는 장르랍니다.

(B) But I can't sleep after watching a horror movie.
하지만 공포 영화를 보면 나는 잠을 잘 수가 없어요.

(C) Great. Horror is best when it's summer.
좋아요. 여름에는 공포 영화가 최고죠.

(D) I didn't know you like scary movies.
당신이 무서운 영화를 좋아하는 줄 몰랐어요.

해설 여자가 공포 영화에 대한 거부감을 표현했으므로 남자도 공포 영화에 대한 자신의 생각을 말하여 화제에 호응하는 것이 자연스럽습니다. (B)는 남자의 말이 여자와 같은 의견이 되는 상황에서 But으로 시작하므로 어색합니다. (C)는 여자가 공포 영화를 보자고 제안하는 상황이라면 가능한 대답입니다.

★ **horror movie** 공포 영화 / **scary** 무서운

3 **W:** May I help you?
도와 드릴까요?

M: Would it be okay if I just look around?
그냥 둘러봐도 괜찮겠습니까?

W: _______________________

(A) Don't forget to pay for it, OK?
돈을 지불하는 것을 잊지 마세요, 아셨죠?

(B) Our store is too crowded with shoppers.
우리 가게는 손님들로 너무 붐빕니다.

(C) Of course. Let's take a look together.
물론이죠. 함께 봅시다.

(D) Do as you please. Take your time.
좋으실 대로 하세요. 천천히 보세요.

해설 남자의 말은 상점에서 점원의 방해를 받지 않고 혼자서 물건을 둘러보기 원한다는 뜻입니다. 친절한 점원이라면 어떻게 대답할지 생각해 봅시다. (C)는 손님이 혼자서 둘러보겠다는 의미로 말하는데 점원이 함께 보자고 응답하고 있으니 답이 될 수 없습니다.

★ **crowded** 붐비는 / **take a look** 보다 / **as you please** 좋으실 대로, 마음껏 / **take one's time** 천천히 하다. 늑장을 부리다 / **look around** 주변을 둘러보다. (가게에서 물건을 사지 않고) 둘러보다. 구경만하다

4 **M:** Would you like to try some raw fish?
생선회를 좀 드시겠어요?

W: Well, I've never eaten anything like that.
글쎄요, 나는 지금까지 그런 것을 먹어본 적이 없어요.

M: _______________________

(A) You're an excellent chef.
당신은 뛰어난 요리사군요.

(B) I cooked it. I'm glad you liked it.
내가 요리했어요. 당신이 좋아하시니 기쁩니다.

(C) I think you don't like it.
나는 당신이 그것을 싫어한다고 생각합니다.

(D) Why not try it? You'll love it.
한번 시식해보세요. 좋아하게 되실 거예요.

해설 생선회를 권하자 여자가 먹어본 적이 없다며 망설이는 상황입니다. 무엇이라고 말할 지 생각해 봅시다.

★ **raw** 날 것의 / **raw fish** 생선회 / **excellent** 뛰어난 / **chef** 요리사 / **Why not ~?** (상대방에게 제안, 권유할 때) ~하는 게 어때요? / **try** 시험 삼아 먹어보다

5 **W:** Could you tell me the way to the City Hall?
시청까지 가는 길을 가르쳐 주시겠어요?

   M: How lucky you are! I'm going there. You can go with me.
운이 좋으시네요! 나도 거기에 가는 중입니다. 저와 함께 가시죠.

   W: _______________________

(A) I agree. It is very far from here.
동의합니다. 그곳은 여기서 아주 멀어요.

(B) Okay. You can use my cell phone.
좋아요. 내 휴대전화를 이용하셔도 됩니다.

(C) I guess we are too late.
내 생각에 우리는 너무 늦은 것 같아요.

(D) That's very kind of you. Thank you.
친절하시군요. 감사합니다.

해설 시청으로 가는 길을 묻는 여자에게 남자가 그곳까지 동행해 주겠다고 말하고 있는 상황입니다. 여자는 감사해야 할 것입니다.

★ That's very kind of you. 친절하시군요.

6 **M:** How about studying together at the library?
도서관에서 함께 공부하는 것 어때?

   W: All right. What time shall we make it?
좋아. 몇 시에 만날까?

   M: _______________________

(A) Let's make it at three o'clock.
3시 정각에 만나자.

(B) Sorry, I am not ready to make it yet.
미안해, 나는 아직 그것을 만들 준비가 되지 않았어.

(C) It takes about two hours to make it.
그것을 만드는 데 약 2시간이 걸려.

(D) Okay. I will be waiting there.
좋아. 거기에서 기다릴게.

해설 'What time shall we make it?(몇 시에 만날까?, 몇 시로 정할까?)'라는 표현의 의미를 오해하지 않도록 조심하세요. 남자는 희망하는 약속시간을 말해야 합니다.

★ make it 정한 시간에 맞춰 대다

7 **W:** How do you like this skirt?
이 치마 어때요?

   M: Wow, that skirt looks great with your jacket.
와, 그 치마는 당신 재킷과 정말 잘 어울려요.

   W: _______________________

(A) Then, what will you choose?
그러면, 당신은 무엇을 고를 거예요?

(B) It's very nice of you to say so.
그렇게 말해주셔서 고맙습니다.

(C) I just bought a new coat.
방금 새 코트를 샀어요.

(D) Thanks for your concern.
당신의 관심에 감사드립니다.

해설 남자가 여자의 치마를 칭찬해 주었으므로 여자는 감사의 말을 하는 것이 좋겠습니다.

★ How do you like ~? (소감이나 느낌을 묻는 말) ~에 대하여 어떻게 생각하세요? / It's very nice of you to ~ (감사의 표현) ~해주시다니 참 친절하시군요. ~해주셔서 감사합니다

8 **M:** Did you call me?
나를 불렀나요?

   W: Yeah, can you give me a hand to move some flowerpots?
예, 화분 옮기는 것을 도와주시겠어요?

   M: _______________________

(A) I was happy I could help you then.
내가 그때 당신을 도와드릴 수 있어서 좋았어요.

(B) Of course. Give me ten minutes.
물론이죠. 10분만 기다려 주세요.

(C) Then can you help me tomorrow?
그러면 내일 나를 도와주실 수 있어요?

(D) I hope so, but I'm not good at gardening.
그러고 싶어요, 그러나 나는 꽃 가꾸는 일을 잘하지 못해요.

해설 여자가 도움을 구했으니 남자는 도와줄 것인지의 여부를 말해야 합니다. (D)가 답이 될 수 없는 것은 여자가 화초재배를 도와달라고 부탁하는 것이 아니라 단지 화분을 옮기도록 도와달라고 부탁하는 것이기 때문입니다.

★ give a hand 도와주다 / gardening 원예, 화초재배

9 **W:** These kids are so cute. Are you among them?
이 아이들 너무 귀엽군요. 당신도 여기에 있나요?

   M: Yes, the picture was taken when I was in kindergarten.
네, 그 사진은 내가 유치원에 다닐 때 찍은 거예요.

   W: _______________________

(A) Wait a minute. Let me find which one is you.
잠깐만요. 누가 당신인지 내가 찾아볼게요.

(B) My son will be a good match for your daughter.
내 아들이 당신 딸과 좋은 짝이 될 거예요.

(C) That's funny. I was in the kindergarten, too.
우습군요. 나도 그 유치원에 있었어요.

(D) I haven't seen you for a long time.
오랜만이군요.

해설 두 사람은 남자의 어릴 적 사진을 화제로 대화하고 있습니다. (A)처럼 말하는 것이 자연스럽습니다. (D)는 오랜만에 누군가를 만났을 때 나누는 인사말입니다. 'Long time no see!'라고 줄여서 말하기도 합니다.

★ kindergarten 유치원

10 **M:** When and where did you buy this book?
언제 어디서 이 책을 샀니?

   W: I bought it on the Internet last month.
지난달에 인터넷에서 샀어.

   M: _______________________

(A) Be careful not to spend too much time on the Internet.

인터넷에 너무 많은 시간을 쓰지 않도록 조심해.

(B) How lucky you are! They are all sold out in the bookstore.
너 참 운이 좋구나! 서점에서는 모두 팔렸더라고.

(C) Why do you prefer going to a local bookstore?
왜 동네 서점에 가는 것을 더 좋아하니?

(D) You're right. Shopping on the Internet isn't always cheaper.
네 말이 맞아. 인터넷 쇼핑이 항상 더 저렴한 것은 아니야.

해설 남자는 인터넷에서 구매한 책을 화제로 이야기하고 있습니다. (A)는 화제에서 벗어나고, (C)와 (D)는 여자가 말한 바와 일치하지 않습니다. (B)처럼 호응해 주는 것이 자연스럽습니다.

★ sold out 매진된, 다 팔린 / local 지역의, 한 고장의

11 **W:** I teach science in a high school.
나는 고등학교에서 과학을 가르칩니다.

M: Can you tell me what made you want to be a teacher?
왜 선생님이 되기를 원했는지 말씀해 주시겠어요?

W: ______________________________

(A) I thought teaching was very rewarding.
나는 가르치는 일이 매우 보람 있다고 생각했어요.

(B) I plan to go to Teachers' College.
나는 교육대학에 갈 계획입니다.

(C) I teach at Hilltop high school.
나는 Hilltop 고등학교에서 가르칩니다.

(D) My father is a scientist, too.
나의 아버지 또한 과학자입니다.

해설 남자가 여자에게 선생님이 된 이유를 묻고 있다는 것을 놓치지 않는다면 쉽게 답을 찾을 수 있습니다.

★ rewarding 보람 있는

12 **M:** May I help you?
무엇을 도와 드릴까요?

W: I bought this skirt here yesterday. But I found a grey stain on it.
여기서 어제 이 치마를 샀어요. 그런데 치마에 회색 얼룩이 있는 것을 발견했어요.

M: ______________________________

(A) This skirt won't shrink when you wash it.
이 치마는 세탁해도 줄어들지 않습니다.

(B) Just bring it back if there's any problem.
어떤 문제가 있거든 가져만 오세요.

(C) Sorry, we can exchange it if you want to.
미안합니다, 원하신다면 그것을 교환해 드리겠습니다.

(D) Okay, let me show you how to take out the stain.
좋아요, 어떻게 얼룩을 제거하는지 보여드릴게요.

해설 여자가 새로 구입한 치마에 문제가 있습니다. 남자가 옷가게 점원이라면 사과하면서 교환이나 환불을 제안하는 것이 마땅합니다.

★ stain 얼룩, 오점 / get stained 얼룩이 지다 / exchange 교환하다 / take out 제거하다

13 **W:** I went to my friend's birthday party. We ate Korean food.
나는 친구의 생일 파티에 가서 한국 음식을 먹었어.

M: What was the food like?
그 음식은 어땠니?

W: ______________________________

(A) It was just great.
대단히 좋았어요.

(B) I think I'm full.
나는 배가 불러요.

(C) It was a lot of fun.
재미있었어요.

(D) I need dessert.
디저트가 먹고 싶어요.

해설 남자는 여자에게 한국 음식을 먹어본 소감을 묻고 있습니다.

★ What is ~ like? (소감을 묻는 말) ~은 어떤가요, ~을 어떻게 생각하세요? / dessert 주된 식사를 마친 후 후식으로 제공되는 음식. 아이스크림 따위

14 **M:** I can't find my wallet.
내 지갑을 찾을 수 없어.

W: Did you have it when you got off the bus?
버스에서 내릴 때 가지고 있었니?

M: ______________________________

(A) Well, taking a taxi is a better bet.
글쎄, 택시를 타는 것이 좋은 방법일 것 같은데.

(B) I'm not sure of it.
그것을 확실히 모르겠어.

(C) I'll get off at the next stop.
다음 정류장에서 내릴 거야.

(D) I forgot to bring my wallet. Can I borrow some money?
지갑을 가져오는 것을 깜박했어. 돈 좀 빌릴 수 있을까?

해설 지갑을 찾고 있는 남자가 버스에서 내릴 때 지갑을 가지고 있었는지 기억하지 못하는 상황이라면 (B)처럼 대답하는 것이 가장 적절합니다. 'I'm not sure.'는 '잘 모르겠어.' 정도의 의미입니다.

★ bet 내기, 내기에 건 돈, 좋은 방법

15 **W:** How do you feel now?
지금은 어때?

M: I feel much better. The fever came down yesterday.
훨씬 나아졌어. 어제 열이 내렸어.

W: ______________________________

(A) Yes, the weather is getting normal.
맞아, 날씨가 정상을 되찾고 있어.

(B) I'm so glad to hear that.
그 말을 듣게 돼서 기뻐.

(C) Thanks for asking me.
내게 물어봐 줘서 고마워.

(D) Be careful you do not hurt.
다치지 않도록 조심해.

해설 남자는 어딘가 아픈 것 같습니다. 여자가 안부를 묻고 남자가 몸이 많이 나아
졌다고 말했으므로 여자는 '다행이다.' 또는 '잘 됐다.' 정도로 호응해 주는 것
이 자연스럽습니다.

★ feel better 몸이 나아지다 / fever 열(병) / normal 정상의

16 **M:** Can I make an appointment to see Dr. White?
Dr. White와의 진료시간을 정할 수 있을까요?

 W: Would next Monday morning be good for you?
다음 주 월요일 아침으로 해도 괜찮을까요?

 M: ___________________________________

(A) Because I have a bad stomachache.
왜냐하면 복통이 심해서요.

(B) Don't forget to see me then.
그때 나를 만날 것을 잊지 마세요.

(C) Can you confirm my reservation?
제 예약을 확인해 주시겠어요?

(D) Can't I see him sooner? My teeth are killing me.
좀 더 일찍 의사 선생님을 볼 수 없을까요? 이가 아파 죽겠어요.

해설 남자가 병원에 전화하여 진료예약을 하는 상황입니다. 여자가 월요일 아침으
로 예약하면 어떨지 묻고 있으므로 그에 대한 대답이 이어져야 합니다.

★ make an appointment 약속 시간이나 장소를 정하다 / stomachache 복통
/ confirm a reservation 예약을 확인하다

17 **W:** How are the final exams going?
기말고사가 어떻게 되어가고 있니?

 M: Okay, but I can't wait to get finished with the tests.
좋아, 하지만 시험이 빨리 끝났으면 좋겠어.

 W: ___________________________________

(A) Be patient! It's almost finished.
참아! 거의 끝났어.

(B) Wow! You have already finished it.
와, 너는 이미 끝냈구나.

(C) I don't understand why it is so delayed.
왜 그렇게 연기되는지 이해할 수가 없어.

(D) Forget it and try your best to improve much more next
time!
잊어버리렴. 그리고 다음에는 훨씬 더 나아지기 위해 최선을 다
해라.

해설 남자가 기말고사가 끝나기를 기다리는 것이 힘들다고 했으므로 이에 대한 호
응으로는 격려의 말이 오는 것이 좋겠군요.

★ the final exams 기말고사 / I can't wait to ∼ ∼하기를 기다릴 수 없다. 몹시
∼하고 싶다 / patient 참을성 있는, 인내하는

18 **M:** I'm going skiing next weekend. You should join me.
다음 주말에 스키 타러 갈 거야. 너도 나와 함께 가야 해.

 W: It sounds fun, but I'm afraid of falling down.
재밌겠구나, 하지만 넘어질까 봐 걱정돼.

 M: ___________________________________

(A) Then what time shall I pick you up?
그러면 몇 시에 내가 데리러 갈까?

(B) It's great that you can teach me how to ski.
나에게 스키 타는 법을 가르쳐주겠다니 굉장한데.

(C) Don't be afraid. It's easy to learn skiing.
겁먹지 마. 스키를 배우는 것은 쉬워.

(D) Sorry to hear that you have another appointment.
다른 약속이 있다니 아쉽구나.

해설 남자가 여자에게 스키를 타러 가자고 권하고 있습니다. 여자가 흥미를 보이면
서도 넘어질까 봐 두렵다고 말하므로 남자는 좀 더 적극 권해야 할 것 같습니다.

★ appointment 만날 약속

19 **W:** Do you know why Ted was absent from school?
Ted가 왜 결석했는지 아니?

 M: He had an accident while riding his bike.
자전거를 타다가 사고가 났어.

 W: ___________________________________

(A) That's terrible. Was he badly hurt?
안 됐구나. 그가 심하게 다쳤니?

(B) Thank you for worrying me. I feel better.
걱정해줘서 고마워. 몸이 나아졌어.

(C) Oh, no! Did he find his bike again?
맙소사. 그는 자전거를 다시 찾았니?

(D) Is there anyone who can know the reason?
이유를 아는 사람 혹시 없니?

해설 여자가 친구의 결석한 이유를 묻자, 남자가 자전거 사고가 났다고 말해주는
상황입니다. 여자의 입장에서는 깜짝 놀라며 많이 다치지 않았는지 물어보는
것이 자연스럽겠군요.

★ hurt 다치다

20 **M:** Did you hear the thunderstorm last night?
지난밤에 천둥과 비바람 소리 들었니?

 W: Yeah, it kept me up most of the night.
그래, 덕분에 거의 밤새도록 깨어있었어.

 M: ___________________________________

(A) I didn't sleep well, either.
나 또한 잠을 잘 잘 수 없었어.

(B) Don't be afraid. I'll be with you.
두려워하지 마. 내가 네 옆에 있어줄게.

(C) No. I didn't listen to the forecast.
아니, 기상예보를 듣지 못했어.

(D) Did you have a nightmare?
너는 악몽을 꾸었니?

해설 지난밤 천둥과 비바람 소리에 거의 잠을 자지 못했다는 여자의 말에 자연스럽
게 호응할 수 있는 말을 찾아야 합니다.

★ thunderstorm 천둥 번개를 동반한 폭풍우 / keep up the night 밤새 깨어
있다 / forecast 예보, 예측 / nightmare 악몽

21 **W:** Are you working at the store today?

오늘 가게에서 일하니?

M: No, today's my day off.

아니, 오늘은 쉬는 날이야.

W: ________________________

(A) Oh, no! I expected you could come to my birthday party today.

맙소사! 난 네가 오늘 내 생일 파티에 올 수 있는 줄 알았어.

(B) If you, please can you help me move to a new apartment?

만약 그렇다면, 부디 내가 새 아파트로 이사 가는 것을 도와줄 수 있니?

(C) Do you mind if I come to the store to meet you?

내가 가게로 너를 만나러 가도 괜찮겠니?

(D) We can't afford to pay for sloppy work.

우리는 변변치 못한 일에 돈을 줄 수는 없어.

해설 여자가 남자에게 오늘 근무가 있는지 묻자, 남자는 마침 쉬는 날이라고 대답합니다. 여자가 왜 물어보았나는지 생각해 봅시다.

★ off (일 또는 근무를) 쉬는 / afford to ~ ~ 할 여유가 있다, ~할 수 있다 / sloppy 엉성한, 변변치 못한, 성실하지 않은

Do you mind if ~? 만약 ~한다면 꺼려하겠습니까? ~해도 괜찮겠습니까?

→ 대답에 주의해야 합니다. 괜찮다는 의미로 말할 때 not을 써야 합니다. 다음의 예를 참고하세요.

Do you mind if I open the window? 창문을 열어도 괜찮겠습니까?

→ Of course not. 물론 괜찮습니다.

22 **M:** What do you think about the movie, Friday the 13th?

13일의 금요일이라는 영화에 대하여 어떻게 생각하니?

W: I don't like such a scary movie. How about you?

나는 그런 무서운 영화는 좋아하지 않아. 너는 어떠니?

M: ________________________

(A) I am crazy about it. It is really thrilling.

나는 그것을 너무 좋아해. 그것은 정말 스릴 있어.

(B) Then shall I go to see it with you?

그러면 내가 너와 함께 그것을 보러 가도 돼?

(C) Me too. I think it is very interesting.

나도 그래. 그것은 아주 재미있다고 생각해.

(D) Sorry. I'm afraid I can't help you.

미안해. 내가 너를 돕지 못할것 같아.

해설 두 사람은 공포영화를 소재로 대화하고 있습니다. 여자는 공포영화를 싫어한다고 말하면서 남자의 의견을 묻고 있으므로, 남자는 공포영화에 대한 자신의 생각을 말해야 합니다.

★ thrilling 오싹하게 하는, 전율하게 하는 / be crazy about ~ ~을 몹시 좋아하다

23 **M:** I couldn't come because of a cold and fever.

나는 감기에 걸리고 열이 나서 오지 못했어.

W: Are you feeling any better today?

오늘은 좀 나았니?

M: ________________________

(A) This one is better than mine.

이것이 내 것보다 좋구나.

(B) Well, I'm not upset about it.

글쎄, 그것 때문에 화난 것은 아니야.

(C) Yes, I feel like myself again.

그래, 다시 평소대로 돌아온 것 같아.

(D) Sorry, I'm terribly busy today.

미안해, 오늘은 몹시 바빠.

해설 여자가 몸이 아팠던 남자의 안부를 묻고 있으므로 남자는 자신의 몸 상태를 말해주어야 합니다.

★ upset 화난, 당황한 / feel like oneself again 평소 상태를 회복하다

24 **M:** Can I help you, ma'am?

부인, 무엇을 도와드릴까요?

W: Do you have these in size 220?

이 제품을 220 사이즈로 주세요.

M: ________________________

(A) They're very stylish. They look good on you.

아주 멋지네요. 당신에게 잘 어울립니다.

(B) You are choosy about what you wear.

입는 것에 대하여 까다로우시군요.

(C) I think we have. Let me go and check for you.

우리가 가지고 있다고 생각해요. 가서 찾아볼게요.

(D) Can you tell me why you ask for a refund?

왜 환불을 원하는지 말씀해 주시겠어요?

해설 신발 가게에서 손님과 점원이 나누는 대화입니다. 손님이 사이즈를 맞춰달라고 부탁할 때 점원이 할 말을 생각해 봅시다.

★ stylish 세련된, 현대식의, 멋진 / look good on ~에 잘 어울리다 / choosy 가리는, 까다로운 / refund 환불(하다)

25 **W:** What did you do to your ankle?

발목에 무슨 문제가 있니?

M: I sprained it while playing soccer.

축구하다가 삐었어.

W: ________________________

(A) It sounds interesting!

흥미 있게 들리는데!

(B) Oh, no. You should have been more careful.

맙소사. 너는 좀 더 주의를 기울였어야 했어.

(C) Can I join your team?

내가 너희 팀에 함께 해도 될까?

(D) Do you have any trouble in writing or eating?

쓰고 먹을 때 이상이 있니?

해설 남자가 축구하다가 발목을 삐었다는 말에 대하여 어떻게 호응할지를 고르는 문제입니다. (D)는 발목을 삔 것과 쓰고 먹을 때의 곤란은 상관이 없으므로 오답입니다.

★ sprain (손목이나 발목을) 삐다 / should have p.p. (과거에 하지 못한 일에 대한 아쉬움이나 후회를 표현하여) ~했어야만 했는데

26 M: It's been so long since I've been up here.
여기에 와본지 정말 오랜만입니다.

W: Yeah, I can't remember the way exactly.
맞아요, 길을 정확히 기억하지 못하겠어요.

M: ___________________________

(A) Excuse me, could you direct me to the Holiday Hotel?
실례합니다, Holiday 호텔에 가는 길을 알려주시겠어요?

(B) You'll see a brown building on the right as you go down the street.
이 길로 가다보면 오른쪽에 갈색 건물을 볼 수 있을 겁니다.

(C) Sorry, I am a stranger here.
미안합니다, 나도 이곳을 잘 모릅니다.

(D) Let's ask that person coming over there for directions.
저기 오는 사람들에게 길을 물어봅시다.

해설 두 사람이 어떤 곳을 오랜만에 방문하여 길을 잘 모르겠다고 말합니다. 그렇다면 지나가는 누군가에게 길을 물어볼 수밖에 없습니다.

★ direct ~ to … ~에게 …로 가는 길을 알려주다

27 M: I'd like to reserve a table at 7 o'clock.
7시에 테이블 하나를 예약하고 싶어요.

W: How many will be with you, sir?
얼마나 많은 분이 동석하실 건가요?

M: ___________________________

(A) A party of 5. And my name is Charles Moore.
일행이 다섯 명입니다. 그리고 내 이름은 Charles Moore입니다.

(B) I'd like to confirm my reservation.
나는 예약을 확인하고 싶어요.

(C) We'll have come by 6:40.
우리가 6시40분까지는 도착할 겁니다.

(D) We have 40 kinds of enjoyable dishes.
우리는 40가지의 맛있는 요리를 선보입니다.

해설 남자가 식당에 테이블을 예약하고 있는 상황입니다. 점원은 일행이 몇 명인지 물었으므로 일행의 수를 말해줘야 합니다.

★ reserve a table (식당 등에서) 테이블을 예약해두다 / party 일행, 모임 / confirm a reservation 예약을 확인하다 / enjoyable 즐길만한, 맛있는

28 M: What can I do for you?
무엇을 도와 드릴까요?

W: I'm looking for this kind of shirt in blue color.
이런 종류의 셔츠를 파란색으로 찾는 중입니다.

M: ___________________________

(A) Good choice! It goes very well with your pants.
훌륭한 선택이십니다. 당신의 바지와 잘 어울립니다.

(B) I'm sorry, but they're all sold out.
미안합니다만, 그것은 다 팔렸습니다.

(C) Go straight two blocks and you will see it on your left.
똑바로 두 블록을 가면 왼편에 보일 겁니다.

(D) I'm afraid the bigger size is not available.
유감스럽지만 더 큰 사이즈는 없습니다.

해설 옷가게에서 손님과 점원이 나누는 대화입니다. 손님이 특정한 색깔의 상품을 찾고 있을 때 점원이 할 수 있는 말을 생각해 봅시다. (A)는 손님이 골라놓은 상품을 보면서 할 수 있는 말이고 지금처럼 원하는 상품이 있는지조차 모르는 상황에서는 적절치 못합니다.

★ choice 선택 / go well with ~ ~와 잘 어울리다 / sold out 다 팔린, 매진된 / available 이용 가능한 / I'm afraid ~ 유감스럽지만 ~합니다.

29 W: What did you do last Sunday, Paul?
Paul, 지난 일요일에 너는 무엇을 했니?

M: I just watched TV all afternoon. What about you?
오후 내내 TV만 보았어. 너는 어땠니?

W: ___________________________

(A) I went camping with my family. It was great.
나는 가족과 캠핑을 갔어. 정말 좋았어.

(B) I also like to watch TV, especially a talk show.
나 또한 TV, 특히 토크쇼 보는 것을 좋아해.

(C) I'm going to watch a movie. Will you join me?
나는 영화 보러 갈 거야. 너도 함께 갈래?

(D) Go easy on yourself and don't work too hard.
너무 무리하거나, 너무 열심히 일하지는 마.

★ go easy on ~ 을 살살 다루다. 너무 심하게 ~하지 않다

해설 남자는 여자에게 지난 일요일에 무엇을 했는지 되묻고 있습니다.

30 M: I had a bone in my foot broken yesterday.
나 어제 발에 있는 뼈 하나가 부러졌어.

W: Did you? How did that happen?
그랬어? 어쩌다 그런 일이 생겼니?

M: ___________________________

(A) I've just had it x-rayed.
나는 방금 발에 엑스레이 촬영을 했어.

(B) It will take four weeks to heal completely.
완전히 낫는데 4주가 걸릴 거야.

(C) Is there another pair of shoes?
다른 신발이 있나요?

(D) I slipped and fell down some stairs.
미끄러져서 계단에서 아래로 굴렀어.

해설 여자가 남자에게 발이 부러진 이유를 물었으므로 남자는 어떻게 발이 부러지게 되었는지를 말해줘야 합니다.

★ have + 목적어 + p.p.(과거완료) : 목적어가 ~되도록 하다, 목적어를 ~ 당하다
  − I had a leg broken. 다리가 부러졌다.(=다리가 부러지는 일을 당했다.)
  − I had my hair cut. 머리를 잘랐다.(=머리가 잘리도록 했다.)

31 W: I can't reach the box on the top shelf.
저 선반 꼭대기에 있는 상자에 손이 닿지 않아.

M: Wait a minute. I'll take it down for you.
잠시만 기다려. 내가 내려 줄게.

W: ___________________________

(A) Thank you for the ride.
태워줘서 고마워.

(B) I'm so happy you remember me.
네가 나를 기억해 줘서 행복해.

(C) Be careful not to drop it. It is so heavy.
떨어뜨리지 않도록 조심해. 아주 무거워.

(D) Because she is too short.
그녀는 키가 너무 작으니까.

해설 여자가 손이 닿지 않아 상자를 내리지 못하자 남자가 도와주겠다고 자청한 상황입니다.

★ shelf 선반

32 **M:** I'm afraid we cannot see Susan for some time.
유감스럽지만 얼마동안 Susan을 만날 수 없어.

W: Why? Did something happen to her?
왜? 그녀에게 무슨 일이 있었니?

M: ______________________________

(A) She suddenly left Korea for home last week.
지난주에 그녀가 갑자기 한국을 떠나 고국으로 갔어.

(B) Let's give a farewell party for her.
그녀를 위해 고별 파티를 해주자.

(C) She really tried to see us several times.
그녀는 몇 차례 우리를 만나려고 노력했어.

(D) You shouldn't say so about her.
그녀에 대하여 그렇게 말하면 안 돼.

해설 남자는 여자에게 당분간 Susan을 만날 수 없는 이유를 설명해야 합니다.

★ farewell party 고별 파티

33 **W:** You look so depressed. What is the matter with you?
너 우울해 보이는구나. 무슨 일 있니?

M: Oh, I failed last week's job interview.
아, 지난주 취업 면접시험에서 떨어졌어.

W: ______________________________

(A) Congratulations on your new job! When do you start?
새 직장 축하해! 언제부터 시작하니?

(B) Don't worry. You'll do better next time.
걱정 마. 다음번에는 더 잘할 거야.

(C) Did you? Why did you leave the job?
그랬어? 왜 그 직장을 그만두었니?

(D) No, I didn't know about the interview.
아니, 그 면접(시험)에 대하여 몰랐어.

해설 남자가 직장을 구하려다 실패한 상황이므로 여자는 위로의 말을 건네는 것이 좋겠습니다.

★ depressed 우울한 / job interview 취업면접시험 / congratulation 축하

34 **M:** May I ask you why you quit the job?
당신이 직장을 그만 두는 이유를 물어봐도 될까요?

W: I just think I need a change.
단지 변화가 필요한 것 같아요.

M: ______________________________

(A) What do you like about the job?
그 일의 어떤 점이 좋습니까?

(B) That's too bad. I hope you will get a new job soon.
안됐군요. 당신이 곧 새 일자리 얻기를 바래요.

(C) And what do you plan to do?
그러면 무엇을 할 계획입니까?

(D) Don't give up and stick to it.
포기하지 말고 끝까지 견뎌보세요.

해설 여자가 무언가 변화가 필요하다고 느끼고 다니던 직장을 그만둔다고 말합니다. 남자가 해줄 수 있는 말이 무엇일지 생각해 봅시다.

★ stick to ~ (어려움을 참고) ~을 계속하다, ~을 고수하다

35 **W:** Hello, Far East airline agent Sharon. What can I do for you?
안녕하세요, Far East 항공사의 Sharon입니다. 무엇을 도와 드릴까요?

M: Something urgent came up. I have to get a ticket to New York tonight.
긴급한 일이 생겼어요. 오늘밤 뉴욕으로 가는 항공권을 구해야 만 합니다.

W: ______________________________

(A) You are lucky. We have just one ticket for leaving tomorrow afternoon.
운이 좋으시군요. 내일 오후에 떠나는 항공권이 한 장 있습니다.

(B) You have to reconfirm your flight 24 hours before.
24시간 전에 비행편 예약을 재확인하셔야 합니다.

(C) Sorry, but all our flights for tonight have already been full.
미안합니다만, 오늘밤 출발하는 모든 항공편이 이미 다 찼습니다.

(D) Oh, no! I'll miss you when you go back to America.
안돼요! 미국으로 돌아가시면 당신이 보고 싶을 거예요.

해설 남자가 급히 항공권을 구하기 위하여 항공사 직원에게 문의하고 있는 상황입니다. 직원은 항공권을 제공할 수 있는지의 여부를 말해야 합니다. 남자는 오늘밤의 항공편을 구하고 있는데 (A)는 내일 오후의 항공권을 가지고 있다고 말하고 있으므로 정답이 될 수 없습니다.

★ airline 항공사 / agent 직원 / urgent 긴급한 / reconfirm 재확인하다. 예약을 재확인하다

36 **M:** Do you remember borrowing 20 dollars from me last Thursday?
지난 목요일 나에게 20달러 빌렸던 것 기억나니?

W: Yeah, but did I pay the money back at school the next morning?
그래, 하지만 다음날 아침 학교에서 그 돈을 갚지 않았니?

M: ______________________________

(A) You're right. It was not 20 dollars but 15 dollars.
네 말이 맞아. 20달러가 아니고 15달러였어.

(B) Try to remember. Last Friday was a holiday, so we didn't

see each other.
기억해보렴. 지난 금요일은 휴일이어서 우리는 만난 적이 없어.

(C) Can you tell me when you will pay the money back?
언제 돈을 갚을 건지 말해줄 수 있니?

(D) I don't want to hurry you but I need the money right now.
너를 재촉하고 싶지는 않지만 지금 당장 돈이 필요해.

해설 남자가 여자가 빌려간 돈에 대하여 이야기를 꺼내자 여자는 이미 돈을 갚은 것으로 생각하고 있습니다. 과연 누구의 기억이 맞는 것인지 두 사람은 서로의 기억을 되짚어봐야 하겠군요.

★ borrow 빌리다 / pay back (돈을) 갚다 / hurry 서두르게 하다, 재촉하다

37 **W:** You don't look so good. What's up?
너 좋아 보이지 않는구나. 무슨 일이니?

M: I didn't sleep all night. This toothache's really killing me.
밤새 잠을 자지 못했어. 치통 때문에 정말 죽을 맛이야.

W: ___________________________

(A) You'd better brush your teeth more carefully.
이를 좀 더 주의 깊게 닦는 것이 좋겠구나.

(B) Hurry to call the police immediately.
즉시 경찰을 부르도록 서두르자.

(C) Maybe you should see a dentist.
아마 치과진료를 받아야 하겠구나.

(D) Then go and have fun.
그러면 나가서 놀자.

해설 남자가 치통 때문에 잠을 잘 수 없었다고 말하므로, 여자는 진료를 받아보도록 권하는 것이 자연스럽습니다. (A)번은 치통과 이를 닦는 것이 반드시 연관있다고 볼 수 없고 (C)와 같이 보다 직접적인 답이 있으므로 정답에서 제외하기로 합니다.

★ What's up? 무슨 일이니? / toothache 치통 / hurry to ～ 서둘러 ～하다 / see a dentist 치과진료를 받다

38 **M:** You are in good shape. Have you worked out?
건강해 보입니다. 운동을 하고 있나요?

W: Actually, I've been on a diet for about 3 months.
사실, 약 석 달 동안 다이어트를 해왔어요.

M: ___________________________

(A) Which fitness center do you go to?
어떤 헬스클럽에 가십니까?

(B) Me too. I also have to lose weight.
나도 그래요. 나 또한 체중을 줄여야 해요.

(C) I'm looking forward to what you will look like in 3 months.
3개월이 지나서 당신이 어떤 모습일지 기대돼요.

(D) Great! You look much slimmer than before.
굉장하군요! 전보다 훨씬 날씬해 보여요.

해설 여자가 석 달 동안 다이어트를 했었다고 말합니다. 석 달 동안 꾸준히 다이어트하는 것은 누구에게나 쉬운 일이 아닙니다. 남자의 칭찬이 이어지는 것이 자

연스럽습니다.

★ be in good shape 건강이 좋다 / work out 운동하다 / go on a diet 다이어트하다, 체중조절하다 / fitness center 헬스클럽 / lose weight 체중을 줄이다 / look forward to ～ ～을 학수고대하다 / slim 날씬한

39 **W:** May I take your order?
주문하시겠습니까?

M: Well, what is today's special?
글쎄요, 오늘의 특별메뉴는 무엇이죠?

W: ___________________________

(A) It's a beef steak with a baked potato.
구운 감자를 곁들인 소고기 스테이크입니다.

(B) Actually, today is our wedding anniversary.
사실 오늘이 우리의 결혼기념일입니다.

(C) Your order will be ready soon.
주문하신 음식을 곧 준비해드리겠습니다.

(D) Sure, the menu is at your choice.
물론이죠, 메뉴는 당신이 선택하세요.

해설 식당에서 이루어지는 대화입니다. 남자가 점원에게 오늘의 특별메뉴를 묻고 있으므로 점원은 메뉴 이름으로 대답해야 하겠습니다.

★ anniversary 기념일 / order 주문

40 **M:** Did you see my wallet? I put it on the table a while ago.
내 지갑 봤니? 조금 전에 그것을 테이블 위에 두었었어.

W: Maybe you've just put it down somewhere else.
아마 그것을 다른 곳에 놓아두었을 거야.

M: ___________________________

(A) Can you lend me some money?
내게 돈을 빌려줄 수 있니?

(B) Yes, I'd better look around.
그래, 주변을 둘러보는 것이 좋겠다.

(C) Thank you for helping me find it.
내가 그것을 찾도록 도와줘서 고마워.

(D) You're right. Who came here when I left?
네 말이 맞아. 내가 자리를 떴을 때 누가 여기에 왔었지?

해설 남자가 지갑을 찾고 있습니다. 여자는 아마 다른 곳에 놓아두고 잊어버린 것 같다고 조언합니다. 남자가 여자의 말을 받아 들여 (B)처럼 주변을 둘러봐야겠다고 말하는 것이 가장 자연스럽습니다.

★ somewhere else 다른 어떤 곳 / look around 주변을 둘러보다

01. (D)	02. (A)	03. (D)	04. (B)	05. (C)
06. (B)	07. (D)	08. (C)	09. (D)	10. (C)
11. (D)	12. (D)	13. (B)	14. (A)	15. (D)
16. (C)	17. (A)	18. (B)	19. (C)	20. (B)
21. (D)	22. (C)	23. (B)	24. (D)	25. (A)
26. (B)	27. (C)	28. (C)	29. (D)	30. (C)
31. (A)	32. (B)	33. (D)	34. (B)	35. (B)
36. (A)	37. (C)	38. (D)	39. (B)	40. (D)

1 **M:** I'd like to have some clothes washed. Here they are.
옷 몇 벌을 세탁하고 싶습니다. 여기 있습니다.

W: Let's see. Shirts are 3 dollars each and pants are 2 dollars each.
어디 보죠. 셔츠는 한 벌에 3달러이고 바지는 한 벌에 2달러입니다.

M: OK. I'll leave two shirts and a pair of pants.
좋아요. 셔츠 두 벌과 바지 한 벌을 맡길게요.

Q: 남자는 얼마나 지불하겠습니까?
(A) 5달러 　　　　　(B) 6달러
(C) 7달러 　　　　　(D) 8달러

해설 세탁소에서의 대화입니다. 셔츠 한 벌에 3달러이고 바지는 한 벌에 2달러인데, 남자는 셔츠 두 벌과 바지 한 벌을 세탁소에 맡겼습니다.

★ **have ～ washed** ～을 세탁시키다 / **leave** 놓고 가다, 맡기고 가다

2 **W:** I can't believe I missed the math class.
내가 수학 수업을 빠뜨렸다는 게 믿을 수 없어.

M: Really? What happened?
정말? 무슨 일이 있었니?

W: I got up late. I'm not sure if my alarm clock went off.
늦게 일어났어. 내 알람시계가 울렸는지 모르겠어.

Q: 여자는 왜 수학 수업에 불참했습니까?
(A) 아침에 늦잠을 잤다.
(B) 그녀의 시계가 느리게 갔다.
(C) 알람시계를 맞춰두지 않았다.
(D) 수업시간을 잘못 알았다.

해설 마지막 말에 따르면, 여자는 알람시계가 울렸는지도 모를 정도로 곤하게 늦잠을 잤습니다.

★ **go off** 발사되다, (경보 등이) 울리다 / **oversleep** 너무 오래 자다

3 **M:** What a surprise! Do you know we don't have to attend school tomorrow?
와우! 내일 우리 학교에 갈 필요가 없다는 것 아니?

W: Really? Tomorrow is the school anniversary?
정말? 내일이 개교기념일이니?

M: No. It's just for heavy snow. School will be closed from tomorrow.
아니. 폭설 때문이야. 학교가 내일부터 휴교할거야.

Q: 남자는 그토록 흥분한 이유는 무엇입니까?
(A) 눈이 많이 올 것이다.
(B) 학교에 입학허가를 받았다.
(C) 내일이 개교기념일이다.
(D) 학교가 며칠간 휴교할 것이다.

해설 남자의 말에 따르면, 내일부터 Snow Day가 시작된다는 것을 알 수 있습니다. Snow Day는 폭설로 인하여 학생들의 등교가 곤란할 때 학교가 임시로 휴교하는 것을 말합니다.

★ **school anniversary** 개교기념일 / **heavy snow** 폭설 / **be admitted to attend the school** 입학을 허락받다

4 **W:** Peter, why are you so blue? It's not like you.
Peter, 왜 그렇게 우울하니? 너답지 않구나.

M: It's because of deadlines. I feel like I am a writing machine.
마감시한 때문이야. 내가 꼭 글 쓰는 기계 같아.

W: Cheer up! Writing an article in a newspaper isn't a job for everyone.
힘내! 신문에 기사를 쓰는 것은 아무나 할 수 있는 일이 아니야.

Q: Peter의 직업은 무엇입니까?
(A) 화가 　　　　　(B) 기자
(C) 작가 　　　　　(D) 기계공

해설 대화를 통해 남자는 신문에 기사를 쓰는 일을 한다는 것을 알 수 있습니다.

★ **blue** 우울한 / **deadline** 최종기한, 마감시한 / **article** 기사

5 **M:** I'm afraid I can't go out until this Friday. I have to prepare for the science exam.
유감스럽지만 이번 금요일까지 밖에 나갈 수 없어. 나는 과학시험을 준비해야 해.

W: You said it would be finished today, didn't you?
오늘 끝날 거라고 말했었잖아, 그렇지 않아?

M: Yes, I did. But because of the snow days, it has been postponed for two days.
그랬었지. 그러나 폭설로 인한 휴일 때문에 시험이 이틀 연기되었어.

Q: 오늘은 무슨 요일입니까?
(A) 월요일 　　　　　(B) 화요일
(C) 수요일 　　　　　(D) 목요일

해설 대화에 따르면, 원래 오늘 치르기로 했던 과학시험이 폭설로 인한 휴일 때문에 이틀 미뤄져서 이번 금요일에 치러진다고 합니다. 그렇다면 오늘은 금요일로부터 이틀 전입니다.

★ **postpone** 연기하다

6 **W:** Help me! I've lost my little girl. She was around the telephone booth just now.
도와주세요! 딸아이를 잃어버렸어요. 그 애는 방금 전에 공중전

화 주변에 있었어요.

M : Take it easy. Can you tell me what your daughter looks like?

진정하세요. 딸아이가 어떤 모습인지 말해주실 수 있나요?

W : Yes. She is wearing a pink T-shirt with Teddy bear printed on it. She has blonde curly hair.

네. 그 애는 테디 베어가 새겨진 분홍색 티셔츠를 입고 있어요. 그 애는 금발의 곱슬머리예요.

Q : 여자는 무엇을 하고 있습니까?

(A) 공중전화 부스로 가는 길을 묻고 있다.

(B) 딸을 찾고 있다.

(C) 셔츠를 사기 위하여 고르고 있다.

(D) 딸이 오디션을 치르도록 하고 있다.

해설 여자는 공중전화 주변에서 잃어버린 딸아이를 찾고 있습니다.

★ **telephone booth** 공중전화 박스 / **Take it easy.** 진정하세요. 침착하세요. / **blonde** 금발의 / **curly** 곱슬머리의

7 M : Can I have popcorn and coke?

내가 팝콘과 콜라를 먹어도 될까요?

W : Actually, I don't like to have something. I just want to focus on the movie.

사실 나는 뭘 먹고 싶지 않아요. 그냥 영화에 집중하고 싶어요.

M : Do you? Well, will it be bothering you if I have popcorn beside you?

그래요? 만약 내가 당신 옆에서 팝콘을 먹으면 방해가 될까요?

Q : 그들은 어디에 있습니까?

(A) 간이식당   (B) 도서관에

(C) 거리에   (D) 영화관에

해설 영화에 집중하기 위하여 팝콘을 먹지 않겠다는 여자의 말이 힌트입니다.

★ **bother** 괴롭히다. 성가시게하다 / **snack bar** 샌드위치처럼 가볍게 먹을 수 있는 음식을 파는 식당

8 W : Shall we go climbing to see the reds and yellows of the trees?

울긋불긋한 단풍을 보기 위해 우리 등산하러 갈까요?

M : Great! Maybe the trees of the mountains are turning their most beautiful colors.

좋지요! 아마 산은 단풍이 절정일겁니다.

W : Then I'll stop by around 7a.m.M tomorrow. Is it OK?

그러면 내가 내일 아침 7시 즈음에 들를게요. 괜찮죠?

Q : 지금은 어떤 계절입니까?

(A) 봄   (B) 여름

(C) 가을   (D) 겨울

해설 단풍을 보러 산에 가자는 여자의 말과 단풍이 절정일 거는 남자의 말이 힌트입니다.

★ **the reds and yellows of the trees** 울긋불긋한 단풍 / **A tree turns the most beautiful colors.** 아름답게 단풍이 들다. / **stop by** ～에 들르다

9 M : Which class do you like the most?

어떤 수업을 가장 좋아하니?

W : I am not sure. Art class is really good. So are science and social studies.

잘 모르겠어. 미술은 정말 좋아. 과학과 사회도 그래.

M : Well, I'm always waiting for physical education. Running on the playground makes me happy.

음, 나는 항상 체육시간을 기다려. 운동장에서 달리는 것이 날 행복하게 해.

Q : 남자가 가장 좋아하는 과목은 무엇입니까?

(A) 미술   (B) 과학

(C) 사회   (D) 체육

해설 남자는 항상 체육시간을 기다린다고 말합니다. Physical Education(체육)이란 단어를 모르더라도 운동장에서 달릴 때 행복하다는 말을 통해 정답을 짐작해 볼 수 있습니다.

★ **social studies** 사회 / **physical education** 체육

10 W : What are you going to bring to Sharon's party tonight?

오늘밤 Sharon의 파티에 무엇을 가져올 거니?

M : I'd like to bring some potato chips. How about you?

약간의 포테이토칩을 가져갈 거야. 너는 어떠니?

W : I am thinking of getting tuna sandwiches. No, on second thoughts, I'll bring some Korean rice cakes.

나는 참치 샌드위치를 가져갈까 생각 중이야. 아니, 다시 생각해보니, 한국 전통 떡을 조금 가져가야겠다.

Q : 여자는 파티에 무엇을 가져갈 것입니까?

(A) 포테이토칩   (B) 참치 샌드위치

(C) 한국 전통 떡   (D) 꽃다발

해설 여자가 처음에는 참치 샌드위치를 생각하다가 곧 생각을 바꾸고 있습니다.

★ **potato chips** 감자를 얇게 썰어 기름에 튀긴 음식 / **tuna** 참치 / **on second thoughts** 다시 생각해보니 / **rice cake** 떡 / **bunch** 다발

11 M : It's dark outside. Shall I drive you home?

밖이 어두워. 내가 집까지 태워다줄까?

W : But you don't have a driver's license!

그러나 너 아직 운전면허증도 없잖아!

M : No. I got a driver's license two years ago when I was twenty.

아니. 내가 20살이던 2년 전에 운전면허증을 땄어.

Q : 남자는 지금 몇 살입니까?

(A) 19살   (B) 20살

(C) 21살   (D) 22살

해설 남자가 20살이던 2년 전에 운전면허를 취득했다고 말하는 것이 힌트입니다.

★ **license** 면허증

12 W : I'm afraid I can't attend our study club this Saturday. I have to visit my grandma's.

난 유감스럽게도 이번 토요일에 있는 우리 스터디 클럽에 나갈

수 없겠어. 할머니 댁을 방문해야 해.

M: Do you? We need to gather together before the finals. Are you able to show up at Sunday's meeting?

그러니? 우리는 기말고사 전에 함께 모여야 해. 일요일 모임에는 나올 수 있니?

W: Well, in the morning I'm going to church. But I'm free in the afternoon.

글쎄, 아침에 교회를 갈 거야. 그러나 오후에는 시간이 있어.

Q: 여자는 남자를 언제 만날 수 있습니까?

 (A) 토요일 아침   (B) 토요일 오후

 (C) 일요일 아침   (D) 일요일 오후

해설 여자는 일요일 오전에 교회에 다녀온 후 오후에는 시간이 난다고 말합니다.

★ **the finals** 기말고사 / **show up** 나타나다, 참석하다

---

13 M: Shall we go camping for our vacation? I know a wonderful place.

우리 휴가 때 캠핑 갈까요? 내가 좋은 장소를 알아요.

W: Well, I'd rather stay home and take a good rest.

글쎄요. 나는 차라리 집에서 푹 쉬겠어요.

M: Hey, honey. I see what you mean. But vacation is for trying something exceptional.

여보, 무슨 말인지는 알겠어요. 하지만 휴가란 뭔가 특별한 것을 해보라고 있는 거예요.

Q: 휴가 중에 여자는 무엇을 하기 원합니까?

 (A) 캠핑 가기   (B) 집에 머물기

 (C) 무언가 특별한 일을 하기 (D) 멋진 곳으로 여행하기

해설 여자는 집에서 푹 쉬고 싶다고 말합니다.

★ **exceptional** 예외적인, 특별한

---

14 W: My car is making a rattling noise. It is getting louder when I speed up.

내 자동차에서 덜컹거리는 소리가 나요. 속도를 높이면 더 심해져요.

M: All right. Let me take a look under the hood. Hmm... Did you replace the fan belt lately?

좋아요. 보닛을 열고 한 번 보겠습니다. 음... 최근에 팬벨트를 교체하셨나요?

W: Yes, I did 3 days ago. Why? Is there any problem?

네, 3일 전에 했어요. 왜 그러시죠? 거기에 무슨 문제가 있나요?

Q: 여자는 어디에 있습니까?

 (A) 자동차 수리점   (B) 세탁소

 (C) 병원   (D) 컴퓨터 수리 센터

해설 여자가 자동차의 덜컹거리는 소음을 문의하고 남자는 자동차의 엔진 덮개(hood)를 열어보고 있습니다.

★ **rattling** 덜컹거리는 / **hood** 자동차의 엔진룸을 덮고 있는 덮개, 보닛(=bonnet) / **replace** 교체하다

---

15 M: I'd like this style of sneakers in black, please.

이런 스타일의 검은색 운동화를 원해요.

W: Sorry, the black ones are all sold out. How about blue ones or red ones?

죄송합니다, 검은색은 다 팔렸어요. 파란색이나 빨간색은 어떠십니까?

M: Then a high-top style is better for me. Show me those high-top sneakers in black, please.

그러면 내게는 목이 높이 올라오는 스타일이 낫겠군요. 검은색 목이 높은 스타일의 운동화를 보여주세요.

Q: 남자는 무엇을 사겠습니까?

 (A) 검은색 운동화   (B) 빨간색 운동화

 (C) 파란색 운동화   (D) 검은색 목이 높은 운동화

해설 신발가게에서 손님과 점원이 나누는 대화입니다. 검은색 운동화가 매진되었다고 말하자 손님은 최종적으로 검은색 목 높은 운동화를 선택하고 있습니다.

★ **sneakers** 운동화 / **sold out** 다 팔린, 매진된

---

16 W: Could you show me a bag, please?

저 가방을 볼 수 있을까요?

M: Sure, the pattern and the colors are in style this season.

물론이죠, 그 모양이나 색깔이 최신 유행입니다.

W: Yes. Let me see the price tag. Oh, I can't afford that.

그래요. 가격표를 좀 볼게요. 오, 나는 이것을 살만한 여유가 없어요.

Q: 여자는 그 가방에 대하여 어떻게 생각합니까?

 (A) 모양이 마음에 들지 않는다.

 (B) 색깔이 그녀가 원하는 것이 아니다.

 (C) 너무 비싸다.

 (D) 유행에 뒤떨어진다.

해설 마지막 말에서 여자는 가방을 살만큼 여유가 없다고 말합니다.

★ **in style** 유행하는, 멋진 / **price tag** 가격표 / **afford** ~할 여유가 있다. ~을 살 수 있는 여유가 있다

---

17 W: Traffic is terrible in this area these days.

요즘 이 지역은 교통체증이 심해.

W: Maybe it's due to that new shopping mall.

아마 저 새로 생긴 쇼핑몰 때문일거야.

M: You can say that again. Traffic has doubled since it opened.

네 말이 맞아. 저곳이 문을 연 뒤로 교통량이 두 배가 되었어.

Q: 그들은 새로 생긴 쇼핑몰에 대하여 어떻게 생각하고 있습니까?

 (A) 교통체증의 원인이다.

 (B) 가격정책이 매우 매력적이다.

 (C) 지역 경제에 이바지한다.

 (D) 많은 동네 가게들이 그것 때문에 문을 닫고 있다.

해설 두 사람은 새로 생긴 쇼핑몰 때문에 부근의 교통흐름이 안 좋아진 것을 불평하고 있습니다.

★ **traffic** 교통(량) / **be due to** ~ 때문이다 / **You can say that again.** (상대방의 말에 동의를 표할 때) 정말 그래요, 당신이 옳아요 / **contribute** ~에 이바지하다, 기여하다

18 W: I replaced a black ink cartridge last week. But today I've found a serious problem inside my printer.

검은색 잉크통을 지난주에 교체했는데요. 그러나 오늘 프린터 안에 심각한 문제가 있는 것을 발견했어요.

M: Could you be more specific about the problem?

그 문제에 대해 좀 더 구체적으로 말씀해 주시겠습니까?

W: I saw large black stains on the bottom of the printer inside. The black ink must be running down.

프린터 내부의 바닥에 커다란 검정 얼룩이 있는 것을 보았습니다. 검은색 잉크가 새고 있음에 틀림없어요.

Q: 여자의 프린터는 무엇이 문제입니까?
(A) 잘 작동하지 않는다.
(B) 검은색 잉크통이 새고 있다.
(C) 검정 잉크를 다 써 버렸다.
(D) 검정 잉크가 종이 위에서 잘 마르지 않는다.

해설 프린터 내부의 바닥면에 검정 얼룩이 생겼다는 여자의 말이 힌트입니다.

★ cartridge 통 / specific 구체적인 / stain 얼룩 / run down 흘러내리다 / leak 유출되다. 새다 / run out of ~을 다 써버리다

19 M: I don't know how to get to the airport. Which is better, taking an airport bus or taking a taxi?

어떻게 공항에 가야할 지 모르겠어. 공항버스를 타는 것과 택시를 타는 것 중에 어떤 것이 나을까?

W: Um, it's been raining all morning. Traffic might be kind of bad.

음, 오전 내내 비가 오고 있어. 교통흐름이 약간 안 좋을 것 같아.

M: You're right. We'd better take the subway.

당신 말이 맞아. 지하철을 타는 편이 나을 것 같아.

Q: 남자는 어떻게 공항으로 가겠습니까?
(A) 공항버스로   (B) 택시로
(C) 지하철로   (D) 걸어서

해설 두 사람이 공항으로 가려고 하는군요. 여자가 비가 와서 교통이 안 좋을 것 같다고 말하자 남자는 지하철로 공항에 가는 편이 낫겠다고 말합니다.

★ kind of 약간, 어느 정도

20 W: Andy, did you forget to take out the garbage?

Andy, 당신 쓰레기 내놓기로 한 것 잊었어요?

M: No, honey. But can't I take it out tomorrow?

아니, 여보. 하지만 내일 내놓으면 안 될까?

W: No, you can't! Tomorrow you are supposed to mow the lawn. And your study is still a junk yard. You promised to clean it up the day before yesterday.

안돼요. 내일은 잔디를 깎아야 해요. 그리고 당신 서재는 아직도 쓰레기장이에요. 당신은 그저께 서재를 청소하겠다고 약속했어요.

Q: Andy의 문제는 무엇입니까?
(A) 잘 씻지 않는다.
(B) 집안일에 부지런하지 않다.
(C) 자신의 잘못을 사과하지 않는다.
(D) 항상 똑같은 변명을 늘어놓는다.

해설 대화를 통해 Andy는 해야 할 집안일을 차일피일 미루는 버릇이 있음을 알 수 있습니다.

★ garbage 쓰레기 / be supposed to ~ ~해야 한다. ~하기로 되어 있다 / mow 깎다 / lawn 잔디(밭) / study 서재 / apologize for ~에 대하여 사과하다 / make an excuse 변명하다

21 M: We're looking for someone who has some experience. Have you worked as a receptionist before?

우리는 경험 있는 사람을 원합니다. 전에 안내 데스크 직원으로 일해본 적 있나요?

W: Yes, I used to work for a company that sold computer equipment.

네, 컴퓨터 장비를 파는 회사에서 일했습니다.

M: How long did you work for the company?

그 회사에서 얼마동안 일했나요?

Q: 여자는 무엇을 하고 있나요?
(A) 사람 찾기   (B) 환영 파티 준비
(C) 컴퓨터 장비 팔기   (D) 구직 면접 치르기

해설 남자가 여자를 고용하기 위하여 여러 가지 질문을 하고 있습니다.

★ receptionist (회사, 호텔 등의) 접수직원, 안내 데스크 직원

22 W: I can't believe you are a middle school student. Seems like just yesterday that you were in a baby carriage.

네가 중학생인 것이 믿기지 않는구나. 네가 유모차를 타던 것이 어제 같은데.

B: Actually, I am not a middle school student any more. I already graduated last Wednesday.

사실, 저는 더 이상 중학생이 아니에요. 지난 수요일에 이미 졸업했는걸요.

W: Yeah, time flies like an arrow. By the way, last Thursday was your birthday, wasn't it?

그래, 시간이 화살처럼 빨리 지나는구나. 그런데 지난 목요일이 너의 생일이었지, 그랬지?

Q: 소년은 언제 중학교를 졸업했나요?
(A) 어제   (B) 지난 화요일
(C) 지난 수요일   (D) 지난 목요일

해설 소년은 지난 수요일에 중학교를 졸업하고 지난 목요일에는 생일을 맞이했습니다.

★ baby carriage 유모차

23 M: Linda, congratulations! I was surprised you won the first prize in the English speech contest.

Linda, 축하해! 영어 말하기 대회에서 네가 일등상을 타서 깜짝 놀랐어.

W: So was I. I feel like I'm on the top of the world.

나도 그랬어. 날아갈 것 같은 기분이야.

M: So what will you do with the prize money?

그래 상금으로 무엇을 할 거니?

Q : Linda의 기분은 어떻습니까?

　　(A) 부러워하는　　　　　　　(B) 기쁜

　　(C) 겁먹은　　　　　　　　　(D) 당황스러운

해설 Linda가 영어 말하기 대회에서 일등상과 상금을 탔습니다.

★ win the prize 상을 타다 / be on the top of the world 세상 꼭대기에 오른 기분이다. 기분이 매우 좋다.

24　W : Who transferred the money to Mr. Wilson's account just now? Was it you or Jeff?

누가 방금 전 Mr. Wilson의 계좌로 돈을 보냈지요? 당신인가요, 아니면 Jeff인가요?

M : I did. Is there something wrong?

내가 보냈는데요. 무슨 잘못된 거라도 있나요?

W : Take a look at it, Brian. This should be 35,000 dollars, not 350,000 dollars! You added another zero by mistake.

한번 보세요, Brian. 이것은 350,000달러가 아니라 35,000달러이어야 해요! 당신이 실수로 0을 하나 보탰어요.

Q : Brian이 다음에 할 행동으로 가장 가능성이 높은 것은 무엇입니까?

　　(A) 서류에서 추가된 영을 지운다.

　　(B) 경찰에 절도 신고를 한다.

　　(C) Jeff를 찾아 사장에게 데려온다.

　　(D) 은행에 연락하여 송금을 취소한다.

해설 Brian이 금액을 잘못 확인하고 거래처에 돈을 보낸 상황입니다. 서둘러 은행에 연락하여 송금 거래를 취소해야 하겠습니다.

★ transfer money 돈을 이체하다. 송금하다 / account 은행계좌 / erase off 지워 없애다 / theft 절도 / cancel 취소하다

25　M : Are you Jessy? Wow, I didn't expect to meet you here.

너 Jessy 맞지? 와, 너를 이곳에서 만날 줄 몰랐어.

W : Oh, my! Harry, Long time no see!

맙소사! Harry, 정말 오랜만이다!

M : Why not go out of this crowded hall and talk over a cup of coffee? I have much to tell you.

이 복잡한 홀에서 나가 커피 한 잔 하면서 이야기하는 게 어때? 너에게 해줄 말이 많아.

Q : 그들이 다음에 할 행동으로 가장 가능성이 높은 것은 무엇입니까?

　　(A) 커피숍으로 간다.

　　(B) 서로에게 작별 인사를 한다.

　　(C) 전화번호를 교환한다.

　　(D) 그 장소에서 약간 더 이야기한다.

해설 마지막 말에서 커피를 마시며 이야기하자는 남자의 말이 힌트입니다.

★ talk over a cup of coffee 커피 마시며 이야기하다

26　W : How about this coat? Does it match well?

이 코트 어때요? 잘 어울리나요?

M : Okay, honey. But that is the 10th coat you've tried on. Why not choose one now?

좋아, 자기야. 하지만 그것이 당신이 입어 본 열 번째 코트야. 이

제 하나 고르는 것이 어때?

W : I'm afraid I'll regret buying it. This expensive kind of coat is not easy to buy again.

사놓고 후회하게 될까 두려워요. 이런 비싼 코트는 다시 사기가 쉽지 않아요.

Q : 그들은 어디에 있나요?

　　(A) 식당에　　　　　　　　　(B) 의류점에

　　(C) 결혼식장에　　　　　　　(D) 병원에

해설 여자가 옷가게에서 코트를 고르는 중입니다.

★ match well 잘 어울리다 / try on 한번 입어보다

27　M : I'm going to get a suit with a tie. Will you come with me?

넥타이와 정장 한 벌을 구입할건데 함께 가주겠니?

W : Later. I'm terribly busy getting my report finished.

나중에. 보고서를 마치느라 너무 바빠.

M : Come on. How I wish you could choose it for me!

그러지 말고. 당신이 정장을 골라 주기를 내가 얼마나 바랬는데!

Q : 여자는 지금 무엇을 하고 있습니까?

　　(A) 정장 구매하기

　　(B) 요리 하기

　　(C) 보고서 작성하기

　　(D) 취업 면접시험을 준비하기

해설 보고서를 작성하느라 바쁜 여자에게 남자가 정장을 사러 함께 가자고 조르는 상황입니다.

★ suit 정장

28　W : Do you know that plastic soda bottles can be made into clothes?

플라스틱 탄산음료 병으로 옷을 만들 수 있다는 사실 아세요?

M : Really? I know broken pieces of glass are used to make the road we drive on.

정말요? 나는 깨진 유리병이 우리가 지나다니는 자동차 도로를 만드는데 사용된다는 것은 알아요.

W : That's amazing! We should not throw away even a paper cup thoughtlessly from now on.

놀랍군요! 이제부터는 종이컵 하나도 생각 없이 버리면 안 되겠어요.

Q : 그들은 무엇에 대하여 이야기하고 있습니까?

　　(A) 화학　　　　　　　　　　(B) 미래 도시

　　(C) 쓰레기 재활용　　　　　　(D) 쓰레기 분리수거

해설 두 사람은 폐품을 재생하는 것에 대하여 자신이 아는 놀라운 사실을 서로에게 소개하고 있습니다.

★ soda 탄산음료 / be made into ~의 재료가 되다 / amazing 놀라운 / from now on 지금부터 계속하여

29　M : I'd like to return this bucket I bought here. It leaks.

여기서 구입한 이 양동이를 물리고 싶어요. 물이 새거든요.

W : Oh, I'm sorry. Would you like a refund?

죄송합니다. 환불해 드릴까요?

M: Actually, I'd prefer to exchange this one for another one.
실은 이것을 다른 제품과 교환하고 싶어요.

Q: 남자는 왜 여자를 방문했습니까?
(A) 양동이를 하나 더 사려고
(B) 양동이에 대하여 환불을 받으려고
(C) 양동이를 수선하려고
(D) 자신이 구매한 물건을 교환하려고

해설 마지막 말에서 남자가 이상 없는 제품으로 교환하고 싶어 하는 것을 알 수 있습니다.

★ leak 새다, 유출되다 / refund 환불 / exchange A for B A와 B를 교환하다

30 W: Wow, you get a brand new bike. I saw a retail store selling the same model at 340 dollars.
와, 새 자전거를 샀구나. 나는 이것과 똑같은 모델을 소매점에서 340달러에 파는 것을 보았어.

M: Really? I bought this online at just 280 dollars. Instead of paying an additional 20 dollars for assembling it, I did it on my own.
정말? 나는 온라인으로 겨우 280달러에 구입했어. 조립하는 비용 20달러를 추가로 지불하는 대신 내가 직접 조립했어.

W: Great! Let me know the Internet address of the store.
굉장한데! 그 가게의 인터넷 주소를 알려줘.

Q: 남자는 자전거 가격으로 얼마를 지불했습니까?
(A) 340달러   (B) 300달러
(C) 280달러   (D) 260달러

해설 여자가 소매상에서 340달러에 파는 것을 보았다는 자전거를 남자는 온라인으로 280달러에 구입했다고 말합니다. 조립비용 20달러 때문에 혼동하지 마세요. 별도로 조립비용 20달러가 더 들었을 텐데 남자 스스로 조립하여 그 비용을 절감했다는 뜻입니다.

★ brand new 신제품의 / retail 소매의 / online 인터넷망을 통하여 / assemble 조립하다 / on one's own 스스로, 혼자서

31 M: Hi, Pamela! Sit here. So are you getting ready for summer?
안녕, Pamela! 여기 앉으세요. 그래, 여름 준비는 하고 있나요?

W: I just bought summer clothes and sandals. Now I want to change my look. Would short hair be well with me?
방금 여름에 입을 옷과 샌들을 샀어요. 이제 내 외모를 바꾸려고요. 짧은 머리가 나랑 잘 어울릴까요?

M: That's a good choice! How would you like the color? Blonde is in fashion this year.
좋은 선택이에요! 머리색을 어떻게 해드릴까요? 금발이 올해의 대세예요.

Q: Pamela는 어디에 있습니까?
(A) 미용실   (B) 옷가게
(C) 미술관   (D) 헬스클럽

해설 두 사람의 대화를 통해 여자는 손님이고 남자는 미용사임을 알 수 있습니다.

★ look 외모 / How would you like ~? (미용실이나 식당 등에서 직원이 손님에게) ~을 어떻게 해드릴까요? / blonde 금발

32 W: Honey, did you check if we left out anything?
여보, 혹시 뭐 빠뜨린 거 있나 확인했어요?

M: Yeah. My passport, my digital camera, credit cards, some medicine, and...
그래요. 내 여권, 디지털 카메라, 신용카드, 약 그리고 ...

W: You didn't mention the flight tickets. Did you get them in your bag?
항공권을 말하지 않았어요. 그거 가방에 넣어 두었나요?

Q: 그들은 무엇을 하고 있습니까?
(A) 항공권 예약
(B) 여행 짐 꾸리기
(C) 분실한 항공권 찾기
(D) 가게에서 선물 고르기

해설 남자가 언급하는 여러 가지 물건들과 항공권을 확인하라는 여자의 말을 통해 두 사람이 여행을 떠나기 앞서 짐을 꾸리고 있음을 알 수 있습니다.

★ passport 여권 / medicine 약 / flight ticket 항공권 / pack up 짐을 꾸리다

33 M: This is awful. According to this article, there's a factory outside the town. That factory is pumping chemicals into the river.
지독하군요. 이 기사에 따르면 도시 외곽에 공장이 하나 있는데, 그 공장이 화학물질을 강에 내보낸다고 하네요.

W: How long has the factory been doing that?
그 공장이 얼마동안 그런 짓을 했는데요?

M: It says the factory has been throwing chemicals for 3 years.
기사에는 그 공장이 3년 동안 화학물질을 버려왔다고 쓰여 있어요.

Q: 남자는 무엇을 하고 있습니까?
(A) 강으로 화학물질을 퍼내기
(B) 영화 보기
(C) 공장에서 일하기
(D) 신문 읽기

해설 남자가 신문 기사를 읽고 여자에게 이야기해주는 상황입니다.

★ article 신문 기사 / chemical 화학물질 / pump 펌프로 퍼내다

34 W: What would you like to have for your birthday present?
생일선물로 무엇을 받고 싶니?

B: My mind is set on one thing. I'm dying for a kitty.
내 생각은 단 하나뿐이에요. 새끼 고양이가 갖고 싶어 죽겠어요.

W: But I can't buy you a kitty. You've got to understand your mom. I'm allergic to cats.
하지만 고양이를 사줄 수는 없어. 넌 엄마를 이해해야 해. 엄마는 고양이 알레르기가 있어.

Q: 그들은 무엇에 대하여 이야기하고 있습니까?
(A) 생일 파티

(B) 생일 선물

(C) 고양이 기르는 법

(D) 고양이 알레르기가 생기는 한 가지 이유

해설 소년이 생일선물로 고양이를 갖고 싶어 하지만 고양이 알레르기가 있는 엄마 때문에 고양이는 안 된다고 달래는 상황입니다.

★ kitty 고양이 새끼 / have got to ~ ~해야 한다(=have to ~) / be allergic to ~에 알레르기가 있다

35 **M :** Sue, you look terribly busy this morning.

Sue, 오늘 아침 매우 바빠 보이는군요.

W : I am. I have a meeting which starts in ten minutes. I also have to mail these letters.

맞아요. 10분 후에 시작하는 미팅이 있어요. 또한 이 편지들을 발송해야 해요.

M : Um, I have a bit of headache. I'm going out to get some aspirin. I could mail the letters if you want.

음, 내가 두통이 있어서 아스피린을 사러 나갈 거예요. 원하시면 내가 편지를 발송해 줄 수 있어요.

Q : 남자는 Sue를 위하여 어떤 일을 하기 원합니까?

(A) 미팅 준비

(B) 편지 발송

(C) 아스피린을 사오는 일

(D) 그녀를 병원으로 데려가는 일

해설 두 사람은 직장 동료인 것 같습니다. 바쁜 여자를 위하여 남자가 외출하면서 편지를 발송해주겠다고 제안하고 있습니다.

★ headache 두통 / aspirin 아스피린 (두통약의 하나)

36 **W :** I'd like to go to your exhibition with my children. Does it open at 10 a.m., right?

아이들과 함께 귀측의 전시회에 가고 싶어요. 오전 10시에 개관이죠. 맞죠?

M : That's only on weekends. On weekdays, you are available from 2 p.m. to 5 p.m.

주말에만 그렇습니다. 평일에는 오후 2시부터 5시까지 이용 가능합니다.

W : I see. Then I have to go this Saturday. I'm not free in the afternoon.

잘 알았습니다. 그럼 이번 토요일에 가야 하겠군요. 오후에는 시간이 없어서요.

Q : 토요일에 여자는 몇 시부터 전시회장에 입장할 수 있습니까?

(A) 오전 10시 　　　　　(B) 오후 12시

(C) 오후 2시 　　　　　(D) 오후 5시

해설 남자는 전시회장의 안내 직원입니다. 여자가 전시회장 문 여는 시간이 오전 10시가 맞는지 문의하자 남자는 주말의 경우에 그렇다고 대답합니다. 여사가 토요일에 전시회장에 간다면 주말 시간대가 적용됩니다.

★ exhibition 전시(회) / weekends 주말 / weekdays 평일 / available 이용 가능한

37 **M :** I'm fed up with preparing for the presentation all day. Let's take a walk for a change.

종일 발표 준비하는 일에 질려버렸어요. 기분 전환을 위해 산책합시다.

W : Good idea! I'd rather cycle around the park. Can I take your bike?

좋은 생각이에요! 나는 공원에서 자전거를 탈래요. 내가 당신 자전거를 가져가도 될까요?

M : Why not? Let's go out together!

물론이죠. 함께 나갑시다!

Q : 말하는 이들은 다음에 무슨 일을 하겠습니까?

(A) 발표를 준비한다.

(B) 시험을 치른다.

(C) 공원에 간다.

(D) 강아지와 함께 논다.

해설 남자가 기분전환을 위하여 산책하자고 하자 여자는 공원에 따라가서 자전거를 타겠다고 말합니다.

★ be fed up with ~에 싫증나다. 물리다 / for a change 기분 전환을 위하여

38 **W :** I left my school bag behind on the subway this morning.

오늘 아침에 내 학교 가방을 지하철에 두고 내렸어요.

M : What does your bag look like?

가방이 어떻게 생겼죠?

W : It's a pink checkered backpack and a little teddy bear is attached to the zipper.

분홍색 체크무늬가 있는 등에 매는 가방인데 작은 테디 베어 인형이 지퍼에 매달려 있어요.

Q : 여자는 어디에 있나요?

(A) 경찰서 　　　　　(B) 교실

(C) 문구점 　　　　　(D) 분실물 보관소

해설 여자가 지하철에 두고 내린 학교 가방을 찾기 위하여 분실물 보관소 직원과 이야기하는 상황입니다.

★ checkered 체크무늬가 있는 / be attached to ~에 부착되어 있다 / stationery 문구 / lost and found (공공장소 등에 설치된) 분실물 보관소

39 **M :** Does it take a long time to get to the Vision Tower by subway?

지하철로 Vision Tower까지 가는 데 한참 걸리나요?

W : Sure, you have to walk from the station over 20 minutes. As for me, I'd take a bus. Bus 34 stops right in front of the building.

물론이죠, 지하철에서 20분 넘게 걸어야 해요. 나라면 버스를 타겠어요. 34번 버스가 그 건물 바로 앞에 섭니다.

M : That's very kind of you. Thanks. I'll take it.

친절하시군요. 감사합니다. 그 버스를 타야겠네요.

Q : 남자가 어떤 것에 탑승할 가능성이 가장 높습니까?

(A) 지하철 　　　　　(B) 버스

(C) 택시 　　　　　(D) 기차

해설 남자가 여자로부터 목적지 건물 바로 앞에 정차하는 버스에 대하여 안내받은 상황입니다.

★ as for ∼에 대하여 말하자면

40 W: It takes so long for me to get to school. I have no time to study.
학교까지 가는 데 너무 오래 걸려. 공부할 시간이 없어.

M: Right. Commuting takes your energy away.
맞아. 통학하는 것이 네 에너지를 다 뺏어가고 있어.

W: So I've found three rooms near the school. I'm going to check them out.
그래서 학교 부근에 방 세 개를 찾아두었어. 그것들을 검토해보려 가는 중이야.

Q: 무엇이 여자의 계획입니까?
(A) 학교를 그만 두는 것
(B) 통학을 위하여 차를 구입하는 것
(C) 학교 기숙사로 입주하는 것
(D) 학교 근처에 방을 얻는 것

해설 마지막에 여자가 학교 부근에 방 셋을 알아두었고 이것을 검토하러 간다고 하는 말이 힌트입니다.

★ commute (학교로) 통학하다, (직장으로) 통근하다 / dormitory 기숙사

PUZZLE 1

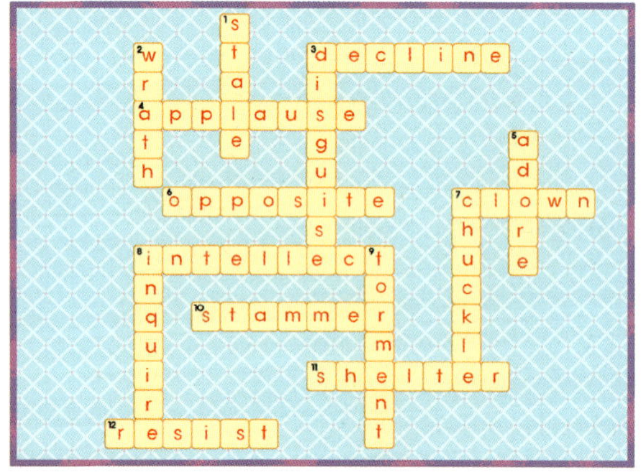

Across

3 (decline) 어떤 것의 질, 양, 또는 중요성에서의 감소
4 (applause) 많은 사람들이 박수 치는 소리
6 (opposite) 가능한 한 어떤 것과 다른,
7 (clown) 재밌는 의상과 화장을 하고 사람들을 웃게 만드는 사람
8 (intellect) 사물을 이해하고 총명하게 생각하는 능력
10 (stammer) 많은 끊김과 반복되는 소리로 말하는 것
11 (shelter) 위험으로부터의 보호 또는 바람, 비, 뜨거운 태양 등으로부터의 보호
12 (resist) 매우 좋아하는 것을 갖거나 하고 싶은 일을 하는 것을 멈추는 것

Down

1 (stale) 먹기에 신선하지 않거나 좋지 않은
2 (wrath) 극도의 노여움, 화
3 (disguise) 외모를 바꾸는 것
5 (adore) 누군가를 매우 사랑하고 자랑스럽게 느끼는 것
7 (chuckle) 조용히 웃는 것
8 (inquire) 누군가에게 정보를 묻는 것
9 (torment) 심각한 정신적 또는 육체적 고통

PART C. Listen and Predict

01. [B]	02. [D]	03. [B]	04. [A]	05. [C]
06. [C]	07. [D]	08. [B]	09. [C]	10. [C]
11. [C]	12. [C]	13. [D]	14. [C]	15. [D]
16. [B]	17. [D]	18. [B]	19. [B]	20. [D]

1 M: Linda is on a trip to London. She checks into a hotel room where she can be connected with the Internet. She needs access to the Internet from her laptop to check e-mail. She follows the instructions for access to the Internet several times, but it doesn't work. She makes a phone call to the front desk at the lobby to ask for some help.
Linda는 런던에서 여행 중입니다. 그녀는 인터넷을 이용할 수 있는 호텔 방에 숙박 수속을 합니다. 노트북 컴퓨터를 통해서 이메일을 확인할 수 있도록 인터넷에 접속해야 합니다. 여러 번 인터넷에 접속하기 위해 지시사항대로 하지만 작동이 되지 않습니다. 호텔 로비에 있는 접수대에 도움을 위해 전화를 합니다.

Q: Linda는 무엇을 물어보겠습니까?
(A) 내 컴퓨터가 작동되는 건가요?
(B) 인터넷에 대한 도움을 받을 수 있을까요?
(C) 룸서비스가 가능합니까?
(D) 아침에 모닝콜을 해 주시겠어요?

해설 인터넷 접속에 대한 도움을 받아야 하는 상황입니다.

2 W: Susan has lived in the downtown by herself for five years. Today, she gets a call from her father. He is also missing his daughter and asks her to visit her hometown this coming Saturday to have family gathering. She promises to her father that she will go, but then realizes that she has to work on that day. So, she decides to ask her co-worker, Helen, a favor.
Susan은 다운타운에 5년 동안 혼자 살고 있습니다. 오늘은 아버지로부터 전화를 받았습니다. 아버지는 Susan을 보고 싶어해서 토요일 가족모임에 고향에 오라고 합니다. 아버지에게 가겠다고 이야기 하지만, 곧 토요일에 근무를 해야 하는 것을 알게 됩니다. 그래서 동료인 Helen에게 부탁을 하기로 합니다.

Q: Helen은 어떻게 대답하겠습니까?
(A) 아버지가 날 많이 보고 싶어 하셔.
(B) 내일 나대신 근무 좀 서 줄 수 있니?
(C) 그들은 다운타운에 사시고 계셔.
(D) 문제없어. 내가 대신 해줄게.

해설 부탁을 받는 Helen의 응답을 고르는 문제입니다. 따라서 (A)와 (B)는 Susan의 대사이므로 답이 될 수 없습니다.

3 **M:** Tomorrow is Helen's birthday. It is such a special day because Helen and one of her classmates, Jane, were born on the same day. They both have a plan for a nice birthday party. They want to invite as many friends as they can and they start making a list for inviting people. First, they make a phone call to the closest friend, Kate. But Kate has another important plan for tomorrow.
내일은 Helen의 생일입니다. Helen과 반 친구인 Jane이 같은 날에 태어났기 때문에 특별한 날이기도 합니다. 그들은 멋진 생일파티를 계획하고 있습니다. 가능한 한 많은 친구를 초대하고 싶어서 초대할 친구들의 명단을 만듭니다. 먼저, 그들은 가장 친한 친구인 Kate에게 전화를 합니다. 하지만 Kate는 내일 중요한 계획이 있습니다.

Q: Kate가 할 말은 무엇이겠습니까?
(A) 문제없어. 난 틀림없이 파티에 갈 거야.
(B) 나도 그러고 싶은데, 다른 약속이 있어.
(C) 정말 우연이다. 우리 생일이 똑같네.
(D) 걱정마. 내가 생일 파티를 취소할게.

해설 다른 약속이 있어서 못가는 말을 전하는 내용입니다.

★ coincidence 우연

4 **W:** Bill and Tom have an English speech contest as a team. This contest is one of the biggest events in the city. However, the day before the contest, Bill caught a severe cold. He went to the hospital to see a doctor, but he does not get well now. Today is the day for the contest. Bill is a little bit frustrated because of his worsening condition. Tom wants to make Bill feel at ease.
Bill과 Tom은 같은 팀으로 영어 말하기 대회에 나갑니다. 이 대회는 도시에서 가장 큰 대회 중 하나입니다. 하지만 대회 전날, Bill이 심한 감기에 걸렸습니다. 그는 병원에 가서 진찰을 받았지만 나아지지는 않았습니다. 오늘은 대회 당일 날입니다. Bill은 안 좋아지는 상태 때문에 약간 짜증나 있습니다. Tom은 Bill을 편하게 해 주고 싶어 합니다.

Q: Tom이 할 말은 무엇이겠습니까?
(A) 걱정마. 모든 것이 잘 될거야.
(B) 내 생각에는 네가 지금 멈춰야 해.
(C) 집에 가서 좀 쉬어라.
(D) 완벽하네. 이제 넌 괜찮아.

해설 상대방에게 힘을 불어 넣어주는 내용을 찾으면 됩니다.

5 **M:** Steven has an appointment with his family for dinner tonight. They decide to go to a well-known steak house. So yesterday he asked his sister, Donna, to reserve 5 seats on-line for his family members, but he forgot to tell her not to pay in advance because he had a mind to pay all expenses this time. When he arrives at the restaurant, he realizes his sister already paid in advance.
Steven은 오늘 저녁 가족과 약속이 있습니다. 그들은 유명한 스테이크 음식점에 가기로 하였습니다. 그래서 어제, 그는 여동생인 Donna에게 인터넷으로 가족을 위해서 다섯 자리를 예약할 것을 부탁했습니다. 하지만 그가 식사 값을 지불하려고 했기 때문에 여동생에게 미리 값을 지불하지 말라고 이야기하는 것을 잊어버렸습니다. Steven이 식당에 도착 했을 때, 그는 여동생이 미리 값을 지불한 것을 알게 되었습니다.

Q: Steven이 할 말은 무엇이겠습니까?
(A) 네 실수야. 다른 곳으로 가자.
(B) 내가 살게. 많이 먹어.
(C) 그러지 않아도 됐는데.
(D) 자리 예약해 줘서 고맙다.

해설 여동생, Donna가 먼저 금액을 지불한 것에 대해 할 수 있는 응답을 고르는 문제입니다.

6 **W:** Mark has been on a diet for 3 months and it has worked well so far. He finds out there are several do's and don'ts. He thinks the best way to lose weight is to eat right and work out regularly. And he tries to stay away from junk food like hamburgers and pizza. Lisa decides to go on a diet with Mark. She is asking some advice to Mark before starting.
Mark는 세 달 동안 다이어트 중입니다. 지금까지는 잘 되어 오고 있습니다. 그는 몇 가지 해야 할 일과 하지 말아야 할 일을 알게 되었습니다. 체중을 줄이는 가장 좋은 방법은 올바르게 식사하고 정기적으로 운동을 해야 한다고 생각합니다. 그리고 그는 햄버거나 피자와 같은 몸에 안 좋은 음식들을 피하기 위해 노력합니다. Lisa는 Mark와 함께 다이어트를 하기로 결심합니다. 그녀는 시작하기 전에 Mark에게 조언을 구합니다.

Q: Mark가 어떻게 대답하겠습니까?
(A) 몇 번 굶으면 알게 될 거야.
(B) 빠른 다이어트는 어떤 때에는 효과가 있어.
(C) 식습관과 규칙적인 운동이 가장 중요해.
(D) 가끔은 너 스스로 여유를 가질 필요가 있어.

해설 Mark는 가장 중요한 것이 식습관과 꾸준한 운동이라고 했습니다.

7 **M:** This year, Ruth becomes a middle school student. Susie, her sister, is planning a surprise party for Ruth. She bought some nice presents and Ruth's favorite food yesterday. But Ruth's brother didn't know Susie was preparing a surprise party. He accidentally told Ruth about a party plan yesterday. Ruth doesn't want to disappoint

Susie. When Susie gives Ruth presents and food, Ruth pretends it is surprising.

올해 Ruth는 중학생이 됩니다. 그녀의 언니인 Susie는 Ruth를 위해 깜짝 파티를 준비합니다. 그녀는 어제 선물도 사고 Ruth가 좋아하는 음식도 샀습니다. 하지만 Ruth의 남동생은 Susie가 깜짝 파티를 준비하는지 몰랐습니다. 그는 어제 우연히 Ruth에게 파티 계획을 이야기했습니다. Ruth는 Susie를 실망시키고 싶지 않았습니다. Susie가 Ruth에게 선물과 음식을 주었을 때, Ruth는 놀라는 척 합니다.

Q : Ruth가 할 말은 무엇입니까?
(A) 이게 흔히 말하는 깜짝 파티이구나.
(B) 난 파티를 좋아하지 않아. 그러니까 가치가 없어.
(C) 네가 계획하고 있는 거 이미 알고 있어.
(D) 정말 놀랐어! 고마워.

해설 알고 있었지만 모르는 체 하는 상황입니다.

8 W : Mike has a final exam today. He almost stayed up late at night, preparing for the final. Today he wakes up a little late and he runs to the school. The exam starts at 9:30. He is barely on time in the classroom and takes a deep breath, getting himself ready for the test. When he starts taking the exam, he realizes he left all his pens at home. So he needs to ask his friend.

Mike는 오늘 기말고사 준비를 합니다. 그는 거의 밤늦게까지 기말고사 준비를 했습니다. 오늘 그는 약간 늦게 일어나서 학교로 달려갑니다. 학교 시험은 9:30에 시작합니다. 그는 간신히 교실에 정시에 들어갔고, 깊은 숨을 쉬며, 시험 준비를 하고 있습니다. 그가 시험을 보려할 때, 그는 모든 펜을 집에 놓고 온 것을 알게 되었습니다. 그래서 친구에게 부탁해야 합니다.

Q : Mike는 무엇을 물어보겠습니까?
(A) 언제 시험이 시작했니?
(B) 쓸 수 있는 연필 하나 빌려도 될까?
(C) 늦게 일어났니?
(D) 내 펜 좀 찾아주겠니?

해설 펜을 빌려야 하는 상황입니다.

9 M : Sam and Minsu have known each other for 5 years. Today Sam is coming to Korea for the first time. Minsu, his Korean friend, is at the airport to pick Sam up at the airport. Minsu already made up some plans for sightseeing for Sam. Minsu is asking what Sam will like to do first. Sam has flown about 13 hours. So he feels very hungry.

Sam과 Minsu는 서로 5년 동안 알고 지냈습니다. 오늘은 Sam이 처음으로 한국에 오는 날입니다. 그의 한국 친구 Minsu는 공항에 Sam을 마중하러 갔습니다. Minsu는 이미 Sam의 관광을 위해서 계획을 짜 놨습니다. Minsu는 Sam에게 무엇을 먼저 하고 싶은지 물어봅니다. Sam은 13시간동안 비행기를 타고 왔습니다. 그래서 그는 매우 배고파합니다.

Q : Sam이 할 말은 무엇입니까?
(A) 행동이 말보다 빨라.
(B) 집과 같은 곳은 없어.
(C) 어느 상황이건, 먹는 것이 먼저야.
(D) 보는 것이 믿는 것이지.

해설 배고플 때 쓸 수 있는 표현을 고르는 문제입니다.

10 W : Robert is watching a documentary program in the living room. It is about the environmental issues including how to discard wastes around us. He is impressed with one of the solutions the program is suggesting, which is recycling and volunteer works. He wants to join the volunteer works. Robert makes a call to Linda and asks her to join together. Linda feels the same as Robert does.

Robert는 거실에서 다큐멘터리 프로그램을 보고 있습니다. 우리 주위의 쓰레기를 어떻게 처리해야 하는지에 대한 환경 문제를 다루는 프로그램입니다. 그는 프로그램이 제안하는 해결 방법 중 하나인 재활용과 자원봉사에 감명을 받습니다. 그는 자원봉사 일에 지원하고 싶어 합니다. Robert는 Linda에게 전화를 해서 같이 가자고 물어봅니다. Linda도 Robert와 같은 생각입니다.

Q : Linda가 어떻게 반응하겠습니까?
(A) 이 프로그램을 녹화해두자.
(B) 그 이상도 그 이하도 아니야.
(C) 재활용이 중요해.
(D) 다큐멘터리는 언제나 심각해.

해설 방송에서 제안하는 해결에 동의를 하고 있으므로 재활용이나 자원봉사에 관한 언급이 있어야 합니다.

11 M : Tom has a meeting with his friends at a cafe after school. They are talking about the school project, how to develop discussion skills. While having talks at the cafe, he finds out a big TV screen on the wall. A big baseball game is on TV. Suddenly there is a shout of joy from Daniel because his team won the game. Daniel feels so happy that he says he will buy pizza for his friends.

Tom은 학교가 끝난 후에 친구들과 카페에서 모임을 갖습니다. 그들은 토론 기술을 발전시키는 방법에 관한 학교 프로젝트에 대해서 이야기 하고 있습니다. 카페에서 이야기 하고 있는 동안, 그는 벽에 큰 TV 스크린을 봅니다. 야구경기가 방영되고 있습니다. 갑자기 Daniel이 환호를 했습니다. 왜냐하면 그의 팀이 이겼기 때문입니다. Daniel은 너무 기뻐서 친구들에게 피자를 사겠다고 말합니다.

Q : Daniel이 할 말이 무엇입니까?
(A) 난 한국 스타일의 음식이 좋아.
(B) 커피 한잔 하자.
(C) 내가 살게. 피자 가게로 가자.
(D) 야구는 내가 가장 좋아하는 운동이야.

해설 피자를 사겠다는 내용을 고르는 문제입니다.

12 W: Terry is the class leader. One of his favorite subjects is Physical Education because he can enjoy many outdoor activities rather than studying theories. When he comes back to the classroom after soccer practice in Physical Education class, Joe, one of his classmates, finds that his money in the wallet has been stolen. Terry and Joe search everywhere but in vain. He cannot help telling this to his teacher.

Terry는 학급 반장입니다. 그가 가장 좋아하는 주제 중 하나가 체육입니다. 왜냐하면 이론을 공부하는 것보다 많은 외부 활동을 즐기는 것을 좋아하기 때문입니다. 체육 시간에 축구 연습을 하고 교실로 돌아왔을 때 반 친구인 Joe가 지갑에 있던 돈이 없어진 것을 알게 됩니다. Terry와 Joe는 모든 곳을 다 찾았지만 허사였습니다. 그는 선생님께 말씀드리지 않을 수 없습니다.

Q: Terry가 할 말은 무엇입니까?
(A) 난 축구 연습을 즐겨.
(B) 너하고 나만 아는 일이야.
(C) 난 이걸 선생님께 말씀드려야 하겠어.
(D) 우리 선생님은 이걸 아시면 혼내실거야.

해설 찾아봤지만 돈이 발견되지 않아 선생님께 말씀드린다는 내용이 나와야 합니다.

13 M: Jack is traveling in Korea. This is his second visit to Korea, but still there are a lot of places for him to go around. Suchan is one of his Korean friends and he is helping Jack enjoy Korean culture. Suchan invites Jack to his home to have dinner together. Jack feels uneasy because there is unfamiliar etiquette he is not used to even though Suchan explains it to Jack kindly. But Jack thinks he is learning by doing.

Jack은 한국을 여행하고 있습니다. 이번이 두 번째 방문이지만 그가 돌아볼 곳은 아직도 많습니다. Suchan은 한국 친구 중에 한 명이고 Jack이 한국 문화를 만끽하도록 도와주고 있습니다. Suchan은 Jack에게 함께 저녁식사를 하자고 그의 집으로 초대합니다. Jack은 Suchan이 친절하게 설명을 해 주지만 아직도 이해하지 못하는 익숙하지 못한 예절 때문에 불편함을 느끼고 있습니다. 하지만 Jack은 그가 행하면서 배우고 있다고 생각합니다.

Q: Jack이 할 말은 무엇입니까?
(A) 난 해외여행을 싫어해.
(B) 문화차이는 중요해.
(C) 문화 충격은 극복하기 힘들어.
(D) 경험은 이해보다 효과가 있어.

14 W: Paul is working at a fast food restaurant as a part time job. When a customer comes in, he usually starts taking an order by saying "How may I help you?" After taking an order, he checks the price of each item the customer orders. A customer pays for a meal and Paul gives some changes back if there is any. And finally Paul asks the customer whether to eat at a restaurant or to bring it out.

Paul은 파트타임으로 식당에서 일하고 있습니다. 손님이 들어오면, 그는 주로 "어떻게 도와드릴까요?"라고 물어보면서 주문을 받기 시작합니다. 주문을 받고 난 후에는, 손님이 주문한 음식의 가격을 확인합니다. 손님이 식사 값을 지불하고 Paul은 잔돈이 있으면 거슬러 줍니다. 마지막으로 Paul이 손님에게 식당에서 먹을 건지 포장할 건지에 대해 물어봅니다.

Q: Paul은 어떻게 물어보겠습니까?
(A) 줄을 서 주시겠어요?
(B) 잠깐 기다리시겠어요?
(C) 여기서 드시고 가실 건가요, 포장하실 건가요?
(D) 음료수를 무료로 더 주나요?

해설 식당에서 먹을 건지 포장할 건지에 대한 표현을 찾는 문제입니다.

15 M: Marie is looking for a book in the bookstore. She has to write a report about a language development theory for an assignment. To finish up her report, she needs to buy a book whose title is "Human language acquisition," by Dr. Brown. She asks a clerk where she can find the book. But the clerk says there isn't any copy of the book left in the bookstore.

Marie는 서점에서 책을 찾고 있습니다. 그녀는 숙제로 언어 발달 이론에 대해 보고서를 써야 합니다. 보고서를 끝내기 위해, 그녀는 Dr. Brown이 쓴 "인간 언어 습득"이라는 제목의 책을 사야 합니다. 그녀는 점원에게 그 책이 어디 있는지 물어봅니다. 하지만 점원은 서점에 남아있는 책은 없다고 말합니다.

Q: Marie가 어떻게 물어보겠습니까?
(A) Dr. Brown을 만날 수 있습니까?
(B) 이 책은 얼마입니까?
(C) 이 책을 어디서 찾을 수 있습니까?
(D) 이 책 주문을 할 수 있을까요?

해설 책의 재고가 없는 상황에서 추가 주문을 하는 내용을 고르는 문제입니다.

16 W: Carol is staying at home during the weekend because of the heavy snow outside. Once it snows in winter, it is difficult to go around the downtown. So Carol relaxes herself at home, playing computer games, watching TV, or reading books. Suddenly, there is a phone call from Tom. Tom wants to show Carol a funny video clip on the Internet. So Carol wants to know where she can find it.

Carol은 폭설 때문에 주말동안 집에 머무르고 있습니다. 일단 겨울에 눈이 오면, 시내를 돌아다니기가 어렵습니다. 그래서 Carol은 컴퓨터 게임을 하거나 TV를 보거나 책을 읽으면서 집에서 쉽니다. 갑자기, Tom에게서 전화가 옵니다. Tom은 Carol에게 재미있는 인터넷 동영상을 보여주고 싶습니다. 그래서 Carol은 어디에서 그것을 찾을 수 있는지 알고 싶습니다.

Q: Carol이 할 말은 무엇입니까?

(A) 도와줄 수 있니?

(B) 그 사이트 주소가 뭐니?

(C) 어쨌든, 고마워.

(D) 내 주소 알려줄게.

해설 동영상을 볼 수 있는 주소를 물어보는 내용을 고르는 문제입니다.

17 M: Alice is living in the school dormitory during the school semester. She is working on the report about music. She needs to finish the report by tomorrow. After she writes down the outline of the report, she goes downstairs to a computer room. When she almost finishes typing, the computer shuts down for unknown reasons. She hasn't saved the file yet. She doesn't know what to do. So she asks for help from an assistant.

Alice는 학기 중에 학교 기숙사에서 살고 있습니다. 그녀는 음악에 대한 보고서를 작성하고 있습니다. 내일까지 보고서를 끝내야 합니다. 보고서의 개요를 적고 나서, 아래층에 있는 컴퓨터 실로 갑니다. 그녀가 거의 타이핑을 끝낼 즈음에 컴퓨터가 갑자기 이유 없이 꺼집니다. 그녀는 아직 파일을 저장하지 못했습니다. 그녀는 어떻게 할지 몰라 합니다. 그래서 조교에게 도움을 청합니다.

Q: Alice가 어떻게 물어보겠습니까?

(A) 파일 저장했나요?

(B) 컴퓨터에 무슨 일이 있었던 건가요?

(C) 보고서 끝내는 거 도와주시겠어요?

(D) 내가 무엇을 해야 하죠?

해설 조교에게 도움을 청할 때 어떻게 해야 할지 모르는 상황에서 쓸 수 있는 표현입니다.

18 W: Eric often goes to an amusement park with his friends on Sunday. There are many exiting and thrilling rides, fantastic parades, and beautiful gardens. He walks around for a whole day with the friends. So he gets tired and decides to have lunch. While he is looking for a good place to have lunch. One girl comes to him and asks if he can take a picture of her and her family.

Eric은 일요일에 친구들과 놀이공원을 갑니다. 그곳에는 재미있고 스릴 있는 놀이기구도 많고 환상적인 퍼레이드도 있고, 아름다운 정원도 있습니다. 그는 친구들과 하루 종일 걸어 다닙니다. 피곤해져서는 점심을 먹으러 갑니다. 점심 먹을 장소를 찾고 있는 동안, 한 소녀가 다가와 그녀와 가족들의 사진을 찍어 줄 것을 부탁합니다.

Q: Eric이 어떻게 반응하겠습니까?

(A) 당신의 친절에 감사합니다.

(B) 물론이죠. 어떤 버튼을 눌러야 하는지 말해 주세요.

(C) 혼자 사진 찍기 싫어요.

(D) 난 이 사진이 가장 좋아요.

해설 가족사진을 찍어줄 것을 부탁하는 소녀에게 할 수 있는 말입니다.

19 M: Ann is enjoying pizza with her friends at a restaurant. She thinks this restaurant is pretty good because it is newly built and clean. Most of all, she likes the service from a waitress. After paying for the price of what they ate, they are headed home. Suddenly she realizes that she didn't leave a tip for the waitress. So she comes back to the restaurant.

Ann은 친구들과 함께 식당에서 피자를 즐깁니다. 그녀는 이 식당이 새로 지었고 깨끗해서 좋다고 생각합니다. 무엇보다, 그녀는 식당 여종업원의 서비스가 마음에 듭니다. 그들이 먹은 식사 값을 내고, 그들은 집으로 향합니다. 갑자기 Ann은 여종업원에게 팁을 주지 않은 것을 알게 됩니다. 그래서 그녀는 식당으로 다시 돌아갑니다.

Q: Ann이 어떤 말을 하겠습니까?

(A) 지금까지 본 최고의 종업원이네요.

(B) 죄송합니다. 팁을 놓고 가는 것을 빼먹었네요.

(C) 죄송한데 요금이 더 나왔는데요.

(D) 이 식당은 날 편안하게 해 주는 군요.

해설 팁을 놓고 간 여자가 할 수 있는 표현을 고르는 문제입니다.

★ overcharge 더 많이 부과하다 / cozy 편안한

20 W: Ryan is 14 years old. He is a music genius. When he was 5 years old, he started playing the piano by himself. He is good at singing as well as he has a clear and refined tone of voice. More surprisingly, once listening to songs, he can pinpoint the exact notes of the songs. He hasn't taken any special music lessons so far. When people ask him about his special talents, he admits he was born with the gift.

Ryan은 14살입니다. 그는 음악 천재입니다. 그가 5살이었을 때, 그는 스스로 피아노를 치기 시작했습니다. 그는 깨끗하고 세련된 음색을 갖고 있을 뿐만 아니라 노래도 잘 부릅니다. 더 놀라운 것은, 일단 노래를 들으면, 그 노래의 정확한 음을 찾아냅니다. 그는 지금까지 특별한 음악 레슨을 받은 것도 아닙니다. 사람들이 그에게 특별한 음악적 재주에 대해 물어보면, 그는 재능을 타고 난 것에 대해 인정합니다.

Q: Ryan이 어떻게 대답하겠습니까?

(A) 밀져야 본전이에요.

(B) 사돈 남 말 하고 있네요.

(C) 저도 알 건 압니다.

(D) 듣는 것으로도 배우고 연주할 수 있어요.

01. (B)	02. (C)	03. (C)	04. (A)	05. (B)
06. (C)	07. (D)	08. (D)	09. (B)	10. (D)
11. (C)	12. (D)	13. (C)	14. (A)	15. (B)
16. (B)	17. (C)	18. (D)	19. (B)	20. (C)

1 **W:** What would you like to have for breakfast?
아침식사로 뭘 드릴까요?

M: I'd like bacon, eggs, and coffee.
베이컨, 달걀 그리고 커피요.

W: How would you like your eggs?
달걀은 어떻게 해드릴까요?

M: Sunny-side up, please.
한쪽만 익혀주세요.

Q: 다음에 이어질 여자의 말은 무엇입니까?
(A) 긍정적으로 생각하세요.
(B) 알았습니다. 10분이면 준비될 겁니다.
(C) 해가 곧 떠오를 거예요.
(D) 당신이 결정하세요.

해설 'sunny side of things'는 '사물의 긍정적인 부분'을 의미하고, 'depend on~'은 '~에게 달려있다'는 뜻입니다. 'sunny-side up'은 '계란을 한 쪽만 익혀서 계란 노른자가 원형을 유지한 상태'를 말합니다.

2 **W:** Do you have anything to declare to customs?
세관에 신고할 것이 있으세요?

M: I have nothing to declare.
신고할 게 없습니다.

W: What's the purpose of your visit?
방문목적은 무엇입니까?

M: I'm here on business.
사업차 왔습니다.

Q: 다음에 이어질 여자의 말은 무엇입니까?
(A) 오, 그래요? 저는 휴가를 보내러 왔어요.
(B) 전 뉴욕에 있는 르네상스호텔에 머물거예요.
(C) 미국에는 얼마동안 머무실 예정입니까?
(D) 제 명함을 드릴까요?

해설 'on holiday'는 '휴가를 보내러'라는 의미이고, 'on business'는 '사업을 하러'라는 뜻입니다.

★ declare 신고하다 / customs 세관

3 **M:** I didn't do well on my history exam yesterday.
어제 역사시험을 잘못 봤어.

W: That's why you have a long face.
그래서 그렇게 기분이 안 좋아 보이는 구나.

M: I'm afraid my parents would be disappointed.
부모님께서 정말 실망하셨을까봐 걱정이야.

W: Keep your chin up! You will be better on the next exam.
기운 내! 다음 시험에는 분명히 잘 할거야.

Q: 다음에 이어질 남자의 말은 무엇입니까?
(A) 시험에 최선을 다 할 필요가 없었어.
(B) 턱을 다쳤어. 그래서 입을 벌릴 수가 없어.
(C) 고마워. 너와 얘기하니 기분이 편해져.
(D) 내가 뭘 잘못했다고 이런 일이 생긴 거야?

해설 'You have a long face.'는 '기분이 안 좋아 보인다.'라는 의미이고, 'Keep your chin up.'은 '기운 내.'라는 의미입니다.

★ chin 턱 / comfort 편안 / deserve 자격이 있다

4 **M:** Did you do anything special over the weekend?
주말에 뭐 특별한 일이라도 있었니?

W: Guess what? I had a blind date!
있잖아. 나 어제 소개팅을 했어!

M: Oh, did you? What was your date like?
오, 그랬어? 데이트 상대는 어땠는데?

W: He looked just perfect, but not my type at all.
정말 완벽했어. 하지만 나의 이상형이 아니야.

Q: 다음에 이어질 남자의 말은 무엇입니까?
(A) 너의 이상형은 어떤 거야?
(B) 네가 이상형을 만났다니 정말 기뻐.
(C) 난 아직도 이상형을 찾고 있어.
(D) 소개팅을 더 하고 싶지 않아.

해설 'ideal type, dream guy, Mr. Right'은 모두 '이상형'이라는 뜻입니다.

★ ideal 이상적인 / blind date 모르는 사람과 하는 데이트 / perfect 완벽한

5 **W:** You've hardly touched your food. What's wrong?
음식에 거의 손을 대지 않았구나. 무슨 일이야?

M: I have lost my appetite lately.
요새 통 입맛이 없어.

W: You probably have spring fever.
춘곤증인가 보구나.

M: Spring fever? What is it?
춘곤증? 그게 뭔데?

Q: 다음에 이어질 여자의 말은 무엇입니까?
(A) 봄에 몸에서 열이 나는 거야.
(B) 봄에 이상하게 몸이 피곤한 걸 말해.
(C) 전염병의 이름이야.
(D) 다가오는 봄을 맞이하는 축제야.

★ tiredness 피곤함 / epidemic 전염성의 / upcoming 다가오는 / appetite
입맛 / spring fever 춘곤증

[Telephone rings 전화벨]

6 **M:** Good morning! Thank you for calling. How can I help you?
안녕하세요! 전화 주셔서 감사합니다. 어떻게 도와드릴까요?

W: I'd like to place an order for boots in size seven.

사이즈 7인 부츠를 주문하고 싶은데요.

M: Do you want knee boots? They are in fashion these days.
무릎까지 오는 부츠를 원하시나요? 요즘 유행인데요.

W: I'd like the ankle boots with a ribbon.
저는 리본이 달린 발목부츠를 원해요.

Q: 남자가 다음에 말할 것은 무엇입니까?
(A) 저는 무릎부츠를 드릴 준비가 돼 있습니다.
(B) 무릎부츠는 모두 사이즈 7입니다.
(C) 죄송하지만 품절되었습니다.
(D) 머리 리본은 판매하지 않습니다.

★ place an order 주문하다 / out of stock 품절된, 재고가 없는

7 **W:** Larry, what are you going to do during Thanksgiving?
Larry, 추석(추수감사절)에 무엇을 할 예정이니?

M: I have no plans at this time. How about you?
지금은 계획이 없어. 너는?

W: I'm going to Beijing with Maria.
난 Maria와 베이징에 갈거야.

M: Oh, really? I envy you. How long will you stay there?
정말? 부럽다. 얼마나 오래 머물거니?

Q: 여자가 다음에 말할 것은 무엇입니까?
(A) 2년 되었어요.
(B) 난 추석을 정말 재밌게 보냈어.
(C) 가는데 5시간 정도 걸려.
(D) 5일 동안 머물 거야.

★ at this time 지금은

[Telephone rings 전화벨]
8 **M:** Hello. Could I speak to William Evans, please?
안녕하세요. William Evans씨와 통화할 수 있을까요?

W: I'm sorry. He's not in at the moment. Would you like to leave a message?
죄송하지만, 그는 지금 자리에 안 계세요. 메시지를 남기시겠습니까?

M: Well, this is Peter Jackson. I was calling to let him know that today's dinner party has been changed from 6:00 this evening to 7:00 tomorrow evening.
네, 전 Peter Jackson입니다. 오늘 저녁 파티 시간이 6시에서 내일 저녁 7시로 변경되었다는 사실을 알려드리려고 전화 드렸습니다.

W: Oh really? But it's already 5:00.
정말요? 그렇지만 지금이 벌써 5시인데요.

Q: 남자가 다음에 말할 것은 무엇입니까?
(A) 그에게 메시지를 전달해 주세요.
(B) Evans씨는 이것에 대해 매우 화가 날거예요.
(C) 오, 다행입니다!
(D) 알아요. 너무 늦게 공지해서 죄송하다고 전해주세요.

9 **W:** Peter, I'm really tired. I can't walk an inch.
Peter, 나 너무 피곤해. 조금(1인치)도 걸을 수가 없어.

M: This park is much bigger than we expected. Look over there, a bike rental shop. How about riding a bike?
이 공원이 생각했던 것 보다 너무 크다. 저기, 자전거 대여소를 봐. 자전거를 타는 게 어떨까?

W: Sounds great. We need two bikes. Let me check the price. $15 for a bike per hour.
좋은 생각이야. 자전거가 두 개 필요해. 가격을 좀 보자. 한 시간에 한 자전거당 15달러인데.

M: For how long do you think we need the bike?
우리 얼마나 오래 자전거가 필요할까?

Q: 여자가 다음에 말할 것은 무엇입니까?
(A) 1시간이면 너무 비싸다.
(B) 2시간이면 이 공원을 돌아보는 데 충분해.
(C) 우선, 대여소를 찾자.
(D) 너무 피곤해서 걸을 수가 없어.

해설 얼마나 오랜 시간 자전거가 필요할지 묻는 질문이므로 2시간이면 충분할 것이라는 대답이 적절합니다.

★ per hour 시간당

10 **W:** I didn't sleep well last night. A man upstairs makes a lot of noise recently.
어젯밤에 잠을 잘 못 잤어. 최근에 윗집의 남자가 너무 소음을 많이 내.

M: Why don't you ask him to be quiet?
그 남자에게 조용하라고 말하는 게 어때?

W: I already did, but it was useless.
이미 했지만, 소용없었어.

M: Then consider moving into my apartment building.
그럼 우리 아파트 건물로 이사 오는 걸 생각해 봐.

Q: 여자가 다음에 말할 것은 무엇입니까?
(A) 솔직해져 봐.
(B) 자기 전에 수면제를 먹어 봐.
(C) 네가 우리 아파트를 좋아하는 걸 알고 있어.
(D) 그리고 싶지만, 너희 아파트는 임대료가 너무 높아.

★ rent 대여료 / sleeping pill 수면제 / move 옮기다, 이사하다

11 **M:** Can you help me find my bag?
내 가방 찾는 것 좀 도와주겠니?

W: Where do you think you saw it last?
마지막으로 어디서 본 것 같니?

M: Well, I was at the bookstore for an hour.
글쎄, 한 시간 동안 서점에 있었는데.

W: Then did you check or call the store?
그럼 가게를 확인하거나 전화는 해봤니?

Q: 남자가 다음에 할 말은 무엇입니까?
(A) 좋은 생각인 것 같지 않다.

(B) 방해하고 싶지 않아.

(C) 응, 그랬었는데 없었어.

(D) 응, 그래서 그들이 갖고 있데.

해설 가방을 찾고 있는 상황이기 때문에 (D)는 답이 될 수 없습니다.

---

12 W: Do you have any special plan for this weekend?
이번 주말에 특별한 계획 있니?

M: Not really. I might stay at home and relax.
아니. 집에 있으면서 쉬려고.

W: Actually Tom and I will go hiking tomorrow.
사실 Tom하고 나하고 내일 하이킹 가려고 하는데.

M: Really? I thought you guys broke up.
정말? 난 너희들 헤어진 줄 알았는데.

Q: 여자가 다음에 할 말은 무엇입니까?
(A) 내가 깨지 않았어.
(B) 하이킹은 나한테 쉽지 않네.
(C) 나는 차라리 집에 있을래.
(D) Kate 덕분에 화해했어.

해설 헤어진 연인이 다시 화해하고 하이킹을 가는 상황입니다.

★ break up (남녀 사이에서) 헤어지다 / make up 화해하다

---

13 M: Hi, Anna. Long time no see.
안녕, Anna. 오랜만이야.

W: Hi, Tom. Good to see you again.
안녕, Tom. 다시 봐서 반갑다.

M: So where have you been? It's been almost three months I saw you last.
어디 갔었니? 마지막으로 본 것이 거의 세 달 전이네.

W: I traveled New Zealand. Can you guess what happened?
뉴질랜드를 여행했었어. 어떤 일이 있었는지 아니?

Q: 남자가 다음에 할 말은 무엇입니까?
(A) 신경 쓰지마. 별 일 아니야.
(B) 사업 때문에 갔다 왔다고?
(C) 좋아, 어떤 일이 있었는지 말해줘.
(D) 정말 우연이다! 너에겐 너무 좋겠구나.

해설 여행에서 발생한 일을 이야기하는 내용입니다.

---

14 W: Excuse me, but do I know you?
죄송합니다만, 우리 아는 사이인가요?

M: Well, I'm not sure. But you look familiar to me.
글쎄요, 잘 모르겠는데. 어디서 뵌 것 같군요.

W: That's what I thought. What city are you from?
저도 같은 생각이에요. 어느 도시에서 오셨나요?

M: I'm originally from San Francisco. How about you?
저는 San Francisco 출신입니다. 당신은요?

Q: 여자가 다음에 할 말은 무엇입니까?
(A) 난 New York에서 태어나서 자랐습니다.
(B) 내가 스무 살 때 프랑스를 여행했었어요.

(C) 이미 근처 호텔에 예약해 놨습니다.

(D) San Francisco에는 아름다운 다리가 있다고 들었습니다.

해설 여자가 어디 출신인지 묻는 지문입니다.

---

15 M: I've never seen such a dolphin show. It is just amazing.
난 이런 돌고래 쇼를 본 적이 없어. 정말 대단하다.

W: You can say that again. They must have practiced a lot.
나도 그래. 연습 정말 많이 했겠다.

M: So where is the next place you can recommend?
그럼 다음 추천해 줄 곳은 어디야?

W: Jane said we should see an international costume parade.
Jane이 우리가 국제 의상 퍼레이드는 꼭 봐야 한다고 했어.

Q: 남자가 다음에 할 말은 무엇입니까?
(A) 이런 종류의 패션쇼를 보고 싶었어.
(B) 재미있겠다. 어디 그리고 시간은 언제니?
(C) 나도 할래. 어디서 옷을 살 수 있는지 알아보자.
(D) 비가 많이 와서 가게는 문을 닫을 거야.

해설 의상 퍼레이드를 하는 데에 대한 내용을 고르는 문제입니다.

---

16 W: Hi, how can I help you?
어떻게 도와드릴까요?

M: Well, I want to get a refund for this camera I bought here last week.
음, 지난주에 이곳에서 산 카메라를 환불하고 싶습니다.

W: OK, is there anything wrong with it?
네, 뭔가 잘못된 것이 있나요?

M: Yes, it hasn't worked since last Friday.
예, 지난 금요일부터 작동이 되질 않네요.

Q: 여자가 다음에 할 말은 무엇입니까?
(A) 현금으로 지불하시겠습니까 아니면 카드로 하시겠습니까?
(B) 죄송합니다. 영수증을 보여 주시겠습니까?
(C) 그럴 리가 없는데요. 어제까지 잘 됐는데요.
(D) 방침에 어긋납니다. 90일이 지났습니다.

해설 환불에 필요한 영수증을 보여 달라는 내용이 적절합니다.

---

17 M: Excuse me, can you tell me how to go to the National Park?
죄송합니다만, 국립공원으로 가는 길을 알려 주시겠습니까?

W: Let's see. First you need to take a subway.
잠깐 볼까요. 우선 전철을 타세요.

M: Is there any subway station around here?
이 근처에 전철역이 있나요?

W: Yes, go down two blocks and turn left.
네, 두 블록만 내려가셔서 좌회전하세요.

Q: 남자가 다음에 할 말은 무엇입니까?
(A) 제가 보여드릴게요. 따라오세요.
(B) 쉽습니다. 꼭 찾으실 겁니다.
(C) 고맙습니다. 도움이 많이 됐습니다.

(D) 그럼 그곳에 버스 정류장이 있겠군요.

해설 길을 묻는 사람과 대답하는 사람의 대화를 혼동해서는 안 됩니다. (A)와 (B)는 길을 알려주는 사람이 하는 대화이기 때문에 답이 될 수 없습니다.

18 **W:** What kind of drinks would you like to have?
어떤 음료를 드시겠습니까?

M: What will you recommend?
어떤 걸 추천해 주시겠습니까?

W: Well, this food is a little bit oily. So coke will be good.
글쎄요, 오늘 음식은 약간 기름집니다. 콜라가 좋을 듯 합니다.

M: But usually I don't drink soda like coke.
하지만 저는 주로 콜라 같은 탄산음료는 먹지 않습니다.

Q: 여자가 다음에 할 말은 무엇입니까?
(A) 콜라를 너무 많이 마시면 건강에 좋지 않습니다.
(B) 알겠습니다, 빨리 콜라 한 잔 갖다 주세요.
(C) 절 믿으세요. 선택하신 것에 대해 후회하실 겁니다.
(D) 그럼 오렌지나 포도 같은 과일 주스는 어떻습니까?

해설 탄산음료를 먹지 않는 손님에게 다른 음료를 권하는 내용이 적절합니다.

19 **M:** You speak English so fluently. What is your secret?
영어를 유창하게 하네. 비밀이 뭐니?

W: I went to America with my family when I was seven. I lived for 10 years there.
내가 일곱 살이었을 때 가족하고 미국으로 갔어. 미국에서 10년 살았어.

M: Really? I didn't know that. How can you speak Korean like a native?
정말? 난 몰랐었네. 한국어도 어떻게 원어민처럼 잘 하니?

W: My parents taught me not to forget Korean.
부모님께서 한국 말 잊지 않도록 가르쳐 주셨어.

Q: 남자가 다음에 할 말은 무엇입니까?
(A) 한국이 더 살기 좋은 나라지.
(B) 그래서 네가 2개 국어를 하는구나.
(C) 한국어 수업을 들어봐.
(D) 한국어를 하는 편이 나을 거야.

해설 한국어와 영어를 둘 다 유창하게 하는 친구에게 할 수 있는 표현을 고르는 문제입니다.

20 **W:** What do you usually do in your free time?
시간이 나면 넌 주로 무엇을 하니?

M: I've been very busy. My graduate school classes started last month.
나 매우 바빴어. 대학원 수업이 지난달에 시작됐거든.

W: Wow, then you must have been busy lately.
와, 그럼 최근에 매우 바쁘겠구나.

M: Yeah, sort of. But today I guess I need a break.
응, 그렇지 뭐. 하지만 오늘 나는 휴식을 취해야 할 것 같아.

Q: 여자가 다음에 할 말은 무엇입니까?
(A) 난 내 보고서를 준비해야 돼.
(B) 네가 쉴 수 있는 시간이 없어.
(C) 그럼 기분전환으로 영화를 보러 가는 건 어때?
(D) 다음 휴게실에 잠깐 들르자.

해설 휴식이 필요하다고 생각하는 친구에게 할 수 있는 표현을 고르는 문제입니다.

★ **for a change** 분위기 전환으로 / **drop by** 잠깐 들르다 / **a rest area** (고속도로상의) 휴게실

PUZZLE 2

Across

3 (crash) 무언가에 맹렬하게 부딪침으로써 차, 비행기 등에서 사고를 내는 것

6 (identical) 정확히 같음 또는 매우 유사한

8 (former) 이전에 발생하거나 존재 함, 지금은 아님

10 (chore) 규칙적으로 해야만 하는 작은 일, 특히 집을 깨끗이 하기 위해 하는 일

11 (epidemic) 사상, 질병, 풍속 등이 동시에 발생하는

13 (foe) 적, 원수

15 (humid) 공기가 매우 습하고 대개 뜨거워서 불쾌한

Down

1 (tranquil) 유쾌하게 고요하고, 정숙하고, 평화로운

2 (privilege) 오직 한 사람 또는 한 무리의 사람들에게만 주어진 특별한 이점

4 (raft) 보통 나무 들이 함께 묶여진 평평하고 물에 뜨는 구조물

5 (revolve) 바퀴처럼 움직이는 것 또는 어떤 것을 바퀴처럼 움직이게 하는 것

7 (conflict) 사람, 단체, 국가, 기타 사이의 의견 차이 또는 논쟁

9 (rejoice) 행복하다는 것을 느끼거나 보여주는 것

12 (mummy) 천으로 감싸 보존되어 온 시체

14 (odd) 이상한 또는 비범한

SECTION II READING AND WRITING

PART A. Error Recognition

01. (C)	02. (B)	03. (A)	04. (A)	05. (B)
06. (D)	07. (D)	08. (D)	09. (B)	10. (B)
11. (C)	12. (C)	13. (D)	14. (B)	15. (D)
16. (B)	17. (A)	18. (C)	19. (A)	20. (D)
21. (D)	22. (A)			

1 작가가 글을 쓰는 목적 중의 하나는 사람들을 설득하는 것입니다. 예를 들어, 신문 편집자는 자신의 의견을 받아들이도록 독자를 설득하려고 노력합니다.

해설 문장에 동사가 없으므로 trying을 try로 고쳐야 합니다.

★ purpose 목적 / persuade 설득하다 / editorial 편집의 / opinion 의견

2 객관식 문제는 세 개 이상의 가능한 답을 가지고 있습니다. 맞는 답을 찾지 못하겠으면, 답이 하나가 남을 때까지 틀린 답을 없애도록 하세요.

해설 three의 수식을 받으므로 answer가 answers로 바뀌어야 합니다.

★ multiple 많은, 다수의 / contain 포함하다 / remove 제거하다

3 많은 사진작가들은 사진의 주제와 상관없이, 새벽이 사진을 찍기에 가장 좋은 시간이라고 주장합니다.

해설 much는 셀 수 없는 것에 사용하는 것이고, 셀 수 있는 경우에는 many를 써야 합니다.

★ argue 주장하다 / dawn 새벽 / regardless of ~에 상관없이

4 연날리기는 공기역학의 원리에 달려있는데, 공기역학은 공기의 이동에 따라 움직이는 힘에 대한 연구를 의미합니다.

해설 'flying kites'는 단수로 취급되므로 depend가 depends로 되어야 합니다.

★ depend 달려 있다 / principle 원칙, 원리 / aerodynamics 공기역학 / force 힘 / action 움직임

5 세 개의 기본적인 노동권리가 있습니다; 단체를 조직할 권리, 단체교섭을 할 권리, 그리고 단체행동을 할 권리입니다.

해설 three의 수식을 받으므로 right가 rights로 되어야 합니다.

★ basic 기본적인 / organize 단체를 조직하다 / collective 집단의 / bargaining 교섭, 협상 / action 행동

6 오스트레일리아는 섬으로 이루어진 대륙으로 오랫동안 세계의 다른 곳과 떨어져 있어서 캥거루와 코알라가 발견되는 유일한 대륙입니다.

해설 '~로부터 따로 떨어져 있다'라는 표현은 'be isolated from~'이라고 해야 합니다.

★ continent 대륙 / isolate 따로 떨어뜨리다

7 공룡 화석은 단단한 암석에 깊이 묻혀 있어서 과학자들은 처음에 화석이 손상되지 않게 암석으로부터 뼈들을 꺼내야 합니다. 이 작업을 위해서는 대단한 인내심이 요구됩니다.

해설 patience는 셀 수 없으므로 동사를 are이 아닌 is로 써야 합니다.

★ fossil 화석 / bury 묻다 / solid 단단한 / scientist 과학자 / damage 손상을 입히다 / enormous 많은 / patience 인내심 / require 요구하다

8 지구에 생명체가 존재할 수 있는 이유는 공기를 가지고 있기 때문입니다. 식물과 동물들은 공기 없이는 살 수 없습니다.

해설 cannot 다음에는 동사의 원형이 와야 하므로 lived가 live가 되어야 합니다.

★ exist 존재하다

9 속담은 간단한 언어로 표현되는 짧지만 현명한 말입니다. 예를 들면, '정직은 최상의 정책이다'가 있습니다.

해설 shorty and wisely는 saying이라는 말을 꾸며주는 말로 사용되었으므로 short and wise로 바뀌어야 합니다.

★ proverb 속담 / language 언어, 말 / example 예 / honesty 정직 / policy 정책

10 세계 대부분의 어린이들은 동물원을 찾아가게 되면 기뻐합니다. 많은 동물원들은 어린이들이 토끼, 오리 다른 순한 동물들을 만져볼 수 있는 어린이들을 위한 구역을 마련해 놓습니다.

해설 '기쁨을 느끼다'라는 의미로는 'feel delighted'라고 합니다.

★ delighting 기쁨을 주는 / section 구역 / especially 특별히 / pat 쓰다듬다 / gentle 온순한

11 외식을 하는 것은 즐거운 일입니다. 그러나 어떤 사람들에게는 집에서 가족을 위해 요리하는 것이 여가시간을 즐기는 방법이기도 합니다.

해설 '그들의 가족'이라는 의미가 되어야 하므로 them이 their로 바뀌어야 합니다.

★ leisure time 여가시간

12 급성 질병은 짧은 기간 동안 지속되고 보통 심한 증상을 보입니다. 그러나 만성 질병은 긴 시간 동안 지속됩니다.

해설 앞에 나와 있는 lasts처럼 have도 has로 바뀌어야 합니다.

★ last 지속되다 / acute 급성의 / severe 심한 / symptom 증상 / chronic 만성적인

13 현대의 발명품들과 새로운 기계들은 우리를 많은 집안일로부터 해방시켰습니다. 예를 들면, 빨래 건조기는 빨랫줄에 빨래를 너는 일로부터 우리를 해방시켰습니다.

해설 hang은 from 뒤에 오므로 hanging으로 모양이 바뀌어야 합니다.

★ invention 발명, 발명품 / machine 기계 / release 해방시키다 / household 가정 / hang 걸다 / laundry 빨래

14 아시아 사람들은 연장자들을 존경하는 경향이 있지만 미국에서는 나이에 별로 존경심을 표하지는 않습니다.

해설 'be inclined to~'는 '~하는 경향이 있다'라는 뜻이고 'the elderly'는 '연세가 많은 사람들'이라는 뜻입니다. to 뒤에 나오는 respecting은 respect로 바뀌어야 합니다.

★ incline 기울다 / elderly 연세가 많은 / bring 가져오다 / respect 존경

15 좌식 생활양식은 많은 시간을 앉아 있고 움직이거나 운동을 많이 하지 않는 것을 가리킵니다. 택시 운전기사, 작가와 같이 주로 앉아 있는 직업에 종사하는 사람들은 운동을 하기 위해 특별히 노력을 해야 합니다.

해설 efforts 앞에 a가 나왔으므로 effort로 바꿔야 합니다.

★ sedentary 좌식의, 앉아 있는 / indicate 가리키다 / occupation 직업 / effort 노력

16 반대말은 반대의 의미를 가진 단어입니다. 예를 들어, '맞는'과 '틀린'은 반대말이고, '긴'과 '짧은'도 마찬가지입니다.

해설 '반대의'라는 의미로 meanings를 꾸며주어야 하므로, oppositely를 pposite로 바꿔야 합니다.

★ antonym 반대말 / oppositely 반대로

17 대도시지역의 높은 빌딩들은 인구가 밀집된 도시의 증가를 가속시킵니다. 예를 들어, 시카고에 있는 시어즈타워에는 16,000명의 사람들이 일을 합니다.

해설 주어가 skyscrapers이므로 동사는 speed가 되어야 합니다.

★ skyscraper 마천루, 높은 빌딩 / overcrowded 인구밀집의

18 컴퓨터는 보고서를 다시 타이핑하는 번거로움 없이, 보고서에서 불필요한 정보를 제거하는 데 편리합니다.

해설 having to 다음에 동사원형이 와야 하므로 type가 되어야 합니다.

★ convenient 편한 / unwanted 원하지 않는 / type 타자로 치다

19 1888년, Edward Bellamy는 유토피아에 대해 썼는데, 그곳은 모든 사람들이 충분한 수입이 있고, 45세까지 일하고, 그 후에 여가시간을 즐기는 곳입니다.

해설 연도를 나타날 때는 연도 앞에 'in'을 사용합니다.

★ utopia 이상향, 유토피아 / income 수입

20 당신이 회사에 항의편지를 쓸 때, 시작하는 부분에 회사에 바라는 당신의 요구를 쓰고, 다시 이 요구를 마지막 부분에서 반복합니다.

해설 시작이라는 명사가 필요한 자리이므로 beginning으로 수정합니다.

★ complaint 불만족 / a letter of complaint 항의편지

21 Joseph Haydn은 고전주의 시대에 살았던 매우 다작을 하는 작곡가였습니다. 그는 다른 음악작품을 하는 동안에 104개의 교향곡을 썼습니다.

해설 104개의 교향곡이라는 의미이므로 symphony는 symphonies가 되어야 합니다.

★ composer 작가

22 사람들은 개를 진정한 동반자라고 여깁니다. 이것은 전통적인 개의 이름 'Fido'에 잘 반영되어 있는데, 'Fido'는 충실한 사람이라는 의미가 담겨 있습니다.

해설 considering을 considered로 바꿔야 합니다.

★ consider 고려하다 / trusty 믿는 / companion 동반자 / reflect 반영하다 / traditional 전통적인

PART B. Sentence Completion

01. [D]	02. [A]	03. [B]	04. [C]	05. [A]
06. [B]	07. [A]	08. [B]	09. [A]	10. [B]
11. [D]	12. [B]	13. [A]	14. [D]	15. [A]
16. [B]	17. [A]	18. [A]	19. [C]	20. [B]
21. [A]	22. [D]	23. [A]		

1 광고는 회사가 우리에게 ____________________ 사용하는 홍보의 중요한 부분입니다.

(A) their products to buy many
(B) their many products to buy
(C) to buy their products many
(D) to buy their many products (그들의 제품을 사도록 하게 하기 위하여)

★ advertisements 광고 / important 중요한 / promotion 홍보 / persuade 설득하다

2 사막에서 길을 잃은 사람들은 그들의 바로 앞에 호수가 있는 것처럼 보이는 _______________.

(A) sometimes experience the illusion (환상을 때로 경험합니다)
(B) experience the illusion sometimes
(C) sometimes experiences the illusion
(D) experiences the illusion sometimes

해설 주어가 people이므로 동사는 experiences가 아니고 experience가 되어야 합니다.

★ experience 경험하다 / illusion 환상

3 발레무용수들은 때로 뛰어 오른 후에 너무 큰 충격으로 착지를 하게 되면 _______________.

(A) break their toes severe
(B) break their toes severely (발가락을 심하게 부러뜨리게 됩니다)
(C) break severe their toes
(D) break their severely toes

해설 '심하게 부러뜨리다'라는 의미로 break를 꾸며주는 말로는 severely를 사용해야 합니다.

★ land 착지하다 / impact 충격, 영향 / leap 뛰어오르다 / severely 심하게

4 _______________ 전설의 유니콘은 종종 사자의 꼬리와 염소의 수염을 가지고 있는 것으로 나타납니다.

(A) a one horn animal with horselike
(B) a horselike with one horn animal
(C) a horselike animal with one horn (하나의 뿔을 가진 말처럼 생긴)
(D) one horn animal with a horselike
★ legendary 전설의 / tail 꼬리 / beard 수염 / horselike 말 같은

5 슈퍼마켓에는 다양한 아침용 시리얼이 있습니다. ____________ 통로의 반을 차지합니다.

(A) so many different kinds (종류가 너무나 많아서)
(B) many so different kinds
(C) so different many kinds
(D) many different so kinds
해설 'a great diversity of~'는 '~가 다양한'이라는 의미입니다.
★ diversity 다양성 / cereal 시리얼 / occupy 차지하다 / aisle 통로

6 미시시피강은 "큰 강"을 ____________ 인디언 말로부터 그 이름이 유래됩니다.

(A) meant   (B) meaning (의미하는)
(C) means   (D) is meaning
★ derive 비롯되다. 유래를 찾다

7 케이크를 구울 때에는 ____________________. 그러면 케이크가 부풀 수 있는 충분한 공간이 있게 됩니다.

(A) Use a deep pan (깊은 팬을 사용하세요)
(B) Use a deeply pan
(C) Use a pan deep
(D) Use a pan deeply
해설 '깊은 팬'은 'deep pan'으로 표현해야 합니다.
★ bake 굽다 / room 여유공간

8 Meryl Streep은 그녀의 첫 번째 아카데미상을 받은 3년 후인, 1982년에 'Sophie의 선택'이라는 영화에서의 역할로 아카데미의 수상자가 ______________.

(A) is   (B) was (되었습니다)
(C) has been   (D) had been
해설 1982년도 과거에 일어난 일이므로 'was'를 사용해야 합니다.
★ award 상

9 Martin Luther King 목사는 사회변화를 위한 싸움에서 ______________ 원칙을 따랐습니다.

(A) without using any violence (폭력을 사용하지 않는)
(B) without use any violence
(C) without to use any violence
(D) without used any violence
★ principle 원칙 / social 사회의 / violence 폭력

10 거미의 거미줄에 있는 어떤 성분이 거미가 잡은 벌레들이 ______________ 만듭니다.

(A) adheres to the web
(B) adhere to the web (거미줄에 들러붙도록)
(C) to adhere to the web
(D) and adhere to the web
해설 make를 사용하면 뒤에 동사가 원형의 형태로 와야 합니다. 여기서 make의 목적어는 'the bugs it catches'로 '거미가 잡은 벌레들'입니다.
★ certain 어떤. 특정의 / thread 실 / bug 벌레 / adhere 들러붙다 / web 거미줄

11 Alexander Graham Bell은 전화기뿐 아니라 사람들을 싣고 다닐 수 있는 ________ 발명했습니다.

(A) and a kite   (B) so a kite
(C) or a kite   (D) but also a kite (연을)
해설 'not only'는 'but also'와 함께 사용합니다.
★ invent 발명하다

12 그녀의 자서전 '내 인생 이야기'에서 Helen Keller는 앞을 볼 수 없고 들을 수 없음에도 불구하고 어떻게 ______________를 이야기하고 있습니다.

(A) is able to learn
(B) was able to learn (배울 수 있었는지)
(C) is able learning
(D) was able learning
★ autobiography 자서전 / despite ~에도 불구하고 / blindness 앞을 볼 수 없음 / deafness 들을 수 없음

13 책, 가구 그리고 목재 집들이 나무로 ______________ 사실을 생각해보세요.

(A) are made from (만들어진다는)
(B) have made from
(C) make from
(D) made from
★ furniture 가구

14 어떤 피자가게 점원은 아이들이 때로 장난전화를 하기 때문에 ______________ 확인하기 위해서 확인전화를 겁니다.

(A) each order
(B) each order real
(C) real each order
(D) each order is real (각 주문이 사실인지)
해설 that 다음에는 문장이 와야 합니다.
★ make sure 확인하다 / joke 농담, 장난

15 _______________ 지하철은 어떤 지하철이라도 마땅히 칭찬을
받아야 합니다.

(A) that is clean and safe (깨끗하고 안전한)
(B) that is cleanly and safely
(C) which are clean and safe
(D) which are cleanly and safely

해설 'any subway system'은 단수 취급을 받아야 합니다.

★ deserve ~받아 마땅하다 / praise 칭찬

16 시계의 바늘이 천천히 2시 30분을 향했을 때, 학생들은 마지막
수업의 끝 종을 기다리다가 한계에 _______________.

(A) seemed reach
(B) seemed to reach (도달한 것처럼 보였습니다)
(C) seemed reaching
(D) seemed to be reached

★ limit 한계

17 결혼반지는 _______________ 부부의 헌신을 보여주기 위해
착용하는 것입니다.

(A) to each other (서로에 대한)
(B) to each others
(C) to one other
(D) to one others

해설 '서로에게'라는 의미는 'each other'를 사용합니다.

★ commitment 헌신, 약속

18 산기슭에 울창한 소나무 숲이 있습니다. 그러나 좀 더 올라가면
나무는 _______________.

(A) become rare (드물게 됩니다)
(B) become rarely
(C) became rare
(D) became rarely

해설 'at the foot of the mountain'은 '산기슭에'라는 의미이고 'become rare'은 '드
물게 되다'라는 뜻입니다.

★ thick 울창한 / pine 소나무 / forest 숲

19 _______________ 해가 없습니다. 그러나 열이나 뻣뻣한 목 증상
과 함께 오게 되면 심각한 질병의 신호가 될 수 있습니다.

(A) Most headache
(B) Almost headache
(C) Most headaches (대부분의 두통은)
(D) Almost headaches

★ harmless 해가 없는 / fever 열 / stiff 뻣뻣한 / serious 심각한 / illness 질병

20 유타 주의 그레이트 솔트레이크에서는 _______________ 누구도
쉽게 물에 잠기지 않습니다.

(A) because the lake's high percentage of salt
(B) because of the lake's high percentage of salt (높은 소금
함량 때문에)
(C) since the lake's high percentage of salt
(D) since of the lake's high percentage of salt

해설 '~때문에'라는 의미로는 'because of~'를 사용합니다.

★ drown 물에 잠기다 / percentage 비율

21 _______________ 하나는 또한 가장 단순한 것 중의 하나입니
다. 그것은 외발자전거로 바퀴가 오직 한 개밖에 없습니다.

(A) of the most difficult vehicles (가장 타기 어려운 탈 것 중의)
(B) of the more difficult vehicles
(C) most difficult than vehicles
(D) more difficult than vehicles

해설 의미상 '~중의 하나'라는 표현은 'one of ~'를 사용합니다.

★ unicycle 외발자전거 / wheel 바퀴 / vehicle 탈 것

22 야행성 동물이기 때문에 올빼미는 낮 동안에는 _______________.

(A) likely to see
(B) unlikely to see
(C) likely to be seen
(D) unlikely to be seen (잘 보이지 않습니다)

해설 의미상 부정문이 되어야 하므로 'unlikely'를 사용해야 합니다.

★ creature 동물 / owl 올빼미, 부엉이

23 외계인이 우주에 존재하는지 아닌지에 대한 문제에 대한 해답에 과
학은 _______________를 제공하지 못합니다.

(A) enough evidence (충분한 증거)
(B) evidence enough
(C) many evidence
(D) evidence many

해설 enough가 명사를 꾸며 줄 때는 명사의 앞에서 사용됩니다.

★ provide 제공하다 / alien 외계인, 이방인 / universe 우주 / evidence 증거

PUZZLE 3

Across

3 (blunder) 부주의 또는 어리석은 실수

4 (cavity) 어떤 것 속의 구멍 또는 공간

8 (humble) 낮은 사회적 계급 또는 지위를 갖는 것

9 (obstacle) 어떤 일을 성취하는 것을 어렵게 만드는 것

10 (comply) 해야만 하는 것 또는 요청받은 일을 하는 것

12 (deliver) 제품, 편지, 소포 등을 특정 장소 또는 사람에게 가져가다

13 (victim) 공격, 강탈, 혹은 살해당한 사람

14 (waterproof) 물이 들어오는 것을 허락하지 않는 것

15 (random) 어떤 정확한 계획, 목적 또는 양식 없이 발생하거나 선택되는 것

Down

1 (furious) 매우 화가 난

2 (accommodation) 누군가가 머무르거나 살거나 일 할 장소

5 (property) 누군가가 소유한 물건

6 (shabby) 단정치 못하고 상태가 양호하지 않은

7 (multiple) 많은, 또는 많은 물건

11 (offspring) 어느 한 사람의 아이 또는 아이들

PART C. Reading and Logical Thinking

01. (A)	02. (B)	03. (C)	04. (C)	05. (A)
06. (D)	07. (A)	08. (A)	09. (B)	10. (A)
11. (B)	12. (A)	13. (B)	14. (D)	15. (A)
16. (B)	17. (B)	18. (C)	19. (A)	20. (A)
21. (B)	22. (D)	23. (A)		

1 형편이 어려운 어린이들에게는 약간의 등록비를 제외하고는 완전히 ___________. 즉 캠프 참가를 위해 돈을 낼 필요가 없다는 의미입니다.

(A) 무료입니다 　　　　　 (B) 비용이 청구됩니다
(C) 이성적입니다 　　　　 (D) 적당합니다

★ registration 등록 / fee 비용 / needy 형편이 어려운 / entirely 완전히 / free 무료의 / chargeable 비용을 청구하는 / reasonable 이성적인, 적당한 / moderate 적당한

2 어린이들에게 ___________ 에 대한 교육을 하기 위해서, 많은 부모들은 자녀에게 가상의 상황에서 무엇을 할지를 물어보는 경향이 있습니다. 예를 들면, 부모들은 낯선 사람이 차를 태워주겠다고 제안하면 어떻게 할지를 자녀들에게 물어봅니다.

(A) 규칙 　　　　　　　　 (B) 안전
(C) 정직 　　　　　　　　 (D) 애국심

★ imaginary 가상의 / situation 상황 / stranger 낯선 사람 / offer 제공하다 / safety 안전 / honesty 정직 / patriotism 애국심

3 Tolstoy가 쓴 '전쟁과 평화'는 다양한 등장인물들의 상세한 인생

이야기를 아주 복잡한 방식으로 엮어낸 길고 ___________ 소설입니다.

(A) 단순한 　　　　　　　 (B) 사실을 담은
(C) 복잡한 　　　　　　　 (D) 현실적인

해설 문장 속에 있는 complicated, detailed 등의 단어가 힌트가 됩니다.

★ weave 짜다, 엮다 / detailed 상세한 / various 다양한 / character 캐릭터, 등장인물 / complicated 복잡한

4 대도시에 사는 사람들은 대도시들이 공기오염이 더 많기 때문에 소도시의 거주자들보다 ___________ 문제에 좀 더 취약합니다.

(A) 교통 　　　　　　　　 (B) 경제
(C) 환경 　　　　　　　　 (D) 인구

★ vulnerable 취약한 / resident 거주자 / pollution 오염 / economic 경제의 / environmental 환경의 / population 인구

5 Mark Twain은 아무도 완전히 독창적일 수 없기 때문에 다른 사람의 생각을 모방하는 것에 대한 비난이 말도 안 된다고 생각했습니다. 그는 "우리는 ___________ : 우리는 단지 모방할 뿐이다."라고 썼습니다.

(A) 창작할 수 없다 　　　　 (B) 글을 쓸 수 없다
(C) 증명할 수 없다 　　　　 (D) 생각할 수 없다

★ charge 비난, 고발 / copy 모방하다 / absurd 바보같은, 말도 안 되는 / original 독창적인 / create 창작하다 / prove 증명하다

6 교사의 할 일 중의 하나는 학생들이 좀 더 열심히 공부하도록 ___________. 그러나 배움에 대한 열정이 없는 학생들을 더 열심히 공부하도록 독려하는 일은 쉽지 않습니다.

(A) 증명하는 것입니다
(B) 반대로 증명하는 것입니다
(C) 좌절시키는 것입니다
(D) 동기 부여하는 것입니다

★ encourage 용기를 주다 / disprove 반증하다 / discourage 좌절시키다 / motivate 동기부여하다

7 선생님이 학생들에게 ___________ 을(를) 쓰게 하면, 그것은 동물이 아닌 사람의 인생이야기를 쓰라는 것을 의미하는 것입니다.

(A) 전기문 　　　　　　　 (B) 소설
(C) 에세이 　　　　　　　 (D) 역사

해설 사람의 인생이야기는 'biography'입니다.

★ biography 전기문 / history 역사

8 1961년도 뉴욕 현대미술관에서 미술작품이 몇 주 동안 거꾸로 전시되어 있었다는 것을 알게 되어 사람들은 ___________ 미술관 관리자들을 놀려 주었습니다.

(A) 부끄러움을 느끼는 　　　 (B) 기뻐하는

(C) 자랑스러워하는 　　　　　　　(D) 자신감에 찬

★ display 전시하다 / upside down 거꾸로 / make fun of ～ ～를 놀리다 /
administrator 관리자

9 가난한 나라를 위한 자원봉사단체인 평화봉사단은 ___________
으로부터 고통을 겪는 나라에서 일할 수 있는 많은 자원봉사자들을
계속해서 파견하고 있습니다.

(A) 오염 　　　　　　　　　　(B) 가난
(C) 지진 　　　　　　　　　　(D) 질병

해설 'the Peace Corps'는 평화봉사단이라는 기관입니다.

★ volunteer 자원봉사자 / organization 기구 / suffer 고통을 겪다 / poverty
가난 / earthquake 지진

10 타이타닉호는 빙하에 부딪힌 후에 바다 밑바닥으로 가라앉았고, 거
의 1,600명의 사망자를 내는 ___________를 일으켰습니다.

(A) 참사 　　　　　　　　　　(B) 돌파구
(C) 전쟁 　　　　　　　　　　(D) 인플레이션

★ strike 치다, 부딪히다 / iceberg 빙하 / bottom 밑바닥 / cause 일으키다 /
disaster 참사, 재난 / breakthrough 돌파구 / battle 전쟁 / inflation 인플레이션

11 어린이들은 그들의 부모의 탄생을 축하하기 위해 깜짝 파티를 준비
하면서 ___________ 활동을 하는 것을 좋아합니다.

(A) 공개되는 　　　　　　　　(B) 비밀스러운
(C) 인기 있는 　　　　　　　　(D) 주의 깊은

해설 'be fond of ～'는 '～를 좋아하다'라는 뜻입니다.

★ prepare 준비하다 / celebrate 축하하다 / birth 탄생 / secret 비밀 /
popular 인기 있는

12 비의 부족으로 인해 용수공급이 상당히 줄어들었으므로 도시의 모
든 거주자들은 당분간 잔디에 ________ 이 허용되지 않습니다.

(A) 물주는 것 　　　　　　　　(B) 자르는 것
(C) 자라는 것 　　　　　　　　(D) 돌보는 것

★ resident 거주자 / lawn 잔디 / shortage 부족 / seriously 심각하게, 상당히
/ reduce 줄이다 / supply 공급

13 영국의 Diana 황태자비는 분명히 매우 ___________. 그녀의
개인적인 약점에도 불구하고, 그녀는 전 세계 사람들의 관심과 애
정을 받았습니다.

(A) 신비로웠습니다 　　　　　　(B) 매력적이었습니다
(C) 사치스러웠습니다 　　　　　(D) 이기적이었습니다

해설 'draw people's attention and affection'은 '사람들의 관심과 애정을 끌다'라는
뜻입니다.

★ obviously 명백히 / in spite of ～에도 불구하고 / personal 개인적인 /
weak point 약점 / affection 애정

14 Mahatma Gandhi는 수백만 명의 인도사람들이 열정적으로 그에

게 동참하여 폭력을 사용하지 않고 국가 문제들에 대한 ___________
해결 방법을 찾도록 격려했습니다.

(A) 정직한 　　　　　　　　　(B) 단순한
(C) 아름다운 　　　　　　　　(D) 평화로운

★ inspire 영감을 주다 / enthusiastically 열정적으로 / solution 해결책 /
violent 폭력적인

15 대부분의 영화배우들은 하룻밤 사이에 _______________ 을(를)
얻을 수 없고, 스타가 되는 길은 멀고도 험합니다.

(A) 명성 　　　　　　　　　　(B) 우정
(C) 관계 　　　　　　　　　　(D) 자유

★ achieve 획득하다 / overnight 하룻밤에 / fame 명성 / friendship 우정 /
freedom 자유

16 해마다 오직 100개의 인형이 만들어진다는 사실은 이 실물크기의
인형이 ___________ 팔리도록 하고 있습니다.

(A) 싼 가격에 　　　　　　　　(B) 비싼 가격에
(C) 많이 　　　　　　　　　　(D) 자주

해설 해마다 정해진 분량의 인형만이 생산되므로 '비싼 가격'에 팔리는 것이 가장
적절합니다.

★ produce 생산하다 / lead 이끌다 / life-size 실물크기의 / cheaply 싸게 /
expensively 비싸게 / frequently 자주

17 산타클로스가 매우 좁은 공간에 있는 것을 두려워하지 않는다는 것
은 정말 다행입니다. 그렇지 않으면, 산타클로스는 굴뚝을 내려오
면서 통과해야 하는 좁은 공간이 너무 ___________것입니다.

(A) 좋을 　　　　　　　　　　(B) 무서울
(C) 좋을 　　　　　　　　　　(D) 가장 좋을

★ fear 두려움 / limited 좁은 / space 공간 / otherwise 그렇지 않으면 /
chimney 굴뚝 / fond 좋아하는 / frightened 두려워하는 / favored 좋아하는

18 할로윈 데이에 아이들은 종종 유령, 마녀의 복장을 하고 이웃들에
게 사탕을 달라고 합니다. 따라서 이 명절은 사탕 제조업체에게는
___________ .

(A) 해가 됩니다 　　　　　　　(B) 피해를 줍니다
(C) 이익을 줍니다 　　　　　　(D) 적당합니다

★ dress up 차려입다 / ghost 유령 / witch 마녀 / neighbor 이웃 /
manufacturer 제조업체 / harmful 해로운 / damaging 피해를 주는 /
profitable 이익이 되는

19 어떤 동화에서는 주로 왕자인 주인공이 괴물에게 ___________
잃어버린 공주를 찾기 위해서 위험한 세계를 탐험합니다.

(A) 납치된 　　　　　　　　　(B) 생산된
(C) 놀란 　　　　　　　　　　(D) 정화된

★ hero 영웅, 주인공 / explore 탐험하다 / dangerous 위험한 / search for

~를 찾다 / missing 잃어버린 / monster 괴물 / kidnapped 납치된 / purified 정화된

20 작가 Stephen King은 그의 책 일부에서 _____________ 이름을 사용하지 않아 독자들이 시판되고 있는 그의 책 중에서 일부는 그가 쓴 것을 모르기도 합니다.

(A) 진짜   (B) 가짜
(C) 가짜   (D) 펜

★ author 작가 / recognize 알아채다 / real 진짜의 / fake 가짜 / false 가짜의 / pen name 필명

21 공원에 사람들이 버린 모든 쓰레기들은 분명히 나무와 꽃들의 아름다움을 _____________ .

(A) 향상시킵니다   (B) 훼손시킵니다
(C) 증가시킵니다   (D) 개선합니다

★ litter 쓰레기 / improve 향상시키다 / damage 손상시키다 / increase 증가시키다 / upgrade 개선하다

22 많은 사람들이 양치를 올바르게 하지 못합니다. 그러나 당신은 충치를 예방하기 위해서 _____________ 양치를 할 수 있도록 노력해야 합니다.

(A) 공허하게   (B) 헛되이
(C) 약식으로   (D) 주의깊게

해설 'make an effort'는 '노력하다'는 뜻입니다.

★ brush 양치하다 / properly 올바르게 / cavity 충치

23 마음의 병을 앓고 있는 일부 사람들은 _____________ 생각을 가질 수 있습니다. 예를 들어, 그들은 TV가 자신에게 말을 하고 있다고 생각하거나 다른 사람들이 자신의 생각을 훔쳐갈 수 있다고 생각하기도 합니다.

(A) 이상한   (B) 적당한
(C) 이상적인   (D) 생생한

★ mentally 정신적으로 / steal 훔치다 / weird 이상한 / vivid 생생한

PART D. Reading and Retelling

01. [A]	02. [B]	03. [B]	04. [D]	05. [D]
06. [B]	07. [B]	08. [A]	09. [B]	10. [A]
11. [A]	12. [C]	13. [B]	14. [D]	15. [C]
16. [A]	17. [A]	18. [B]	19. [B]	20. [A]
21. [A]	22. [B]	23. [D]	24. [A]	25. [C]
26. [A]	27. [C]	28. [A]	29. [D]	30. [B]
31. [C]	32. [A]	33. [D]	34. [A]	35. [A]
36. [B]	37. [B]	38. [B]	39. [B]	40. [B]
41. [A]	42. [B]	43. [D]	44. [C]	45. [C]
46. [A]	47. [B]	48. [A]		

1 1174년에 이탈리아, 피사의 주민들은 성당의 종탑을 건설하기로 결정했습니다. 그들은 두 명의 유명한 건축가를 찾아내어 탑을 설계하도록 부탁했습니다. 설계에 맞게 일꾼들은 탑을 건설하기 시작했습니다. 곧, 그들은 건설에 치명적인 실수가 있다는 것을 발견하게 되었습니다. 그들은 탑의 아래 지반이 탑을 견디기에는 너무 약하다는 것을 간과했었습니다. 마침내 탑은 한쪽으로 가라앉기 시작했습니다. 공사는 중단되어야 했고, 탑은 150년이 넘도록 미완성인 채로 남아있습니다. 피사의 사탑은 아직도 서 있습니다. 하지만 계속해서 해마다 조금씩 더 기울어지고 있습니다.

★ cathedral 성당 / renowned 유명한 / architect 건축가 / design 설계하다 / critical 치명적인 / overlook 간과하다

해설 'determine to~'는 '~하기로 결심하다'는 뜻이고, 'in accordance with~'는 '~에 따라, 맞춰'라는 뜻입니다.

Q : 피사의 사탑은 왜 한쪽으로 기울어지고 있습니까?

(A) 지반이 너무 부드럽기 때문입니다.
(B) 아직 완공되지 않아서 입니다.
(C) 오래전에 만들어져서 입니다.
(D) 설계에 맞게 만들어지지 않아서 입니다.

2 소금은 인체에 필수적인 것이지만, 너무 많은 소금은 건강에 이상을 가져올 수 있습니다. 대부분의 미국인들은 정말 필요한 것보다 20배 이상의 소금을 섭취합니다. 어디에서 소금을 섭취할까요? 우선 한 가지, 가공식품이 더 많은 소금을 섭취하게 하는 주요 공급원입니다. 왜냐하면 식품회사들이 식품을 생산하면서 지나치게 많은 소금을 사용하기 때문입니다. 또한 사람들은 자기 음식에 소금을 조금 더 추가하는 경향이 있습니다. 사실, 대부분의 식품은 이미 요리되기 전에 많은 양의 소금을 함유하고 있습니다. 이러한 식습관은 건강에 해롭습니다. 따라서 식습관이 달라져야 합니다. 우리는 소금이 적은 가공식품을 선택하도록 하고 식품에 소금을 더 추가하지 않도록 해야 합니다.

★ essential 필수적인 / processed 가공처리의 / excessive 지나친

Q : 소금 섭취를 줄이기 위해서 우리는 무엇을 해야 합니까?

(A) 가공식품을 좀 더 삽니다.
(B) 소금이 적은 가공식품을 사도록 합니다.
(C) 식품에 소금을 더 뿌립니다.
(D) 음식물의 소금을 아무것도 섭취하지 않도록 합니다.

★ take in 섭취하다

3 사우디아라비아와 같은 건조지역에는 마시거나 작물을 재배할 물이 충분하지 않습니다. 여러 해 동안, 과학자들은 이러한 건조 지역에 물을 공급하는 방법을 연구해왔습니다. 그들이 제안한 해결책은 남극해에서 사우디이라비아 사막으로 빙하를 옮겨오는 것입니다. 어떻게 거대한 빙하 덩어리를 바다를 건너 사막으로 옮길 수 있을까요? 어떤 연구자들은 거대한 배와 헬리콥터를 사용하여 빙하를 이동시키는 것이 가능하다고 주장합니다. 그러나 다른 과학자들은 성공 가능성에 대해 회의적입니다. 그들은 빙하의 대부분이 따뜻한 바닷물에 녹게 될 것이라고 주장합니다.

(C) 잦은 충전   (D) 공기 오염 줄이기

★ raise 기르다 / crop 작물 / region 지역 / suggest 제안하다 / chunk 덩어리
/ skeptical 회의적인 / melt 녹다

Q : 이 글에 따르면 무엇이 사우디아라비아에 물을 공급할 수 있다고
합니까?

(A) 배와 헬리콥터   (B) 빙하
(C) 바다   (D) 사막

해설 남극해에 있는 빙하를 옮겨와 사우디아라비아에 물을 공급하는 방법에 대해
이야기하고 있습니다.

4 우리는 해마다 우리의 어머니에게 사랑을 전하기 위해 어머니의 날
을 축하합니다. 어머니의 날의 유래는 1908년 5월 10일로 거슬러
올라갑니다. 그날, Anna Javis는 2년 전에 돌아가신 그녀의 어머
니에게 감사를 전하기 위해 교회에서 특별한 예배를 드리고 있었
습니다. 그때부터 Anna는 이 생각을 전국적으로 전하기 시작했습
니다. 그녀는 사람들이 해마다 자신의 어머니들에게 존경을 표
할 수 있는 날을 하루 정해야 한다고 주장했습니다. Anna의 제안
은 대중의 관심을 얻었습니다. 1910년, 미국의 세 개 주에서 공식
적으로 어머니의 날을 휴일로 선포했습니다. 지금은 미국에서 가장
중요한 휴일 중의 하나가 되었습니다.

★ origin 기원, 유래 / spread 퍼뜨리다 / nationwide 전국적으로 / honor 존
경을 표하다 / proclaim 선포하다

해설 'date back'는 '날짜를 거슬러 올라가다'라는 뜻이고, 'pay respect to~'는 '~
에게 존경을 표하다'라는 의미이고, 'set aside'는 '따로 남겨두다'라는 의미입니다.

Q : 어머니의 날에 대한 Anna의 제안은 무엇이었습니까?

(A) 그녀의 어머니에게 존경을 표하기
(B) 어머니들을 위해 교회에서 특별 예배를 보기
(C) 대중의 관심을 끌기
(D) 어머니들을 존중하기 위한 공식적인 날을 갖기

해설 어머니들을 존중하기 위해 일년에 하루를 정해야 한다는 것이 Anna의 제안이
었습니다.

5 전력에 의해 움직이는 전기자동차는 새로운 생각이 아닙니다. 사
실, 전기 자동차는 1899년도에 최초로 발명되었습니다. 그러나 전
기 자동차는 몇 가지 결점이 있어서 관심을 끌지 못했습니다. 한 가
지 약점은 자동차의 가격이 매우 비싸, 15,000달러가 넘는다는 것
입니다. 또한 휘발유 차에 비해 상대적으로 속도가 느리다는 것입니
다. 더욱이 전기자동차는 60마일마다 충전되어야 합니다. 그러나
많은 사람들은 아직도 전기자동차를, 공기오염을 줄일 수 있고 비싸
지는 휘발유 값과 줄어드는 휘발유 공급문제를 해결할 수 있는 실행
가능한 현실적인 방법으로 여기고 있습니다.

★ electric 전기의 / automobile 자동차 / limitation 제약점 /
disadvantage 약점 / relatively 상대적으로 / recharge 충전하다 /
workable 실행 가능한 / practical 현실적인 / decline 줄어들다

Q : 전기자동차가 인기를 끌지 못하는 이유가 아닌 것은 무엇인가요?

(A) 높은 가격   (B) 느린 속도

6 미국 올림픽위원회는 운동선수들을 훈련시키기 위한 새 코치를 고
용하기로 결정했습니다. 그것은 컴퓨터였습니다. 위원회는 올림픽
에 참가할 미국 선수들의 기술적인 능력을 향상시키기 위해 컴퓨터
를 사용하고 있습니다. 컴퓨터가 선수들의 실력을 테스트하는 데
매우 효과적임이 드러나고 있습니다. 컴퓨터 테스트는 배구, 역도,
펜싱, 육상, 경륜과 같이 적합한 기술을 익히는 것이 중요한 종목에
서 사용됩니다. 컴퓨터를 사용함으로써 과학자들은 운동선수들이
팔이나 다리를 살짝 이동하는 것만으로도 매우 긍정적인 결과를
가져올 수 있다는 것을 알게 되었습니다.

★ committee 위원회 / hire 고용하다 / participate in 참가하다 / competition
경쟁, 대회 / effective 효과적인 / shift 이동

Q : 운동선수를 훈련시키는 데 컴퓨터가 왜 유용한가요?

(A) 컴퓨터는 운동선수들의 신체적인 문제를 찾아낼 수 있습니다.
(B) 컴퓨터는 운동선수들의 기술적인 실력을 테스트할 수 있습니다.
(C) 컴퓨터는 운동선수들의 신체적인 조건을 확인하는 데 유용합니다.
(D) 컴퓨터는 운동선수들을 훈련시키는 비용을 절감할 수 있습니다.

7 Ernest라는 이름의 웨이터는 취미로 매우 독특한 수집을 하고 있
었습니다. 그는 유명인사들의 사진과 사인을 수집하는 것을 좋아했
습니다. Ernest는 40년 이상을 유명인들과 우편으로 연락을 취했
었습니다. 그가 죽은 후에 그의 아파트를 찾았던 사람들은 전세계
유명 인사들의 수천 개에 달하는 기념품들을 발견하였습니다. 사람
들은 Ernest의 많은 기념품들이 가치가 있다는 것을 알게 되었습
니다. 어떤 것은 경매에서 각각 200달러가 넘는 가격에 팔렸습니
다. 하지만 우리는 Ernest가 돈을 벌기 위해서 사인을 수집하지 않
았다는 것을 명심해야 합니다. 그는 유명하고 인기 있는 낯선 사람
들과 연락을 한다는 것이 그저 재미있어서 그랬던 것입니다.

★ collection 수집 / celebrity 유명인사 / memento 기념품 / souvenir 기념품
/ valuable 가치 있는 / auction 경매

해설 'keep in mind'는 '명심하다'는 뜻이고, 'exchange correspondence with'는
'편지(연락)를 교환하다'라는 뜻입니다.

Q : Ernest는 왜 유명인사들의 사인을 수집했나요?

(A) 돈을 벌기 위해서
(B) 그들과의 교류가 즐거워서
(C) 가치 있는 기념품을 모으기 위해서
(D) 유명해지고 인기를 얻기 위해서

8 의미가 같은 두 개의 단어를 동의어라고 합니다. 새로운 단어의
뜻을 설명하는 가장 쉬운 방법은 동의어를 사용하는 것입니다.
congregate와 gather라는 단어를 살펴봅시다. congregate를 정
의하는 한 가지 방법은 뜻이 'gather'라고 말하는 것입니다. 어휘 시
험에서 대부분의 문제는 어려운 단어에 대한 최상의 동의어에 관한
것입니다. 따라서 새 단어의 동의어를 알아 두면, 어휘 시험에서 좋
은 점수를 받을 것입니다. 동의어를 아는 것은 당신이 읽는 것의 이
해를 높이는 데에도 매우 도움이 됩니다. 글을 읽다가 어려운 단어

를 만나게 되면, 동의어로 바꾸게 되면 글의 내용을 훨씬 더 잘 이해할 수 있게 됩니다.

★ synonym 동의어 / congregate 모이다 / gather 모이다 / define 정의하다 / vocabulary 어휘 / enhance 강화하다 / comprehension 이해 / encounter 우연히 만나다

Q : 우리는 왜 동의어를 알아야 할까요?

(A) 어려운 단어를 쉽게 이해하기 위해서
(B) 긴 책을 읽기 위해서
(C) 읽은 내용을 요약하기 위해서
(D) 읽기의 단순한 단어들을 설명하기 위해서

★ summarize 요약하다

[9-10]

당신은 수퍼마켓에서 두 가지 종류의 제품을 만나게 됩니다: 유명브랜드 제품과 자가브랜드 제품. 유명브랜드제품은 유명한 회사가 제조한 상품입니다. 반면, 자가브랜드 제품은 당신이 쇼핑을 하고 있는 수퍼마켓의 주문에 의해 제작된 상품입니다. 자가브랜드 제품은 보통 경쟁사인 유명브랜드 제품보다 가격이 저렴합니다. 그러나 고객들은 가격이 더 저렴한 자가브랜드 제품보다 유명브랜드 제품을 종종 선택합니다. 그들은 유명브랜드 제품의 품질이 자가브랜드 제품보다 더 높을 것이라고 생각합니다. 그들은 유명브랜드 제품의 성분이 자가브랜드 제품과는 다를 것이라고 생각합니다. 사실, 많은 자가브랜드 제품은 유명브랜드 제품을 생산하는 동일한 회사가 생산하므로 상품의 내용은 동일합니다. 단지 상표가 다를 뿐입니다. 그러나 여전히 많은 소비자들은 자가브랜드 제품을 사기를 주저합니다. 그들이 잘 알고 있는 유명브랜드 제품에서 더 편안함을 느낍니다. 유명브랜드 제품은 광고를 통해 소비자의 마음 속에 깊이 새겨져 있습니다.

★ category 항목, 품목 / product 제품 / manufacture 제조하다 / competitor 경쟁자 / ingredient 성분, 재료 / content 내용 / hesitate 주저하다 / imprint 새기다

9 자가브랜드 제품과 유명브랜드 제품의 차이는 무엇입니까?

(A) 성분   (B) 가격
(C) 질   (D) 가게(판매처)

해설 자가브랜드 제품이 보통 유명브랜드 제품보다 저렴하다고 했으므로 가격에 있어 차이를 보입니다.

10 소비자들은 왜 유명브랜드 제품 구매를 더 선호하나요?

(A) 유명브랜드 제품이 더 친근해서
(B) 유명브랜드 제품이 더 저렴해서
(C) 유명브랜드 제품의 품질이 너 좋아서
(D) 유명브랜드 제품의 성분이 더 좋아서

★ contain 함유하다

[11-12]

전화기를 누가 발명했는지 아십니까? Alexander Graham Bell입니다. 또한 전화기가 그의 가장 큰 실패작이었다는 것을 아십니까? Bell

은 들을 수 있는 사람들을 위한 도구를 만들려는 의도가 전혀 없었습니다. 그는 그의 직업과 전 생애에 걸쳐, 청각장애인을 도와주는 데 헌신하려 했습니다. 청각장애인을 향한 Bell의 동정은 그의 가족과 관련이 있습니다. 그의 어머니는 청각장애인이었고, 이는 그가 사람들이 말하는 법을 어떻게 배우는지에 관심을 갖게 했습니다. 그런 후에 그는 청각장애 어린이들에게 말하기치료를 하는 일을 전문적으로 시작하였습니다. 후에, 그는 청각장애인 여성과 사랑에 빠져 그녀와 결혼하였습니다. Bell은 청각장애인들의 조용한 세상을 바꾸겠노라고 결심하였습니다. 그는 그가 만약 소리파장을 보이게 하는 기계를 개선한다면 청각장애인들이 들을 수 있는 사람들처럼 말을 인식할 수 있을 거라고 생각했습니다. 불행히도, Bell은 청각장애인을 위한 기계장치를 완성하지 못했습니다. 그는 절망했습니다. 마침내 그는 그의 설계를 거의 집어던져버렸습니다. 그러나 Bell의 기계장치의 개념은 전화기를 개발하는 데 사용되었습니다. 전화기는 그러나 Bell에게 진정한 행복을 가져다주지는 않았습니다. 왜냐하면 그 발명품은 이미 들을 수 있는 사람들에게만 소리를 전달하니까요.

★ failure 실패 / compassion 동정 / therapy 치료 / visible 눈에 보이는 / perceive 인식하다 / despair 절망

해설 'be committed to~'는 '~에 헌신하다'라는 뜻이고 'specialize in'은 '전공하다. 전문적으로 다루다'라는 의미입니다. 'fall in love with~'는 '~와 사랑에 빠지다'라는 의미입니다.

11 Bell은 평생에 걸쳐 어디에 중점을 두었습니까?

(A) 청각장애인을 돕는 일
(B) 세계를 변화시키는 일
(C) 전화기를 발명하는 일
(D) 비 청각장애인을 위한 도구를 발명하는 일

★ non-deaf 비 청각장애의

12 Bell은 왜 전화기에 만족하지 못했습니까?

(A) 그가 전화기를 사용할 수가 없어서
(B) 그의 어머니가 전화기를 사용하기 전에 돌아가셔서
(C) 그것이 청각장애인을 위한 것이 아니어서
(D) 충분히 가격을 받지 못해서

[13-14]

1752년 6월 Benjamin Franklin은 번개가 전기의 일종이라는 것을 증명하기 위한 특별한 실험을 했습니다. 실험에서 그는 뇌우가 치는 동안에 줄 끝에 열쇠를 매단 연을 날렸습니다. 실험을 하기 전에 많은 사람들은 번개는 초자연적인 힘이라고 믿고 있었습니다. 그의 실험이 성공하고 나서, Franklin은 번개가 폭풍 속에서 연으로 이끌려진다면, 집에 장착된 금속막대를 통해 번개가 지면으로 유도될 수 있다고 추정했습니다. 그의 생각은 많은 의심에 직면하지만 그는 될 것이라는 확신에 차 있었습니다. 곧, 미국의 집들과 건물들에서 피뢰침을 볼 수 있게 되었고, 후에 유럽에서도 볼 수 있게 되었습니다. Franklin의 연을 이용한 실험은 그에게 국제적인 명성과 존경을 가져다주었습니다. 그는 다른 명예와 함께 런던 왕립협회와 프랑스 과학아카데미 회원에 선출되었습니다.

★ experiment 실험 / electricity 전기 / supernatural 초자연적인 / infer 추정하다 / confront 직면하다 / doubt 의심 / confident 확신에 찬 / fame 명성 /

elect 선출하다 / honor 명예

해설 'be confronted with~'는 '~와 직면하다'는 뜻입니다.

13 Franklin은 연을 이용한 실험으로 무엇을 증명했습니까?

   (A) 연은 뇌우 속에서도 날 수 있다.
   (B) 번개는 전기 에너지이다.
   (C) 번개는 위험하다.
   (D) 번개는 초자연적인 힘이다.

14 Franklin은 실험의 성공으로 무엇을 얻었습니까?

   (A) 확신과 경제적인 지원   (B) 성공과 부
   (C) 의심과 불신   (D) 명성과 사회적 지위

[15-16]

많은 사람들이 Abraham Lincoln이 대통령으로서 처음부터 공개적으로 노예를 반대했던 것으로 생각합니다. 사실은 그렇지 않습니다. 그의 개인적인 생각이 어떠했든, 그는 공개적으로 노예제도를 비판하지 않았습니다. 그는 연방에서 남쪽의 주들이 나갈 것을 두려워하여 남부의 노예를 소유할 권리를 존중하겠다고 맹세했습니다. 그는 또한 정부는 남부의 탈주 노예법을 존중하겠다고 서약했습니다. 이 법에 따르면, 모든 미국 시민들은 노예를 주인에게 돌려보내야 한다고 되어 있습니다. Lincoln은 나라가 분리되는 것을 원하지 않는 것이 분명했습니다. 그러나 1862년 9월 22일에 Lincoln대통령은 남부의 모든 노예는 해방되어야 한다는 노예해방을 선언했습니다. 남부의 주들이 이미 연방에서 탈퇴했기 때문에, 남부의 주들은 노예해방선언을 무시했습니다. 그러나 노예해방선언은 북부의 군사력을 강화하였습니다. 대부분 노예였던 약 200,000명의 흑인이 연방군대에 등록하였습니다. 2년 후에 13차 헌법수정을 통해 미국 전역에서 노예제도는 막을 내렸습니다.

★ object 반대하다 / criticize 비판하다 / slavery 노예, 노예제도 / pledge 맹세하다 / runaway 달아난 / master 주인 / separate 분리하다 / emancipation 해방 / proclamation 선언 / state 명시하다 / set free 해방시키다 / withdraw 탈퇴하다 / ignore 무시하다 / enhance 강화하다 / enlist 등록하다 / amendment 수정 / constitution 헌법

해설 'for fear of~'는 '~를 두려워하여'이고, 'the Emancipation Proclamation'은 '노예해방선언'을 말합니다.

15 노예제도에 대한 Lincoln의 초기 공식적 태도는 어떠했습니까?

   (A) 그는 강력하게 노예제도에 반대했습니다.
   (B) 그는 공식적으로 노예제도에 대해 아무런 언급을 하지 않았습니다.
   (C) 그는 노예제도에 동의했습니다.
   (D) 그는 노예제도를 비난했습니다.

해설 Lincoln은 공식적으로 노예제도를 비난하지 않았지만, 남부의 노예제도를 존중한다고 맹세했다는 것으로 판단할 수 있습니다.

16 Lincoln은 왜 노예제도를 비판하지 않았습니까?

   (A) 그는 나라가 분열되는 것을 원하지 않았습니다.

   (B) 그는 개인적으로 노예제도를 지지했습니다.
   (C) 그는 북부의 군대를 강화하기를 원했습니다.
   (D) 그는 흑인노예에 대한 편견을 가지고 있었습니다.

★ prejudice 편견

[17-18]

공룡을 생각하면, 대부분의 사람들은 거대한 공룡을 떠올립니다. 그러나 작은 공룡들도 많이 있었습니다. 작은 공룡들은 큰 공룡들이 그랬던 것처럼 그들의 생김새를 묘사하는 라틴 이름을 가지고 있습니다. 작지만 빠른 공룡은 Saltopus였는데, '뛰어오르는 발'이란 의미를 가지고 있습니다. Saltopus는 다 자라도 몸무게가 약 2파운드밖에 되지 않았고 키가 2피트 정도였습니다. 스코틀랜드에서 유일하게 화석이 발견되었습니다. 또 다른 작은 공룡은 Compsognathus라는 재미있는 이름을 가지고 있는데, 의미는 '예쁜 턱'입니다. Saltopus와 키가 같은 Compsognathus는 몸무게는 세 배 더 나갔습니다. Compsognathus의 유해가 프랑스와 독일에서만 발견되었기 때문에, 두 공룡들이 서로 알았을 가능성은 거의 제로입니다. 또 다른 작은 공룡은 Lesothosaurus로 의미는 "레소토 도마뱀"입니다. 이 이름은 도마뱀을 닮은 생김새에서 유래되었지만 이름의 앞부분은 유적이 발견된 장소인 남부 아프리카의 레소토에 기원을 둡니다.

★ enormous 거대한 / species 종 / leaping 뛰어오르는 / weigh 무게가 나가다 / jaw 턱 / remains 유적, 유해 / originate 기원하다 / appearance 생김새

해설 'be originated from~'는 '~에서 유래하다'이고, 'be based on~'은 '~에 기반을 두다'라는 뜻입니다.

17 큰 공룡의 이름은 무엇을 묘사합니까?

   (A) 생김새   (B) 서식지
   (C) 좋아하는 것   (D) 생활방식

해설 큰 공룡들은 생김새를 묘사하는 라틴이름을 가지고 있다고 했습니다.

★ habitat 서식지

18 Saltopus와 Compsognathus가 서로 알았을 가능성이 왜 없을까요?

   (A) 그들의 몸무게가 달랐기 때문에
   (B) 서로 다른 장소에 살았기 때문에
   (C) 서로 다른 시기에 살았기 때문에
   (D) 그들이 작은 공룡이었기 때문에

해설 'Saltopus'는 스코틀랜드에서 서식했고, 'Compsognathus'는 프랑스와 독일에서 서식했습니다.

[19-20]

기상상태에 대한 과학적 학문인 기상학은 기압을 측정하는 기압계, 온도계, 공기 중의 습도를 측정하는 습도계 및 기상도와 같이 정확한 기상 측정 기구들이 개발된 후에야 탄생했습니다. 과학자들은 이러한 기본 요소들의 측정값과 바람, 구름, 강수량과 같은 다른 대기 조건 사이의 관계를 연구하기 시작했습니다. 그러나 완전한 일기예보에는 충분하지 않았습니다. 나중에 전신의 발명이 전 세계의 정보를 신속하게 전할 수 있게 보장함으로써 일기예보를 완벽하게 했습니다. 오늘날, 기상학자들의 예보는 국제적인 노력으로 이루어집니다. 전 세계에 수천 개의 기상 관측소가 있어서 기상 정보를 보내줍니다. 이 정보는 국가 기상국으

로 전해져 기상학자들이 분석하게 됩니다. 분석된 정보는 신문, TV와 라디오방송국을 통해서 대중들에게 제공되게 됩니다.

★ meteorology 기상학 / accurate 정확한 / barometer 기압계 / atmospheric 대기의 / thermometer 온도계 / hygrometer 습도계 / moisture 수분 / telegraph 전신, 전보 / forecast 예보 / meteorologist 기상학자 / bureau 단체, 부서

19 무엇이 일기예보를 과학적으로 만들었나요?

(A) 대기 조건의 관찰　　　　(B) 측정기구들의 발명
(C) 전 세계의 기상관측소　　(D) 전신의 발명

해설 기상학이 기상측정기구들의 개발과 함께 탄생했다는 대목에서 힌트를 얻을 수 있습니다.

20 사람들은 어떻게 기상정보를 얻을 수 있습니까?

(A) 대중매체를 통해서　　　(B) 기상관측소를 통해서
(C) 기상조건을 연구해서　　(D) 대기 조건을 확인해서

해설 대중들에게는 신문. TV, 라디오 방송을 통해서 전해진다고 언급되어 있습니다.

[21-22]
글을 읽다가 의미를 모르는 단어를 만나게 되면, 어떻게 하시겠습니까? 사전에서 단어를 찾아보는 것이 가장 좋은 방법일 것입니다. 사전은 알파벳 순서로 단어의 정의를 제공하는 책입니다. 찾아보기 말이 각 지면의 최상단에 있어, 그 지면에 수록된 첫 번째 단어와 마지막 단어를 보여줍니다. 두 개의 찾아보기 말 사이에 있는 모든 단어들은 알파벳 순서대로 그 지면에 수록됩니다. 단어들은 알파벳 순서대로 열거되어 목표 단어들을 신속하고 쉽게 찾을 수 있도록 도와줄 것입니다. 사전에는 발음, 개별 음절, 품사, 복수형 또는 기본형에서 바뀌게 되는 동사의 형태 등과 같은 다른 사항들도 수록되어 있습니다. 어떤 사전들은 상당히 많은 정보를 제공합니다. 예를 들어, Tormont Webster's Illustrated Encyclopedic Dictionary는 두 페이지마다 용어에 대한 많은 컬러 그림, 발음기호, 사전을 효과적으로 사용하는 방법에 대한 서문을 싣고 있습니다.

★ definition 정의 / order 순서 / guide word 색인, 찾아보기 말 / arrange 배열하다 / locate 찾다 / target 목표 / pronunciation 발음 / syllable 음절 / part of speech 품사 / plural 복수의 / base word 기본형 / introductory 서문의

21 찾아보기 말은 무엇을 위한 것입니까?

(A) 지면의 단어의 배열을 보여주기 위해서
(B) 사전의 효과적인 사용법을 설명하기 위해서
(C) 각 단어의 발음법을 보여주기 위해서
(D) 각 단어의 정확한 정의를 제공하기 위해서

22 왜 단어들은 알파벳 순서대로 배열됩니까?

(A) 사용자들이 단어를 더 잘 이해할 수 있도록 하기 위해
(B) 사용자들이 단어를 빠르게 찾을 수 있도록 돕기 위해
(C) 단어의 배열이 더 좋아 보이도록 하기 위해

(D) 가능하면 더 많은 단어들을 수록하기 위해

[23-24]
초기 음악은 종교와 밀접하게 연결되어 있던 것으로 믿어집니다. 고대 사람들은 세상이 다양한 신들의 영향 아래에 놓여있다고 믿었습니다. 노래는 신에게 경외를 표하는 최선의 방법 중에 하나였습니다. 노래는 아직도 대부분의 종교에서 중요한 부분을 차지합니다. 종교적이든 아니든, 노래를 불러봤다면, 노래가 재미있다는 것을 알 것입니다. 노래로부터 비롯되는 기쁨이나 환희의 감정은 고대 사람들을 더없이 행복하게 만들었을 것입니다. 노동가 또한 고대의 전형적인 노래 형식이었습니다. 이집트 노예들은 피라미드를 짓기 위해서 무거운 돌들을 나르면서 노래를 불렀습니다. 군인들은 전쟁터로 행진해가면서 노래를 불렀습니다. 농부들은 씨를 뿌릴 때나 수확을 할 때 노래를 불렀습니다. 노래는 일하는 사람들을 덜 힘들게 했을 것이 분명합니다. 노래를 부르는 동안에는 힘든 노동의 고통으로부터 탈출할 수 있었습니다. 때로 노래는 그들이 따라야 할 일에 대한 지시를 포함하고 있었습니다. 노래 안에 있는 지시를 따르면서 사람들은 일을 더 수월하게 하였습니다.

★ religion 종교 / ancient 고대의 / blissful 행복한 / typical 전형적인 / march 행진하다 / harvest 수확하다 / instruction 지시사항

23 노래의 종교적인 목적은 무엇입니까?

(A) 재미있기 위해
(B) 종교적 의식을 신성하게 하기 위해
(C) 종교 지도자를 축복하기 위해
(D) 신을 영예롭게 하기 위해

해설 신에게 경외를 표하기 위해 노래를 한다고 하였습니다.

24 고대 사람들은 노동가를 부를 때, 어떤 기분이었습니까?

(A) 그들은 잠시 고통을 잊을 수 있었습니다.
(B) 그들은 더 고통을 느꼈습니다.
(C) 노래 때문에 부담을 느꼈습니다.
(D) 일을 하기가 더 어려웠습니다.

★ burdensome 부담스러운

[25-26]
바이올린 음악에 대해 아는 것이 있으면, 당신은 아마도 스트라디바리우스라는 말을 들어봤을 것입니다. 스트라디바리우스는 세계의 가장 위대한 바이올린들의 이름입니다. 그 이름은 그 바이올린을 만든 Antonio Stradivari의 이름을 따서 지어졌습니다. Stradivari는 1644년 북부 이탈리아에서 태어났습니다. 그가 살았던 마을인 크레모나는 바이올린을 만드는 것으로 유명한 곳이었습니다. Stradivari는 아주 어릴 때부터 바이올린 연주하는 것을 배우기 시작했습니다. 자라면서 그는 바이올린 연주보다는 만드는 일에 더 관심을 갖게 되었습니다. Stradivari가 살던 시대에는 바이올린이 새로운 악기였기 때문에 바이올린의 표준 형태나 크기가 없었습니다. 따라서 사람들은 서로 다른 크기와 형태의 바이올린을 만들었고, 서로 다른 목재를 사용하였습니다. Stradivari는 바이올린을 위한 최상의 목재를 고르는 탁월한 능력이 있었다고 전해집니다. 그는 또한 목재에 광택을 내는 방법을 알고 있었습니다. 이러한 특별한 능력이 세상에서 가장 멋진 악기를 만들어내는 데 도움을 주었습니다.

★ **standard** 표준 / **superior** 뛰어난 / **polish** 광택을 내다 / **contribute** 공헌하다, 도움을 주다 / **magnificent** 뛰어난

25 Stradivari가 살던 시대에 사람들은 왜 서로 크기가 다른 바이올린을 만들었나요?

   (A) 바이올린 음악이 유행하지 않아서
   (B) 바이올린이 동일한 모양으로 만들기 힘들어서
   (C) 바이올린을 만들기 시작하던 단계였기 때문에
   (D) Stradivari가 다양한 형태의 바이올린을 원했기 때문에

해설 'Since violins were new instruments during Stradivari's time, they had no standard size or shape.'를 보면 바이올린이 이제 만들어지기 시작하는 악기였음을 알 수 있습니다.

26 Stradivari가 바이올린장인이 되는 데 무엇이 가장 큰 도움이 되었습니까?

   (A) 그는 목재를 다루는 방법을 알았습니다.
   (B) 그는 북부 이탈리아에서 태어났습니다.
   (C) 그는 바이올린 연주하는 법을 배웠습니다.
   (D) 당시에 바이올린은 새로 전해진 악기였습니다.

[27-28]

젖소는 우유를 생산하기 위해 길러집니다. 젖소가 우유를 생산할 수 있는 것은 첫 번째 송아지를 낳고 난 이후입니다. 소는 보통 한 마리의 송아지를 낳아서 젖을 먹이기 위해 많은 우유를 생산합니다. 송아지가 생후 이틀이 되면, 엄마소로부터 떼어 놓습니다. 그 후에, 소는 하루에 두 번씩 우유를 짜냅니다. 젖소의 우유생산량은 항상 일정하지는 않습니다. 소가 임신 중일 때는, 우유생산량이 점차 줄어듭니다. 송아지가 태어나기 전 두 달 동안은 젖소의 젖이 마른 시기로 우유를 짜지 않습니다. 이는 사람과 같이 젖소가 섭취하는 대부분의 양분이 태어나지 않은 송아지에게 양분을 공급하는 데 사용되기 때문입니다. 축산업자들은 이 시기에 소에게 더 많은 음식을 제공하여 엄마소와 태어날 소가 모두 영양분을 잘 공급받을 수 있도록 합니다. 다시 말하면 사람과 마찬가지로 영양 상태가 좋은 엄마소가 건강한 아기소를 낳을 확률이 높습니다.

★ **dairy cow** 젖소 / **calf** 송아지 / **pregnant** 임신한 / **nourish** 양분을 공급하다 / **well-nourished** 영양 상태가 좋은

27 젖소의 젖이 마르면 무슨 일이 생기나요?

   (A) 우유를 일정하게 생산할 수 없습니다.
   (B) 송아지를 낳을 수 없습니다.
   (C) 우유를 전혀 생산할 수 없습니다.
   (D) 임신을 할 수 없습니다.

28 젖소의 젖이 마르게 되는 이유는 무엇입니까?

   (A) 태어날 송아지에게 영양을 공급하기 위해
   (B) 다시 임신하기 위해
   (C) 더 질 좋은 우유를 생산하기 위해
   (D) 더 음식을 섭취하기 위해

[29-30]

신문이 탄생하기 전에 사람들은 중요한 소식을 도시를 걸어 다니며 소식을 읽어주는 '거리에서 소식을 알리는 사람'으로부터 들었습니다. 최초의 신문은 사람들이 읽을 수 있도록 손으로 써서 도심에 게시한 게시문이었습니다. 최초의 진정한 신문은 1609년 독일에서 시작한 주간 신문이었습니다. 그것은 Johann Gutenberg가 활자를 발명하여 가능한 것이었습니다. 최초의 영어 신문 중의 하나인 The London Gazette는 1665년 영국에서 처음으로 인쇄되었습니다. Gazette는 고대 영어로 "공식적인 출판"이라는 뜻입니다. 따라서 아직도 많은 신문사가 신문 이름에 그 단어를 사용하고 있습니다. 미국에서는 최초의 성공적인 신문인 The Boston News Letter가 1704년에 인쇄를 시작했습니다. 최초의 1센트 신문인 The New York Sun은 1833년에 출간되었습니다. 그 신문은 실제로 가격이 1센트였습니다. 1센트 신문은 오늘날의 신문과 매우 비슷합니다. 즉, 1센트 신문들은 최신 소식을 신문에 실었고, 광고를 최초로 인쇄했으며, 가판대에서 신문을 팔았고, 최초로 가정으로 배달되었습니다.

★ **town crier** 거리에서 소식을 알리는 사람 / **movable type** 활자 / **publication** 출판 / **newsstand** 가판대 / **deliver** 배달하다

29 왜 아직도 gazette라는 단어가 신문의 이름에 사용됩니까?

   (A) 고대 영어이기 때문에
   (B) 사람들이 그 단어를 좋아하기 때문에
   (C) 단어가 신문을 의미하기 때문에
   (D) 단어의 의미가 출판과 관련이 있기 때문에

해설 'Gazette is an old English word that means "official publication," so many newspapers still use the word, gazette, in their names.'를 보면, 'gazette'의 의미가 출판과 관련이 있어서 사용되고 있다는 것을 알 수 있습니다.

30 첫 번째 1센트 신문은 어떤 점에서 중요했습니까?

   (A) 가격이 1센트였습니다.
   (B) 현대적인 신문의 탄생이었습니다.
   (C) 뉴욕에서 출간되었습니다.
   (D) 일주일에 한 번 인쇄되었습니다.

해설 'The penny newspapers were very similar to today's papers.'에서 1센트 신문이 현대의 신문과 유사하다는 것을 알 수 있습니다.

[31-32]

눈표범은 멸종될 위기에 처해 있습니다. 그들이 사는 땅은 점점 사람들이 정착하고 있습니다. 사람들은 그들의 양이나 염소를 먹이기 위해 땅을 넓히려고 눈표범을 죽입니다. 사람들이 눈표범을 사냥하는 또 다른 이유는 모피입니다. 사냥꾼들은 모피를 팔아 많은 돈을 벌 수 있습니다. 사람들에게 모피를 사지 않도록 독려하는 것이 매우 중요합니다. 사람들이 모피를 사지 않으면, 사냥꾼들은 눈표범 사냥을 멈출 수밖에 없을 것입니다. 다행히 많은 기관들이 눈표범을 도우려 하고 있습니다. 국제 눈표범단체라 불리는 조직은 눈표범을 살리기 위한 많은 다양한 생각들을 가지고 있습니다. 국제 눈표범단체와 같은 단체들은 멸종위기에 처한 동물에 관심이 있는 사람들로부터 기금을 모금하여, 도움이 된다고 생각하는 방식으로 돈을 사용합니다. 예를 들어, 국제 눈표범단체는 눈표범을 추적하는 사람들을 돕기 위해 기금을 사용합니다. 기금은 또한

눈표범에 의해 죽임을 당한 가축들의 주인인 지역 농부들에게 지급되어 농부들이 눈표범을 죽이지 않도록 하고 있습니다.

★ snow leopard 눈표범 / extinction 멸종 / extend 확장하다 / fur 모피 / raise 모금하다 / endangered 위험에 처한, 멸종위기에 처한 / track 추적하다 / local 지역의

해설 'in danger of~'는 '~의 위험에 처한'이라는 의미이고, 'come up with~'는 '~가 떠오르다'라는 뜻입니다.

31 우리는 사냥꾼들이 모피를 얻기 위해 눈표범을 죽이는 것을 어떻게 중단시킬 수 있습니까?

  (A) 사냥꾼들을 대신해서 모피를 팔아서
  (B) 사냥꾼들에게 많은 돈을 주어서
  (C) 사람들에게 모피를 사지 말라고 말해서
  (D) 눈표범을 사냥한 것에 대해 처벌하여서

해설 'It is important to encourage people not to buy the fur. If people don't buy the fur, hunters couldn't help stopping hunting snow leopards.' 이 내용을 통해 사람들에게 모피를 사지 말라고 독려해야 함을 알 수 있습니다.

32 지역 농부들에게 왜 돈이 지급됩니까?

  (A) 농부들의 양이나 염소를 잃은 것을 보상하기 위해
  (B) 사람들로부터 기금을 모금하기 위해
  (C) 눈표범을 죽이기 위해
  (D) 농부들을 부유하게 하기 위해

해설 피해를 입은 농부들에게 보상을 해줘서 눈표범을 죽이지 않도록 하기 위함입니다.

[33-34]
수백 년 전에는 바다로 여행하는 것이 위험하였습니다. 해적들(pirates, privateers, buccaneers)에게 공격을 받거나 살해될 수도 있는 위험이 있었습니다. Pirates는 해적이었습니다. 그들은 배를 공격하여 물건을 훔쳐갔습니다. 때로 그들은 해안가에 살고 있는 사람들을 공격하기도 했습니다. Pirates는 자신들이 훔친 것을 모두 자신들이 가졌습니다. Privateers는 한 나라의 정부로부터 고용되어 전쟁 중인 다른 나라의 배를 공격하였습니다. 그들이 훔친 물건을 그들을 고용한 정부와 나누었습니다. 때로 Privateers는 돈을 더 많이 벌기 위해 Pirates가 되었습니다. 두 나라 간에 평화협정이 체결되면, Privateers는 협정은 자신들과 상관이 없다고 주장했습니다. 그러면 그들은 Buccaneers가 되었는데, 이는 정부로부터 급여를 더 이상 받지 않는 Privateers를 말합니다. Buccaneers는 단독으로 배들을 공격하기 시작했습니다. 그들은 자신들이 Pirates보다 우월하다고 생각했습니다. 그러나 실제로는 Pirates, Privateers와 Buccaneers 사이에는 차이가 거의 없었습니다. 그들을 구별하는 것은 매우 어렵습니다.

★ agreement 협정 / claim 주장하다
해설 'tell A from B'는 'A와 B를 구별하다'라는 뜻입니다.

33 Privateers는 어떤 이유로 Pirates가 되었습니까?

  (A) 전쟁을 끝내고 싶어서
  (B) 다른 나라에 돈을 줄 수 있기 때문에
  (C) 다른 나라에 고용될 수 있기 때문에
  (D) 정부와 훔친 물건을 나눌 필요가 없기 때문에

해설 'They shared the goods they stole with the government that had hired them. Privateers Often became pirates to make more money.'에서 돈을 더 벌기 위해서 'Pirates'가 되었다는 것을 알 수 있습니다.

34 Buccaneers는 Pirates에 대해 어떻게 생각했습니까?

  (A) Pirates가 자신들보다 더 못하다고 생각했습니다.
  (B) Pirates가 Privateers보다 더 못하다고 생각했습니다.
  (C) Privateers가 Pirates보다 더 못하다고 생각했습니다.
  (D) Pirates가 Privateers보다 더 낫다고 생각했습니다.

[35-36]
동굴은 어둡고 축축합니다. 그러나 동굴은 기온이 일정하기 때문에 좋은 피난처가 될 수 있습니다. 수천 년 동안, 동굴은 사람과 동물들에게 피난처를 제공했습니다. 오늘날에도 세계의 어느 곳에선가는 사람들이 동굴에 살고 있습니다. 과거에 사람들은 동굴을 죽은 사람을 위한 무덤으로 사용했습니다. 시신을 야생동물로부터 보호하기 위해, 동굴을 거대한 돌이나 불로 막아 놓았습니다. 사람들은 여전히 동굴 안에 집을 짓고 있습니다. 제2차 세계대전 동안에 몰타섬의 사람들은 주변에서 터지는 폭탄으로부터 자신을 보호하기 위해 동굴에 살았습니다. 프랑스의 어떤 지역에서는 절벽의 아랫부분에 있는 동굴이 영구 주택으로 변경되었습니다. 호주 남부에서는 Coober Pedy라 불리는 도시가 인공 동굴에 완전히 지하로 건설되었습니다. Coober Pedy의 사람들은 뜨겁고 건조한 날씨로부터 자신을 보호하기 위해 지하에서 살면서 일하고 있습니다.

★ damp 축축한 / shelter 피난처 / consistent 지속적인 / explode 폭발하다 / permanent 영원한 / man-made 인공의 / climate 기후

35 어떤 점이 동굴을 좋은 피난처로 만드나요?

  (A) 동굴의 기온은 계절에 따라 달라지지 않습니다.
  (B) 동굴은 어둡고 축축합니다.
  (C) 동굴은 여름에는 덥고, 겨울에는 춥습니다.
  (D) 동굴은 사람들의 집에 가깝습니다.

해설 'Caves are dark and damp, however, they can be a good shelter as the temperature is consistent.'에서 기온이 일정해서 좋은 피난처가 될 수 있다는 것을 알 수 있습니다.

36 왜 불이나 돌이 동굴 앞에 놓였나요?

  (A) 시체가 마르고 변하지 않게 하기 위해서
  (B) 야생 동물들이 시체를 손상시키는 것을 막기 위해서
  (C) 동굴을 더 아름답게 보이게 하기 위해서
  (D) 다른 사람들로부터 동굴을 보호하기 위해서

해설 'To protect the dead body from wild animals'에서 이유를 알 수 있습니다.

[37-38]

지구는 표면 아래에서 작동하는 힘 때문에 항상 변하고 있습니다. 과학자들은 지각이라 불리는 지구의 단단한 상층이 9개의 주요 판으로 이루어졌다고 믿고 있습니다. 이러한 판들은 지구 깊은 곳에서 천천히 회전하고 있는 맨틀이라 불리는 단단한 뜨거운 암석 위에서 움직이고 있습니다. 맨틀의 움직임은 판들을 움직이게 합니다. 판들은 움직여 떨어지고 서로 충돌하게 됩니다. 이러한 움직임은 거대한 암석층이 솟아나게 만듭니다. 솟아난 암석층은 바람, 물, 기후변화에 노출되어 암석 안에 묻혀 있는 화석이 드러나게 합니다. 많은 화석들이 이 암석층에서 발견되었습니다. 암석지형이 화석이 발견되는 유일한 곳은 아닙니다. 암석지형이 아닌 곳에서도 종종 화석이 발견됩니다. 예를 들어, 호박은 내부에 곤충 화석을 지니고 있습니다. 때로 우리는 동굴에서도 화석화된 동물을 발견할 수 있습니다.

★ **crust** 지각 / **plate** 판 / **solid** 고체의 / **rotate** 회전하다 / **expose** 노출시키다 / **fossil** 화석 / **amber** 호박

37 무엇이 지구를 계속해서 변하게 합니까?

　(A) 단단한 뜨거운 암석층
　(B) 지구 표면 아래에서 작동하고 있는 에너지
　(C) 단단한 상층
　(D) 지구의 표면

해설 'Earth is always changing because of forces working beneath its surface.'를 보면, 지구 표면 아래에서 작동하고 있는 힘이라는 것을 알 수 있습니다.

38 암석층에 있는 화석이 드러나도록 하는 직접적인 원인은 무엇입니까?

　(A) 동굴의 동물들　　　　　(B) 바람, 물과 기후변화
　(C) 암석이 아닌 지형　　　　(D) 맨틀

해설 'They are exposed to wind, water, and changing temperature, uncovering fossils buried within the rock.'를 보면, 바람, 물, 기후변화 등이 직접적인 원인임을 알 수 있습니다.

[39-40]

최초의 가발은 고대 이집트인에 의해 수천 년 전에 사용되었습니다. 가발은 두 가지의 목적이 있었습니다. 가발은 가발 착용자에게 높은 사회적 지위를 제공했고, 뜨거운 태양으로부터 보호했습니다. 영국과 프랑스의 귀족이 가발을 착용하기 시작하면서 가발은 1600년대와 1700년대에 인기를 끌었습니다. 영국의 엘리자베스1세의 경우에는 화학샴푸 사용과 화장으로 인해 머리가 빠지기 시작했으므로 가발 착용이 반드시 필요했습니다. 여왕이 가발을 쓴다면 자신들도 써야 한다고 모든 사람들은 생각했습니다. 프랑스의 루이14세도 엘리자베스여왕과 유사한 문제를 가지고 있었습니다. 루이왕은 항상 그의 곱슬머리로 칭송받았었습니다. 머리가 빠지기 시작하면서 그는 가발을 착용하기 시작했습니다. 이것은 남자들에게 새로운 패션의 시작이었습니다. 가발의 크기는 사회적 지위를 나타내주는 것 같았습니다. 더 큰 가발은 더 고귀한 신분을 상징했습니다. 프랑스의 마리 앙뜨와네트와 같은 사람에게는 키가 커보이게 하기 위해 가발이 중요했습니다. 마리 앙뜨와네트는 가발에 금속지지대를 달아 그녀의 키가 커보이게 했습니다. 오늘날 많은 사람들이 대머리를 숨기기 위해 또는 그들의 헤어스타일에 변화를 주기 위해 가발을 착용합니다.

★ **purpose** 목적 / **status** 지위 / **royalty** 귀족 / **chemical** 화학적인 / **makeup** 화장 / **symbolize** 상징하다 / **baldness** 대머리 / **alter** 변화시키다

39 고대 사람들은 왜 가발을 착용했습니까?

　(A) 대머리를 숨기기 위해
　(B) 사회적 신분을 나타내기 위해
　(C) 비로부터 머리를 보호하기 위해
　(D) 머리가 빠지는 것으로부터 보호하기 위해

해설 본문은 가발에는 두 가지 목적이 있었다고 말합니다. 한 가지는 높은 사회적 지위를 보여주기 위해서였고, 또 다른 한 가지는 태양으로부터 보호하기 위함이었습니다.

40 프랑스의 루이14세는 왜 가발을 착용했습니까?

　(A) 엘리자베스여왕과 같아지기 위해
　(B) 대머리를 숨기기 위해
　(C) 화학샴푸를 사용하기 위해
　(D) 키가 커 보이기 위해

[41-42]

비행기는 위대한 공학 작품입니다. 비행기에 관해 항상 받게 되는 질문은 "어떻게 수백 톤의 무게가 나가는 물건이 공기 중에 떠있을까요?"입니다. 아마도 비행기의 가장 중요한 부분은 날개일 것입니다. 각 날개의 상단 부분은 곡선이고 하단은 평평합니다. 공기 중에 떠 있기 위해서 비행기 밑에서 위로 작용하는 압력이 필요합니다. 공기는 비행기 날개의 곡선으로 처리된 상단 부분 위에서, 아래의 평평한 부분에서보다 더 빨리 더 먼 거리를 이동합니다. 날개의 상단에서 빠르게 움직이는 공기는 기압이 떨어지게 합니다. 그래서 날개 위의 공기는 날개 아래의 압력보다 낮아집니다. 이러한 기압차가 비행기가 위로 떠오르도록 만듭니다. 그러면 공기 중에 떠오릅니다. 비행기가 떠오르기 위해서는 높은 속도를 만들어 내야 합니다. 비행은 세상을 더 좁은 곳으로 만들었습니다. 어딘가에 도착하는 데 몇 주나 몇 달이 걸리는 대신에 지금은 단지 몇 시간 또는 며칠이 걸립니다. Columbus가 카나리아제도에서 바하마까지 항해하는데 10주가 걸렸습니다. 오늘날 그 여행은 비행기의 발명으로 겨우 몇 시간이 걸립니다.

★ **lift** 양력(밑에서 위로 작용하는 압력) / **generate** 만들어내다 / **thanks to** ~덕분에 / **invention** 발명, 발명품

41 무엇이 비행기를 떠오르게 합니까?

　(A) 기압의 차이　　　　　　(B) 높은 기압
　(C) 낮은 기압　　　　　　　(D) 높은 속도

42 Columbus가 카나리아제도에서 바하마까지 여행하는 데 왜 10주가 걸렸습니까?

　(A) 여행할 시간이 충분했습니다.
　(B) 비행기가 아직 발명되지 않았습니다.
　(C) 비행기 표를 살 수 없었습니다.
　(D) 여행 중에 길을 잃었습니다.

[43-44]

고릴라와 침팬지는 인간과 아주 가깝습니다. 두 영장류는 인간과 생김새도 비슷하고 행동도 비슷합니다. 둘 다 상당히 지능이 높고, 다른 무리와 함께 하는 것을 좋아하는 가족형 동물입니다. 인간은 고릴라와 대략 98%의 유전자가 동일하고 침팬지와는 거의 99%가 동일합니다. 여러 해 동안, 침팬지는 동물원이나 서커스에서 공연을 하도록 했습니다. 그러나 사람들이 이 동물들에 대한 이해를 하게 되면서, 그들을 자연적인 환경에서 키우는 것이 중요하다는 것을 알게 되었습니다. 전 세계적으로 동물구조 단체는 서커스용 침팬지나 애완용 침팬지를 보호구역으로 돌려보내기 위해 일을 하고 있습니다. 고릴라는 크지만 온순한 동물입니다. 그러나 매우 힘이 셉니다. 이러한 이유로 그들은 침팬지처럼 공연을 하도록 만들어지지는 않았습니다. 그러나 그들이 받은 대우는 잔인합니다. 불법 사냥꾼들이 고릴라와 침팬지를 죽여서 불법적으로 그들의 신체 부위를 팔고 있습니다.

★ ape 영장류 / intelligent 지능적인 / company 함께 있음 / genetic 유전의 / rescue 구조하다. 구조 / protection 보호 / creature 동물 / treatment 대우 / cruel 잔혹한

43 동물구조단체는 침팬지를 위해 무엇을 하고 있나요?

(A) 동물원에서 공연을 하게 합니다.
(B) 자연적인 환경으로부터 벗어나게 합니다.
(C) 서커스로 돌려보냅니다.
(D) 보호구역으로 데려다 줍니다.

44 왜 고릴라는 서커스에서 공연하게 되지 않았습니까?

(A) 고릴라는 온순한 동물입니다.
(B) 고릴라는 침팬지와 같습니다.
(C) 고릴라는 거대하고 힘이 셉니다.
(D) 고릴라는 인간과 유사합니다.

[45-46]

그래피티는 공공장소의 외관에 글을 쓰거나 그림을 그리는 것인데 보통 허가를 받지 않고 이루어집니다. 젊은이들은 다른 사람의 건물에 이름이나 메시지를 칠해 놓습니다. 어른들은 이를 범죄행위로 생각합니다. 사실, 물어보지도 않고 다른 사람의 건물에 그림을 그리는 것은 불법입니다. 그러나 요사이 많은 사람들이 그래피티를 예술의 한 형태로 받아들이고 있습니다. 도시의 벽과 건물에 칠해진 그림과 글자들은 자기표현의 형태로 가치를 부여받습니다. 이제, 그래피티 작가들은 그래피티-아트 프로젝트의 일환으로 건물의 외관을 장식하도록 요청을 받습니다. 그래피티-아트 프로젝트는 도시를 에너지가 가득한 곳으로 만드는 데 도움을 줍니다. 이 프로젝트는 젊은 작가들의 작품을 사람들이 볼 수 있는 곳에 전시합니다. 어떤 곳에서는 젊은 그래피티 작가들에게 수업과 재료를 제공합니다. 많은 그래피티 작가들은 힘든 생활을 해왔습니다. 그러나 지금은 그래피트-아트 프로젝트 때문에 희망에 찬 생활을 하고 있습니다. 어떤 이들은 가게 간판과 벽화를 그리는 일을 찾게 되었습니다. 다른 사람들은 전문적으로 미술을 공부하게 되었습니다.

★ illegal 불법의 / property 자산. 건물 / graffiti 그래피티 / professionally 전문적으로

45 그래피티가 무엇입니까?

(A) 젊은 작가들에게 수업을 제공하는 것
(B) 도시 벽 위에 글이나 그림을 지우는 것
(C) 그림을 통해 공공장소에 자신의 생각을 표현하는 것
(D) 다른 사람들에게 자신의 건물에 무언가 그려달라고 요청하는 것

46 그래피티-아트 프로젝트 덕분에 도시에 어떤 혜택이 주어집니까?

(A) 도시가 좀 더 활기차집니다.
(B) 도시의 사람들을 좀 더 근사하게 보이게 합니다.
(C) 범죄자가 줄어듭니다.
(D) 도시가 더욱 커집니다.

[47-48]

어린이들은 듣는 것으로부터 말하는 것을 배웁니다. 아이들이 듣지 못한다면, 그들의 발달에 심각한 영향을 미치게 됩니다. 그러므로 아기들의 청력을 테스트하는 것이 중요합니다. 이런 방식으로 발생할 가능성이 있는 모든 청력손상을 일찍 감지할 수 있습니다. 청력장애가 있는 어린이는 도움을 받지 못하고 방치될 경우에 학교에서 뒤처지게 됩니다. 그러나 적절한 조치로 도움을 받으면 청각장애 어린이도 학교생활을 훌륭하게 할 수 있습니다. 교실에서 청각 장애 어린이를 지원하기 위해 할 수 있는 일들이 많이 있습니다. 대부분은 매우 간단합니다. 교사는 아이들에게 할 일을 말로 지시할 뿐만 아니라 칠판에 지시사항을 적을 수 있습니다. 청각장애 어린이를 맨 앞자리에 앉게 하는 것은 소음을 차단하는 데 도움을 줄 수 있습니다. 말을 할 때 청각장애 아이를 바라보게 하는 것이 아이들이 입술을 읽도록 도움을 줄 수 있습니다. 교사와 급우들은 수화를 배울 수 있습니다. 때로는 개인교사나 통역사가 도움을 줄 수도 있습니다.

★ affect 영향을 미치다 / development 개발 / detect 감지하다 / fall behind 뒤처지다 / aid 돕다 / instruction 지시사항 / tutor 개인교사 / interpreter 통역사

47 아기의 청력을 테스트하는 것이 왜 중요합니까?

(A) 그들의 발달에 심각하게 영향을 미치기 위해서
(B) 청각 이상을 조기에 발견하기 위해서
(C) 학교에서 뒤처지도록 하기 위해서
(D) 학교생활을 잘 하도록 하기 위해서

48 청각장애 어린이와 대화를 할 때 왜 그들을 바라보면서 해야 합니까?

(A) 사람들의 입술을 읽을 수 있도록 도와주기 위해서
(B) 소음을 없애기 위해서
(C) 수화를 배우기 위해서
(D) 무엇을 해야 힐지 말로 지시하기 위해서

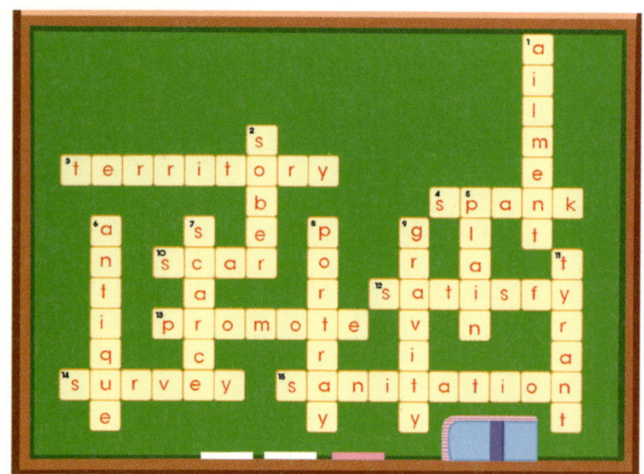

Across

3 (territory) 특정 국가 혹은 지도자에 의해 소유된 혹은 통제되는 땅

4 (spank) 벌로써 손바닥으로 아이의 엉덩이를 치는 것

10 (scar) 칼에 베거나 상처를 입은 후 피부에 남는 흔적

12 (satisfy) 어떤 사람이 원하는 것을 함으로써 그 사람이 기쁘게 느끼게 만드는 것

13 (promote) 어떤 것이 발전하거나 증가하도록 돕는 것

14 (survey) 많은 사람들에게 그들의 태도나 의견을 찾아내기 위해 질문을 하는 것

15 (sanitation) 쓰레기나 오수 등을 제거하고 처치함으로써 공공의 건강을 보호하는 것

Down

1 (ailment) 그렇게 심각하지 않은 병

2 (sober) 취하지 않은

5 (plain) 평평하고 건조한 넓은 지역의 땅

6 (antique) 오래되고 종종 가치 있는

7 (scarce) 이용 가능한 것이 많지 않은

8 (portray) 특정한 방법으로 누군가를 또는 어떤 것을 묘사하거나 보여주는 것

9 (gravity) 어떤 것을 땅으로 떨어지도록 야기시키는 힘

11 (tyrant) 완전한 힘을 가지고 그 힘을 잔인하고 불공정한 방법으로 사용하는 지도자

PART D. Reading and Retelling

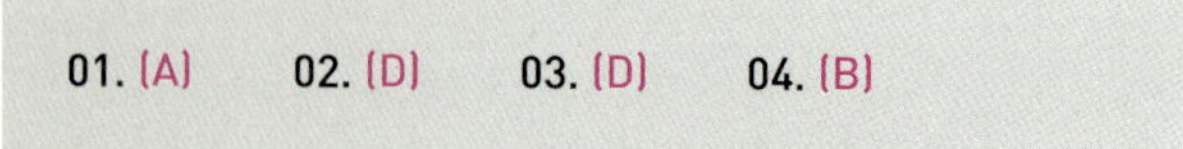

01. [A]   **02.** [D]   **03.** [D]   **04.** [B]

[1]

연령과 성별에 따른 주당 평균 인터넷 사용시간

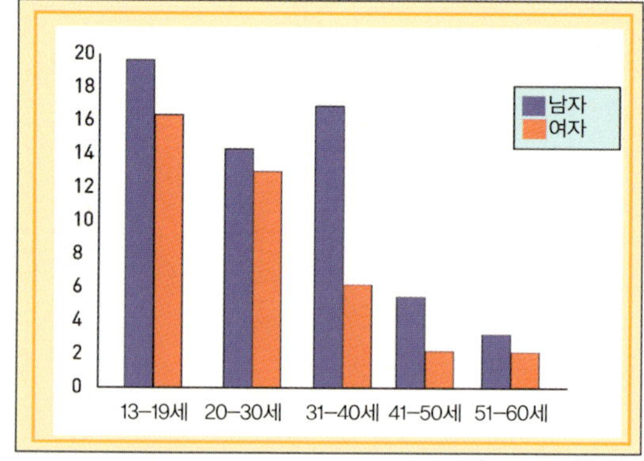

1 차트에 따르면, 다음 중 무엇을 알 수 있습니까?

(A) 여자들은 남자들보다 인터넷을 덜 사용합니다.

(B) 51세 이상의 남자들은 인터넷을 가장 적게 사용합니다.

(C) 남자들은 나이가 들면서 인터넷을 사용하는 시간이 적어집니다.

(C) 31-40세 집단은 성별에 따른 차이가 가장 적습니다.

[2]

5학년생의 성별에 따른 주간 독서 시간과 독해 시험 성적 간의 상관관계

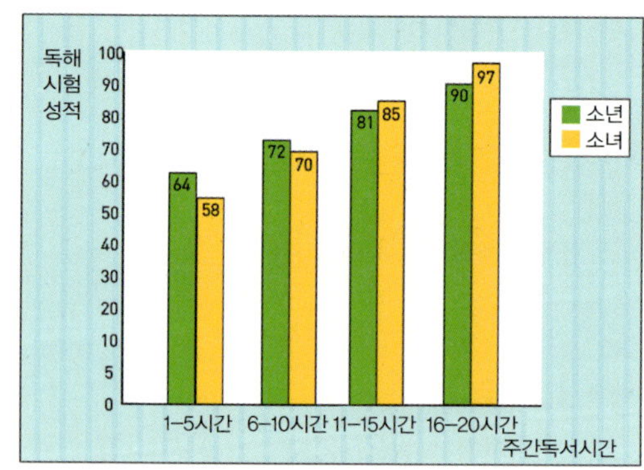

2 여학생의 경우, 어느 그룹이 가장 높은 시험성적을 보이고 있습니까?

(A) 주당 1-5시간 책을 읽는 여학생 그룹

(B) 주당 6-10시간 책을 읽는 여학생 그룹

(C) 주당 11-15시간 책을 읽는 여학생 그룹

(D) 주당 16-20시간 책을 읽는 여학생 그룹

[3]

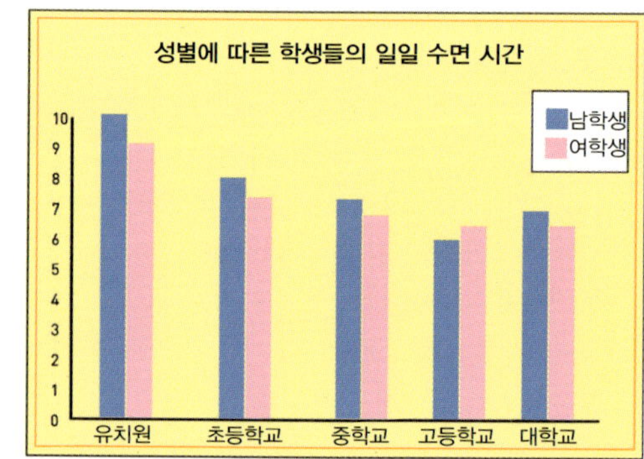

3 어떤 학생들이 다른 그룹의 일반적인 경향을 따르지 않고 있습니까?

    (A) 유치원   (B) 초등학교
    (C) 중학교   (D) 고등학교

해설 고등학교에서만 여학생이 남학생보다 수면시간이 더 긴 것을 알 수 있습니다.

[4]

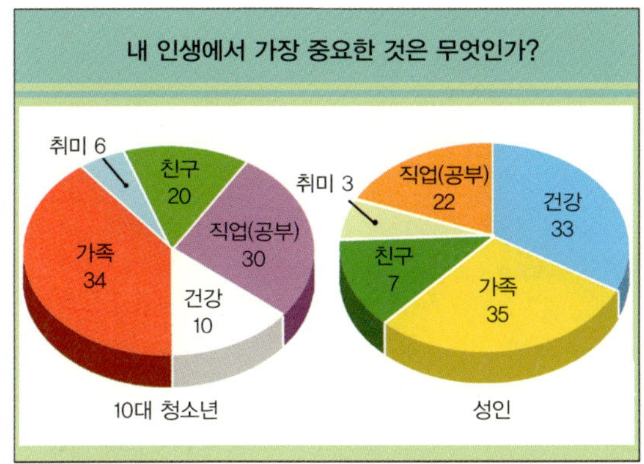

4 어떤 항목에서 성인과 10대 청소년 사이에 가장 큰 차이를 보이고 있습니까?

    (A) 가족   (B) 건강
    (C) 직업(공부)   (D) 친구

PART E. Read and Write

01. ⑧	02. ⑥	03. ①	04. ②	05. ①
06. ⑥	07. ⑤	08. ④	09. ②	10. ④
11. ⑦	12. ⑥	13. ⑧	14. ⑥	15. ③
16. ④	17. ⑧	18. ④	19. ②	20. ①
21. ③	22. ⑥	23. ⑥	24. ②	25. ⑧
26. ①	27. ②	28. ⑤	29. ③	30. ⑥
31. ⑧	32. ②	33. ⑥	34. ①	35. ①
36. ⑤	37. ②	38. ⑦	39. ④	40. ⑧

[1-4]

우리는 모두 다릅니다. 심지어는 일란성 쌍둥이도 다른 성격과 의견을 갖고 있습니다. 우리와 정확하게 똑같은 사람을 찾기란 불가능합니다. 우리는 어느 한 면이나 다른 면에 있어서 더 낫거나 나쁘기도 합니다. 우리는 아주 쉽게 우리 스스로를 철저하게 불행을 느끼도록 비교합니다. 내 동생은 나보다 더 아름답습니다. 나보다 더 부자인 친구를 부러워합니다. 자신을 파괴하는 비교에 다른 사람이 필요 없기도 합니다. 우리를 과거나 미래의 나와 비교하는 것도 똑같은 결과를 초래합니다. 행복은 오늘 우리의 모습 그대로 우리 스스로를 괜찮다고 보는 데서 옵니다.

★ identical twins 일란성 쌍둥이 / nature 자연, 천성 / downright 곧은 철저한 / misery 비참함, 불행 / destructive 파괴하는, 부정적인 / comparison 비교

요약: 어떤 누구도 일란성 쌍둥이라 하더라도 똑같은 성품이나 의견을 갖고 있지는 않습니다. 우리는 다른 사람들과 우리를 2.___⑥___ 방법으로 1.___⑧___를 하는 경향이 있습니다. 우리의 과거와 미래도 비교 3.___①___이 될 수 있습니다. 이러한 비교를 벗어나기 위해서는 있는 그대로의 우리 스스로를 4.___②___합니다.

① 대상   ② 받아들이다   ③ 비교하다   ④ 권리
⑤ 비참, 고통   ⑥ 파괴적인   ⑦ 긍정적인   ⑧ 비교

[5-8]

일부 연구에 따르면, 신체 활동이 근력 트레이닝 형태로 체중 관리 프로그램에 추가되어야 한다고 합니다. 여성 두 그룹에 대한 실험이 시행되었습니다. 두 그룹 모두 다이어트를 했지만 한 그룹은 역기 운동을 했고 다른 그룹은 하지 않았습니다. 양쪽 그룹 모두 평균적으로 13파운드가 빠졌지만 근력 트레이닝을 한 그룹은 지방만 빠졌습니다. 하지만, 역기 운동을 하지 않은 그룹은 지방뿐만 아니라 근육도 빠졌습니다. 근육은 우리의 건강을 유지하는 데 매우 중요해서 체중 관리 프로그램은 어떤 형태이든 근력 트레이닝을 포함해야 합니다.

★ physical activity 신체 활동 / weight training 근력(웨이트) 트레이닝 / consist of 구성하다 / lift weight 역기를 들다 / on average 평균적으로 / muscle 근육

요약: 어떠한 형태로든지 근력 트레이닝 활동을 포함하는 체중 관리 프로그램은 그렇지 않은 프로그램보다 훨씬 5.___①___입니다. 두 여성그룹을 통해서 실험이 6.___⑥___었습니다. 근력 트레이닝과 함께 수반된 체중 관리 프로그램이 8.___④___만을 빼는 데 도움을 주었다고 7.___⑤___었습니다.

① 효과적인   ② 근육
③ 건강   ④ 지방
⑤ 증명된   ⑥ 시행된
⑦ 위험한   ⑧ 반대의증명이 된

[9-12]

사람들은 뉴스는 언제나 옳다고 생각하곤 합니다. 그러나 항상 그런 것은 아닙니다. 뉴스가 사실에 근거한 것처럼 보이지만, 이 사실들은 매체가 보고하고 싶은 방법으로 보도될 수 있습니다. 예를 들면, 뉴스처럼 보이는 정보가 사실이 아닌 의견에만 의존한 것일 수 있습니다. 게다가, 많은 언론인들과 리포터들은 이야기를 흥미 있게 만들기 위해서 뉴스 현상을 비틀기도 합니다. 그 결과 사실을 왜곡시키고 관련된 사람들의 화를 불러일으키기도 합니다. 뉴스의 소비자로서 우리는 반드시 뉴스, 매체, 그리고 사실이 무엇인지에 관해 비판적으로 생각하도록 배워야 합니다.

★ media 매체 / report 보고하다 / opinion 의견 / besides 게다가 / journalist 언론인 / twist 비틀다 / involved 관련된 / consumer 소비자

요약: 뉴스가 항상 9.___②___것은 아닙니다. 사실, 뉴스는 가끔 매체의 10.___④___에 근거합니다. 일부 언론인들은 11.___⑦___이야기를 더하거나 일부를 변형할 수 있습니다. 따라서 뉴스를 12.___⑥___관점에서 받아들이는 것을 강력히 추천합니다.

① 부정적인   ② 사실인   ③ 비틀다   ④ 관점
⑤ 잘못의   ⑥ 객관적인   ⑦ 주관적인   ⑧ 의견

[13-16]

경쟁은 건강할 수 있습니다. 경쟁은 우리를 발전하게 만들며 높은 단계로 도달하게 합니다. 경쟁 없이 우리는 우리 스스로를 얼마만큼 추진시킬 수 있는지를 알 수 없습니다. 사업의 세계에서는, 경제를 더욱 크게 성장시킬 수 있습니다. 하지만 우리는 경쟁의 다른 면을 볼 수 있습니다. 다른 사람과 비교해서 자기 이미지를 만드는 방법으로 경쟁을 사용한다면, 한 사람 안에 있는 최악의 것이 나올 수 있습니다. 경쟁은 다른 사람을 이기려고만 사용하면 어두운 면을 갖게 됩니다. 이러한 방법으로 사람들을 평가하도록 배운 아이들은 종종 어른이 되어서도 오직 승자만이 사랑과 존경을 받을 자격이 있다고 생각합니다.

★ competition 경쟁 / drive 이끌다 / means 방법 / defeat 이기다 / measure 평가하다 / deserve ~할 자격이 있다

요약: 경쟁이 13. ⑧ 방법으로 사용이 된다면 우리를 14. ⑥ 도움이 됩니다. 하지만 동시에 15. ③ 면도 있습니다. 경쟁적으로 쓰이게 되면, 우리는 다른 사람들을 이기는 데에만 관심을 갖게 됩니다. 이러한 사람들은 16. ④ 는 어느 것도 받을 자격이 없다고 생각합니다.

① 밝은　　　　② 파괴하다　　　③ 어두운　　　④ 패배자
⑤ 긍정적으로　⑥ 발전시키다　⑦ 승리자　　　⑧ 건강한

[17-22]

어떤 사람들은 교실에서 선생님이 학생들을 관리할 수 있도록 체벌이 허용되어야 한다고 주장합니다. 그들은 다른 사람에 대해서는 전혀 신경을 쓰지 않는 버릇없는 학생들이 있다고 생각합니다. 그 학생들이 다른 학생들을 방해하는데, 다소 폭력성이 있다 해도 효과적으로 제지하지 않는다면, 다른 학생들은 피해자가 될 것입니다. 그러나 다른 사람들은 어떤 형태의 체벌도 교실에서 사용되어서는 안 된다고 생각합니다. 체벌은 그것이 폭력을 정당화한다는 점에서 교육적인 철학에 위배되는 것입니다. 체벌은 또한 학생의 인권을 심각하게 침해합니다. 학생이 폭력적으로 처벌을 받게 되면 그것은 오랫동안 학생들의 정신 상태에 부정적인 영향을 미칠 것입니다.

★ corporal punishment 체벌 / ill-behaved 행실이 나쁜 / interrupt 방해하다 / intervention 개입 / victim 피해자 / philosophy 철학 / justify 정당화하다 / violence 폭력 / invade 침해하다 / negatively 부정적으로

A학생의 의견: 윗 글과 관련하여 나는 체벌이 나쁘다고 생각하지 않습니다. 선생님들은 통제가 불가능한 문제 학생들을 18. ④ 행동하도록 체벌을 통해서만 17. ⑧ 수 있습니다. 인권에 대해서 말하자면, 다른 선량한 학생들과 선생님의 인권이 행실이 좋지 않은 학생들의 인권보다 더 19. ② 야만 한다고 생각합니다.

B학생의 의견: 윗 글과 관련하여 나는 교실에서 체벌을 사용하는 것에 반대합니다. 체벌은 21. ③ 손상뿐 아니라 마음의 20. ① 을 불러옵니다. 아무도 다른 사람의 신체나 마음을 다치게 할 권리를 부여받지 않았습니다. 학생들의 행동은 폭력을 통해 교정될 수는 없습니다. 그들은 단지 더 큰 처벌을 피하기 위해 변화한 것처럼 단지 22. ⑥ .

① 병　　　　　② 존중되어　　　③ 신체의　　　④ 잘, 바르게
⑤ 나쁜　　　　⑥ 위장하다　　　⑦ 필요한　　　⑧ 훈육하다

[23-28]

논란을 일으키고 있는 문제 중의 하나가 학교에서 핸드폰 사용을 허용하느냐 마느냐 하는 문제입니다. 많은 사람들은 몇 가지 이유로 학생들이 학교에서 핸드폰을 사용할 수 있다고 주장합니다. 첫째, 위급상황 시 아무 때나 아이들과 연락을 할 수 있기 때문에 부모들이 편안함을 느낍니다. 10대들의 경우에는 핸드폰은 다른 사람과 교류하는 가장 중요한 도구입니다. 그들은 사생활을 계속해서 즐길 수 있습니다. 다른 사람들은 핸드폰 사용에 대해 다른 의견을 가지고 있습니다. 그들은 핸드폰사용이 교실에서 학생들의 공부에 대한 관심과 주의를 산만하게 한다고 생각합니다. 게다가, 핸드폰에 대한 의존은 더욱 심각해질 것이라고 합니다. 그들은 점점 더 많은 10대들이 핸드폰을 만지지 않으면 불안해한다고 지적합니다.

★ controversial 논쟁 중인 / permit 허용하다 / interact 교류하다 / distract 산만하게 하다 / reliance 의존 / irritated 불안해하는

A학생의 의견: 윗 글과 관련하여, 나는 핸드폰이 학교에서 사용될 수 있다는 생각에 동의합니다. 대부분의 학생들은 다른 사람에게 피해를 주지 않으면서 학교에서 어떻게, 언제 핸드폰을 사용해야 하는지를 알고 있다고 생각합니다. 핸드폰은 개인적인 23. ⑥ 물품이 아니고 학생들에게 조차도 현대사회의 24. ② 중의 하나가 되었습니다. 학생들의 개인생활을 지나치게 25. ⑧ 않는 것이 중요합니다.

B학생의 의견: 윗 글과 관련하여, 나는 학교에서의 핸드폰 사용에 대해 강력하게 26. ① 니다. 10대들은 이미 게임, 음악듣기, 비디오 보기 등과 같이 너무 많은 시간을 핸드폰을 사용하며 보내고 있습니다. 핸드폰이 다른 사람과의 27. ③ 도구라고 하지만, 10대들은 28. ⑤ 핸드폰 때문에 다른 사람과의 교류가 더 적어지는 것으로 나타납니다.

① 반대하여 (반대함)　　　　② 필수품
③ 의사소통하는　　　　　　④ ~위한
⑤ 역설적으로, 반대로　　　⑥ 선호
⑦ 격려하는　　　　　　　　⑧ 제한하다

[29-34]

지하철에는 노약자를 위한 지정석이 있습니다. 어떤 사람들은 그것이 필요하다고 하고, 또 어떤 사람들은 그것이 필요하지 않다고 합니다. 노약자 지정석에 찬성하는 사람들은 그것이 우리가 얼마나 연장자를 존중하고 몸이 아픈 사람들을 배려하고 있는지를 보여준다고 말합니다. 그것은 우리의 미풍양속을 미래의 후손들에게 전해줄 것입니다. 반대로, 다른 사람들은 노약자지정석이 필요없다고 말합니다. 많은 젊은이들은 이미 노약자 지정석 표지를 무시하고 있습니다. 다른 사람에게 자리를 양보하는 것은 강요될 수 없습니다. 그것은 마음에서 우러나오는 행동이어야 합니다. 게다가, 그것이 연장자나 몸이 불편한 사람을 위한 것이라고 해도, 몸이 불편한 젊은 사람은 실제로는 소외되어 있다는 것이 문제입니다.

★ reserved 예약된, 지정된 / custom 풍습 / generation 세대 / ignore 무시하다 / yield 양보하다 / compel 강요하다 / exclude 소외시키다, 배제하다

해설 'the aged'는 'aged people'로 '나이가 많은 사람들'이란 뜻이고, 'the sick'은 'sick people'로 '아픈 사람들'이라는 뜻입니다. 'in contrast'는 '반대로'라는 의미입니다.

A학생의 의견: 윗 글과 관련하여, 나는 좌석이 노약자를 위해서 지정되어야 한다고 생각합니다. 그들이 지하철에서 서있는 것이 아무리 힘들어도 다른 사람에게 자리를 29.___③___ 해달라고 부탁하는 것은 불가능합니다. 노약자 지정석은 사막의 30.___⑤___ 와 같을 것입니다. 노약자 지정석을 보유하는 것은 또한 젊은 세대들에게 훌륭한 인생의 31.___⑧___ 이 될 것입니다.

B학생의 의견: 윗 글과 관련하여, 나는 지정석을 시행하는 것은 좋은 관례가 아니라고 생각합니다. 33.___⑥___ 자리를 젊은 사람들로 하여금 그곳에 앉지 말라고 강요하는 것은 32.___②___ 것이라고 생각합니다. 그것에 대한 34.___①___ 으로, 젊은 사람들이 노약자 지정석이 아닌 곳에서는 자리를 양보하지 않으려고 하기도 합니다. 공경은 단지 연장자에게가 아니라 훌륭한 인격을 갖춘 사람에게 표해야 하는 것입니다.

★ **practice** 관례, 시행

① 반작용　　② 우스꽝스러운　　③ 양보　　④ 차지된, 점유된
⑤ 오아시스　　⑥ 텅 빈　　⑦ 행동　　⑧ 교훈

[35-40]

사형제도는 남아 있어야 합니까? 이것은 윤리적인 논쟁거리입니다. 어떤 사람들은 사형제도는 즉시 폐지되어야 한다고 주장합니다. 공권력이라 할지라도 사람의 목숨을 빼앗을 권리는 없습니다. 더욱이 아무도 무엇이 옳고 그른지 완벽하게 심판할 수는 없습니다. 사형을 당한 사람들의 절반 이상이 사후에 죄가 없음이 밝혀지고 있습니다. 이것은 말도 안 되는 상황입니다. 그러나 다른 사람들은 사형제도가 흉악 범죄가 늘어나지 않도록 하는 데 결정적인 역할을 해왔다며 존속되어야 한다고 주장합니다. 사형제도가 없다면 우리가 사는 세상은 흉악무도한 범죄로 가득할 것입니다. 사형제도는 흉악범죄의 희생자들에게 보상할 수 있는 유일한 방법입니다.

★ **capital punishment** 사형제도 / **ethical** 윤리적인 / **hot potato** 논쟁거리 / **voice** 주장하다 / **abolish** 폐지하다 / **authority** 권한 / **judge** 심판하다 / **execute** 사형집행하다 / **innocent** 무죄의 / **brutal** 흉악한 / **criminal** 범죄자 / **cruel** 잔인한

A학생의 의견: 이 글과 관련하여, 나는 사형은 곧 종식되어야 한다고 생각합니다. 사형은 국가에 의해서 35.___①___ 가장 잔인한 행위이고, 이것은 정부 권력의 36.___⑤___ 입니다. 사람이 잘못된 37.___②___ 에 의해 살해된다면, 누가 생명의 손실에 대해 보상을 해줄 것인가요? 사형이 중범죄를 감소시키는 데 유용했다면, 우리는 왜 아직도 많은 범죄자를 볼 수 있을까요?

★ **death penalty** 사형 / **compensate** 보상하다 / **offense** 범죄 /

B학생의 의견: 이 글과 관련하여, 나는 사형제도가 필요하다는 생각에 동의합니다. 이 세상에는 인간성을 39.___④___ 38.___⑦___ 범죄가 분명히 존재합니다. 이러한 흉악한 범죄의 희생자들을 생각해보세요. 정부는 이러한 흉악한 행동에 대해 40.___⑧___ 조치를 취해야 합니다. 그것은 바로 사형입니다.

★ **humanity** 인간성

해설 'take action for ∼'는 '∼에 조치를 취하다'라는 뜻입니다.

① 행하는　　② 판결　　③ 개선하는　　④ 파괴하는
⑤ 남용　　⑥ 완벽한　　⑦ 용서할 수 없는　　⑧ 합법의

PUZZLE 5

Across

1 (banner) 글씨가 쓰여진 긴 천 조각

3 (blame) 누군가 또는 어떤 일이 안 좋은 일에 책임이 있다고 말하거나 생각하는 것

6 (lavish) 큰, 인상적인, 또는 비싼

9 (alien) 다른 나라 또는 종족에 속하는 것

10 (velocity) 특정한 방향으로 움직이는 어떤 것의 속도

11 (steep) 높은 각도의

13 (brook) 작은 개울

15 (fad) 단기간 동안 유행하는 어떤 것

16 (eccentric) 비범하고 대부분의 사람과는 다른 방식으로 행동하는 것

Down

2 (replace) 어떤 것이 이전에 있었던 곳에 되돌려 놓는 것

4 (miserable) 극단적으로 불행한

5 (scent) 어떤 것의 기분 좋은 냄새

7 (hazard) 위험하거나 사고 또는 문제를 야기 할 수 있는 어떤 것

8 (fragile) 쉽게 깨지거나 손상됨

12 (prey) 다른 동물에게 사냥 되거나 먹히는 동물, 새 등

14 (oath) 공식적이고 매우 심각한 약속

SECTION I   LISTENING AND SPEAKING

01. (C)	02. (A)	03. (C)	04. (D)	05. (B)
06. (D)	07. (B)	08. (A)	09. (C)	10. (B)
11. (B)	12. (A)	13. (B)	14. (D)	15. (A)
16. (B)	17. (D)	18. (B)	19. (C)	20. (A)
21. (C)	22. (C)	23. (C)	24. (C)	25. (D)
26. (D)	27. (B)	28. (A)	29. (D)	30. (A)

SECTION II   READING AND WRITING

01. (A)	02. (A)	03. (C)	04. (C)	05. (A)
06. (B)	07. (D)	08. (C)	09. (B)	10. (A)
11. (A)	12. (C)	13. (B)	14. (C)	15. (C)
16. (C)	17. (B)	18. (D)	19. (A)	20. (D)
21. (A)	22. (B)	23. (A)	24. (A)	25. (C)
26. (A)	27. (C)	28. (A)	29. (D)	30. (B)
31. ⑥	32. ⑦	33. ③	34. ①	35. ⑥
36. ⑧	37. ⑦	38. ③	39. ②	40. ①

SECTION I   LISTENING AND SPEAKING

1 **M:** You have two blouses and a skirt. It will cost about 10 dollars.
   블라우스 두 장에 치마가 하나군요. 10달러입니다.

   W: Okay. When can I pick up my laundry?
   네. 세탁물을 언제 가지러 오면 되나요?

   M: _______________________________

   (A) It must be a lie.
   분명 거짓말입니다.

   (B) Monday is the day when people feel tired.
   월요일은 사람들이 피곤한 날이야.

   (C) The day after tomorrow.
   내일 모레요.

   (D) You need not have done it.
   그걸 할 필요는 없었어요.

   ★ must ～임에 틀림이 없다.

2 **M:** I am so sorry. I am late.
   너무 죄송해요. 늦었어요.

   W: What took you so long?
   뭐 때문에 그렇게 오래 걸렸나요?

M: _______________________________

(A) I had a car accident on the way.
   오던 길에 자동차 사고가 났어요.

(B) I am looking forward to seeing him in person.
   저는 그를 직접 만나길 고대합니다.

(C) This is the room where I sleep.
   여기는 제가 잠을 자는 방이에요.

(D) The rumor may be true.
   그 소문이 사실일지도 몰라.

★ take so long 장시간 걸리다 / look forward to ～를 학수고대하다

3 **M:** I think his song is mixed with Jazz.
   그의 노래는 재즈와 섞여 있는 것 같아.

   W: Wow. You've got an ear for music.
   와. 넌 음악을 듣는 귀가 있구나(음악을 들을 줄 아는구나).

   M: _______________________________

   (A) There is no accounting for taste.
   취향도 참 가지가지야(취향에 대해 설명할 수 없다).

   (B) I don't have any problem with my ear.
   내 귀에는 아무 문제가 없어.

   (C) Oh, thank you.
   어, 고마워.

   (D) It is worth seeing.
   볼만해.

해설 'There is no accounting for taste.'는 직역하면 '취향에 대한 설명은 없다 (취향은 설명할 수 없다)'는 의미로, 다양한 취향을 다 설명할 수 없다는 표현입니다.

★ be mixed with ～과 혼합된 / be worth ～ing ～할 가치가 있다

4 **M:** Are you being helped?
   지금 도움을 받고 계신가요(도와 드릴까요)?

   W: No, I'm not. Where are turtle-neck sweaters?
   아니요. 목이 긴 스웨터는 어디에 있나요?

   M: _______________________________

   (A) I'm being helped.
   저는 도움을 받고 있어요.

   (B) Oh, certainly.
   네, 물론이죠.

   (C) I am headed for home.
   집을 향해 가고 있습니다.

   (D) It's on the next aisle.
   다음 칸에 있어요.

해설 'Are you being helped(도움을 받고 계신가요)?'는 상점에서 점원이 고객에게 도움을 주려고 할 때 사용하는 표현입니다.

5 **M:** I haven't seen David recently.
   최근에 David를 통 못 봤어.

   W: Didn't he come to the party last night?

어제 밤에 파티에 안 왔어?

M: _______________________

(A) I cannot thank you enough.
매우 감사합니다(더 이상 감사할 수 없습니다).

(B) No. He never showed up.
아니. 전혀 나타나지 않았어.

(C) It is difficult to find a good person.
좋은 사람을 찾기란 어려워.

(D) You had better go there to see him.
네가 그를 만나러 거기에 가 보는 것이 좋을 것 같아.

★ show up 나타나다, 출현하다

6 M: Hi, Lisa.
안녕, Lisa.

W: Hi, Ted. You look so pale, today. What's wrong?
안녕, Ted. 너 오늘 창백해 보인다. 무슨 일 있어?

M: _______________________

(A) I cannot help accepting the offer.
그 제의를 받아들일 수밖에 없어.

(B) It is no use trying to excuse yourself.
변명하는 것은 소용이 없어.

(C) Things are looking great.
그것들은 멋져 보인다.

(D) I don't know. I ache all over today.
모르겠어. 오늘 전신이 다 아파.

★ can't help ～ing ～할 수밖에 없다 / excuse 변명하다 / ache all over
전신이 아프다, 몸살나다

[Telephone rings 전화벨]
7 W: Hello. This is ABC Electronics.
안녕하세요. ABC전자입니다.

M: My name is Jack Smith. I am returning your call.
전 Jack Smith입니다. 전화가 와 있어서 했습니다.

W: _______________________

(A) Jack is a busy person.
Jack은 바쁜 사람입니다.

(B) Oh, Mr. Smith. I called for your interview.
오, Smith씨. 면접 때문에 전화 드렸습니다.

(C) Don't tell me like that on the phone.
전화로 그런 식으로 말하지 마세요.

(D) I don't have the slightest idea.
조금의 생각도 없어(아무 생각도 안나).

★ return the call 전화가 와 있어서 전화를 걸다 / the slightest 가장 적은, 가장
가벼운(slight의 최상급)

8 M: There are two different roads from here.
여기서부터 두 개의 다른 길이 있어.

W: So which way do we go?

그래서 우리는 어느 길로 가니?

M: _______________________

(A) Actually, it doesn't make any difference.
사실, 별 상관은 없어.

(B) As far as I know, it is not true.
내가 알기론, 그건 사실이 아니야.

(C) She can speak two different languages.
그녀는 2개 국어를 할 수 있어.

(D) Please tell me which bus to take.
어느 버스를 타야 하는지 말해주세요.

★ make a difference 변화를 만들다 / as far as I know 내가 아는 바로는

9 M: It was a long day. I am so tired.
너무 긴 하루였어. 너무 피곤해.

W: Me too. I feel so sleepy.
나도 그래. 너무 졸려.

M: _______________________

(A) Why don't we go to the park to play baseball?
공원에 가서 야구나 할래?

(B) I am so full. I think I ate too much.
너무 배불러. 너무 많이 먹었나봐.

(C) Let's wrap it up now and get some rest.
이만 여기서 끝내고 좀 쉬자.

(D) You had a blind date.
너 소개팅을 했구나.

★ wrap something up ～를 마무리 짓다, ～를 포장하다

10 M: I tossed and turned all night.
나 밤새 뒤척거렸어.

W: Really? What's wrong?
왜? 뭐가 잘못됐니?

M: _______________________

(A) It took me an hour and a half.
한 시간 반이나 걸렸어.

(B) I had a digestion problem.
소화 장애가 있었어.

(C) It is high time that you should get up.
너 이제 일어나야 할 시간이야.

(D) Heavy snow kept me from traveling.
폭설은 내가 여행하는 것을 막았어 (폭설 때문에 여행을 못했어).

★ toss and turn (잠을 이루지 못하고) 뒤척거리다 / digestion 소화 / keep
someone from ～ 누군가 ～하는 것을 막다

11 W: What do you want to be when you grow up?
넌 크면 뭐가 되고 싶니?

M: I want to be a cook. I love cooking. How about you?
난 요리사가 되고 싶어. 요리하는 것을 좋아하거든. 넌 어때?

W: I like teaching kids. I want to be a teacher.

난 아이들을 가르치는 것을 좋아해. 난 교사가 되고 싶어.

Q : 그들은 무엇에 대해 말하고 있습니까?
(A) 가계도 　　　　　　(B) 장래 직업
(C) 좋아하는 요리법 　　(D) 현재 직업

[Telephone rings 전화벨]

12 W : ABC Dental Clinic. How may I help you?
ABC 치과입니다. 뭘 도와드릴까요?

M : This is Jack Davis. I made an appointment this Friday, but I don't think I can make it on Friday.
전 Jack Davis입니다. 금요일에 약속을 했었지만, 그 날 못 갈 것 같아서요.

W : Okay. Then when is available for you?
좋습니다. 그럼 언제가 가능하시죠?

Q : 남자는 왜 전화를 합니까?
(A) 약속을 변경하기 위하여 　　(B) 약속을 확정하기 위하여
(C) 약속을 정하기 위하여 　　　(D) 약속을 지키기 위하여

★ **make an appointment** 약속을 하다 / **available** 가능한. 이용 가능한

13 W : Paul, it's time for bed. Turn off the computer.
Paul, 잘 시간이다. 컴퓨터를 끄렴.

B : What time is it, Mom?
지금 몇 시예요, 엄마?

W : It's 10:30.
10시 30분이야.

Q : 소년은 무엇을 하고 있습니까?
(A) TV 보기 　　　　　(B) 컴퓨터 하기
(C) 잠자기 　　　　　　(D) 침대정리하기

14 M : My fingers can't work for my math homework. It has big numbers. Can I borrow your calculator?
수학 숙제하는 데 손가락을 쓸 수가 없어. 너무 큰 숫자라서 말이야. 네 계산기를 좀 빌려도 될까?

W : Sorry, mine doesn't work. Why don't you use your laptop or cell phone?
미안해, 내 것은 고장이 났어. 노트북컴퓨터나 휴대폰을 사용하는 게 어때?

M : Oh, I left my laptop at home, but I can use my cell phone instead.
오, 노트북컴퓨터는 집에 두고 왔지만, 대신에 휴대폰을 쓰면 되겠다.

Q : 남자는 숙제를 하기 위해 무엇을 사용할까요?
(A) 노트북 컴퓨터 　　　(B) 손가락
(C) 계산기 　　　　　　(D) 휴대폰

★ **laptop(computer)** 무릎 위에 놓고 쓰는 컴퓨터. 노트북컴퓨터

15 W : Tommy, take an umbrella with you.
Tommy, 우산 가져가렴.

B : Why, mom? It's sunny outside!
왜요, 엄마? 밖은 맑아요!

W : I know, but it's going to rain this afternoon.
안다, 하지만 오후에 비가 올 거야.

Q : 지금 날씨는 어떻습니까?
(A) 맑은 　　　　　　(B) 비오는
(C) 더운 　　　　　　(D) 추운

16 M : Excuse me, I'm looking for a mystery novel.
실례합니다, 미스터리 소설을 찾고 있는데요.

W : Sorry, we don't have any books here. We only have DVDs and CDs.
죄송합니다, 저희는 책은 가지고 있지 않아요. 저희는 DVD와 CD만 가지고 있습니다.

M : Oh, I didn't know that. Thank you anyway.
오, 몰랐네요. 어쨌든 감사합니다.

Q : 남자는 무엇을 찾고 있나요?
(A) DVD 　　　　　　(B) 책
(C) CD 　　　　　　　(D) 신문

17 W : Mike, I give up on my science report.
Mike, 난 과학 보고서를 포기할거야.

M : Science report? Why? It's due this Friday. You have more days!
과학 보고서? 왜? 그거 이번 금요일까지잖아. 이틀이나 더 남았는데!

W : I know. But I think the topic is too difficult for me.
알아. 하지만, 주제가 나에게는 너무 어려워.

Q : 여자는 보고서를 왜 포기합니까?
(A) 이틀 전까지가 기한이라서.
(B) 시간이 충분히 없어서.
(C) 이번 금요일에 바빠서.
(D) 보고서가 어려운 주제를 가지고 있어서.

★ **due ~** ~가 기한인

18 M : How would you like your hair done?
머리를 어떻게 하기를 원하시나요?

W : I'd like it permed. I don't like straight hair.
파마를 하고 싶어요. 생머리가 싫어요.

M : Great. I think curly hair will look great on you.
좋습니다. 파마 머리가 잘 어울리실 것 같아요.

Q : 여자가 원하는 스타일은 무엇입니까?
(A) 생머리 　　　　　　(B) 파마머리
(C) 앞머리가 있는 짧은 머리 　　(D) 묶은 머리

19 W: Matthew, Hurry up! You will be late.

　　Matthew, 서둘러! 너 늦겠다.

B: Mom, I'm not feeling good today. I have a sore throat.

　　엄마, 오늘 기분이 좋지 않아요. 목이 따가워요.

W: Oh, you also have a fever. You need to see a doctor before you go to school.

　　오, 너 열도 나는구나. 학교 가기 전에 진료를 받아야겠다.

Q: 소년이 다음에 할 것은 무엇입니까?

(A) 학교에 간다.　　　　(B) 수업을 듣는다.

(C) 병원에 간다.　　　　(D) 엄마를 돕는다.

20 W: Oh, no. I left my bag at home!

　　앗. 가방을 집에 놓고 왔네!

M: Do you have time to go back and get it?

　　돌아가서 가져올 시간은 있어?

W: No. The exam starts within 10 minutes. I should be on time.

　　아니. 시험이 10분 내로 시작해. 제 시간에 가야 해.

Q: 여자가 다음에 할 것은 무엇입니까?

(A) 시험 보기　　　　　(B) 집에 돌아가기

(C) 가방을 가지고 오기　(D) 점심 먹기

21 M: Brian is a team leader in his office. Recently he has a new project, so every member in his team is busy and tired. It is 10 p.m. Friday, but he is still in his office working on the project with his members. It is too late and he feels tired. All of his team members also look exhausted. Brian thinks that he has to let the team members go home and get some rest.

　　Brian은 사무실에서 팀장입니다. 최근 그는 새로운 프로젝트를 맡아, 그의 팀의 모든 부원들이 바쁘고 피곤합니다. 금요일 밤 10시이지만, 그는 여전히 부원들과 사무실에서 일을 하고 있습니다. 너무 늦었고 그는 피곤함을 느낍니다. 그의 부원들도 모두 지쳐 보입니다. Brian은 부원들을 집에 보내어 좀 쉬도록 해야 한다고 생각합니다.

Q: Brian은 부원들에게 뭐라고 말할까요?

(A) 그것에 익숙해질 겁니다.

(B) 당신은 훌륭한 사람의 지도하에 있습니다.

(C) 오늘은 이만 끝냅시다.

(D) 모든 순간을 즐깁시다.

★ **in good hands** 훌륭한 지도 아래 있는 / **call it a day** 하루를 끝내다

22 W: Jamie is now busy writing his school paper. He needs to finish the paper by next week. He is supposed to spend the whole weekend working on it. By the way, his friend, Bill is planning a camping trip to a national park this weekend. Bill wants Jamie to join the trip. Jamie knows he has to work, but he also wants to go camping with Bill. Jamie wants to consider the trip more because he doesn't want to lose the chance to experience wildness.

　　Jamie는 학교의 보고서를 쓰느라고 바쁩니다. 그는 다음 주까지 이 보고서를 마쳐야 합니다. 그는 보고서를 쓰기 위해 온 주말을 다 보내려고 합니다. 한편, 그의 친구 Bill은 이번 주말에 한 국립공원으로 캠핑여행을 떠날 계획을 세우고 있습니다. Bill은 Jamie가 이번 여행에 함께 하기를 바랍니다. Jamie는 보고서를 써야 한다는 것을 알고는 있지만, Bill과 캠핑여행도 가기를 원합니다. 야생을 경험할 수 있는 기회를 놓치고 싶지 않은 Jamie는 여행에 대해 더 생각해 보고 싶습니다.

Q: Jamie는 Bill에게 무엇이라고 말할까요?

(A) 행운을 빌어!

(B) 네가 나를 위해 보고서를 써 주길 원해.

(C) 좀 기다려 줘. 좀 더 생각해 볼게.

(D) 안 될 것 같아. 할 일이 너무 많거든.

★ **give something a thought** ～에 대해 생각해보다

23 M: Julia is now on summer vacation. She is traveling to Beijing, China. She goes to a souvenir shop to buy some gifts for her sister. There she meets one of her old friends, Yuna. Yuna is now visiting her brother working in Beijing. Julia is so surprised to see her in a small shop in Beijing. Julia says hello to Yuna and has a short conversation with her.

　　Julia는 지금 여름방학 중입니다. 그녀는 중국의 베이징을 여행하고 있습니다. 그녀는 여동생(언니)의 선물을 사기 위해 기념품점에 갑니다. 거기서 그녀는 그녀의 오랜 친구인 Yuna를 만납니다. Yuna는 베이징에서 일하는 오빠(남동생)를 방문하고 있는 중입니다. Julia는 베이징의 작은 가게에서 그녀를 만나서 너무 놀랍니다. Julia는 Yuna에게 인사를 하고 그녀와 짧은 대화를 나눕니다.

Q: Julia는 Yuna에게 무엇이라고 말할까요?

(A) 참 처량하기도 하지!

(B) 나머지는 네 상상에 맡길게.

(C) 여기서 널 만날 거라고는 기대하지 않았어. 세상 참 좁다!

(D) 물건들이 너무 비싸. 딴 가게로 가.

★ **say hello to ～** ～에게 인사하다. ～에게 안부를 전하다 / **pathetic** 애처로운. 처량한 / **imagination** 상상

24 W: Peter has a final exam next week. He goes to the library to prepare for the exam. It is the final exam period. There are so many people studying that he can't find any empty seats in the library. After he looks around the library for five minutes, he finally finds a seat next to a girl reading a biology book. The seat looks empty but Peter wants to make sure that there is no one in that seat.

　　Peter는 다음 주에 기말고사가 있습니다. 그는 시험을 준비하기 위해 도서관으로 갑니다. 기말고사 시험기간이라 공부하는

사람들이 너무 많아서, 도서관에서 빈자리를 찾을 수 없습니다. 5분 정도 도서관을 둘러본 후, 그는 결국 생물 책을 읽고 있는 여학생 옆에 빈자리를 발견합니다. 그 자리는 비어 보였지만 Peter는 그 자리에 아무도 없는지 확인하기를 원합니다.

Q: Peter는 그 소녀에게 뭐라고 말할까요?
(A) 전화를 해 주시겠어요?　　　(B) 모두 여기 있나요?
(C) 이 자리 주인 있나요?　　　(D) 집까지 태워 주실래요?

25 M: Lisa thinks that her best friend, Alice, looks so sad these days. Lisa wants to know what is wrong with Alice. So Lisa asks Alice to have lunch together. Having lunch, Lisa says that she is so worried about Alice. Alice tells her secret story to Lisa. Lisa is so surprised to hear that, but Alice doesn't want anybody but Lisa to know about her secret.
Lisa는 그녀의 가장 친한 친구 Alice가 요즘 슬퍼 보인다고 생각합니다. Lisa는 Alice에게 무슨 일이 있는지 알고 싶습니다. 그래서 Lisa는 Alice에게 같이 점심을 먹자고 합니다. 점심을 먹으면서 Lisa는 Alice가 너무 걱정된다고 말합니다. Alice는 Lisa에게 자신의 비밀 이야기를 합니다. Lisa는 그 이야기를 듣고 나서 너무 놀랐지만, Alice는 Lisa 이외의 그 누구도 그녀의 비밀에 대해 알기를 원하지 않습니다.

Q: Alice는 Lisa에게 뭐라고 말할까요?
(A) 바보 같은 일이야!　　　(B) 동감이야.
(C) 축배를 들고 싶어.　　　(D) 너만 알아둬.
해설 'keep something to oneself'는 '~에게만 (비밀로) 간직해두다'는 뜻으로 쓰이는 표현입니다.

★ ridiculous 우스운, 어리석은 / toast 축배

26 M: What do we eat for dinner tonight?
저녁으로 뭘 먹을까?
W: What about going to a sushi bar? I love sushi.
스시 바에 가는 거 어때? 난 스시를 좋아해.
M: Jenny. I'm sorry, but I don't eat sushi.
Jenny. 미안해, 난 스시를 못 먹어.
W: Why? What's the problem?
왜? 뭐가 문제야?

Q: 남자가 다음에 할 말은 무엇입니까?
(A) 입에 침이 고이고 있어.
(B) 일본 음식은 단순하고 깨끗해.
(C) 그건 네 탓이야.
(D) 난 날생선에 알레르기가 있어.

★ watering 군침이 도는 / blame 탓하다 / be allergic to ~에 알레르기가 있다

27 M: Which one do you have in mind?
무엇이 맘에 들어?
W: I like the black drawers over there.
저 쪽에 있는 검은색 서랍이 좋아.

M: Looks good. How much is the price on the tag?
좋아 보이네. 가격표에 붙은 가격은 얼마야?
W: Oh, no. It's over 500 dollars.
어머나. 500달러가 넘어.

Q: 남자가 다음에 할 말은 무엇입니까?
(A) 재촉하지 마. 난 준비가 안 됐어.
(B) 가격이 우리 예산 이상이다.
(C) 창피한 줄 알아야지.
(D) 그게 좋은 점이야.

★ drawer 서랍 / rush 재촉하다 / budget 예산

28 M: Did you hear about Judy?
Judy 소식 들었니?
W: No. What's wrong with her?
아니. 무슨 일인데?
M: Judy is now suffering from depression because of the stress from her mom.
Judy가 엄마로부터의 스트레스 때문에 지금 우울증을 앓고 있대.
W: Poor Judy. I knew that her mom always pushed her about her school life and the test scores.
불쌍한 Judy. 그녀의 엄마가 항상 학교생활과 시험성적에 대해 그녀를 압박한다는 것은 알고 있었어.

Q: 남자가 다음에 할 말은 무엇입니까?
(A) 도가 지나치셨구나.
(B) 한번 시도해보고 싶어.
(C) 오늘 아침은 춥다. 그렇지 않니?
(D) 기분이 좀 더 나아진다.

★ suffer from ~를 앓다 / depression 우울증 / go too far 도가 지나치다

29 M: How was my performance on the stage?
무대에서 내 공연 어땠어?
W: You are such a brilliant guitar player! It was cool!
넌 천재적인 기타연주가야! 너무 멋졌어!
M: Really? Thank you.
정말? 고마워.
W: How did you learn it?
어떻게 배웠니?

Q: 남자가 다음에 할 말은 무엇입니까?
(A) 그는 동안이야.
(B) 난 아무 걱정 없어.
(C) 내가 여기 온 지 3년이 됐어.
(D) 솔직히 말하면, 독학했어.

★ baby face 동안 / teach oneself 스스로 가르치다. 독학하다

30 W: Jake. You are great at cooking! I really enjoyed the meal.
Jake. 넌 요리를 정말 잘 한다! 식사 정말 맛있게 먹었어.
M: Thanks. It's my pleasure.

고마워. 내 기쁨이야.

W: The beef steak was the best. How do you cook this well?

비프스테이크가 최고였어. 어떻게 이렇게 요리를 잘 하니?

M: I don't know. My father was a top chef at a hotel restaurant. I think it's thanks to my father.

모르겠어. 아버지가 호텔 레스토랑의 최고 요리사이셨어. 아버지 덕택인 것 같아.

Q: 여자가 다음에 할 말은 무엇입니까?

(A) 핏줄은 못 속이는 구나.   (B) 멋진 세상이야!
(C) 뭐가 맘에 들어?   (D) 우린 해냈어.

해설 'It runs in the family(blood).'는 '그것은 집안 내력이다(핏속에 흐르고 있다),' 즉, '유전적인 것이다.'라는 의미로 쓰이는 표현입니다.

SECTION II READING AND WRITING

1 효과적으로 의사소통하기 위해서, 당신은 학문에 관련된 청중이 기대하는 형태를 인지하고 있어야만 합니다.

해설 effective는 to 부정사구의 동사인 communicate를 꾸미고 있으므로 부사 형태를 띠어야 하므로 effectively가 맞습니다.

2 대부분의 미국 원주민들은 다른 나라로부터 북미로 온 사람들과 가치관, 믿음, 생활 방식에 있어서 동일합니다.

해설 부사인 almost는 명사인 American Indians를 꾸밀 수 없습니다. 명사를 꾸미는 것은 형용사입니다. 여기에서는 almost 대신 most를 사용하면 적절합니다.

★ **identical** 동일한

3 다음의 연습문제들은 독해의 문맥이 새로운 어휘의 의미에 실마리(힌트)를 제시할 수 있는 방식들의 개요를 제시합니다.

해설 관계부사 how 대신 사용하는 that으로 대체해야 합니다.

★ **summary** 요약, 개요 / **clue** 실마리, 힌트

4 심리학의 전문가들은 많은 사람들에게 '부'가 사회 내에서의 그들의 힘과 영향력을 상징한다고 믿습니다.

해설 (C)는 that절의 동사 자리입니다. wealth를 주어로 하고 strength와 influence를 목적어로 취하는 동사 symbolizes를 취해야 맞습니다.

★ **psychology** 심리학 / **influence** 영향

5 고대 천문학의 몇 가지 이론들은 인디언들에 대해 증명된 그것들(이론들)보다 훨씬 더 매혹적입니다.

해설 주어가 복수인 some theories이므로, 동사인 seem의 s는 빠져야 맞습니다.

★ **astronomy** 천문학 / **theory** 이론 / **fascinating** 매혹적인, 황홀케 하는 / **proven** 증명된

6 몇몇의 유명인사들은 세계평화를 _________ 비정부조직에게 돈을 기부합니다.

(A) seek   (B) seeking (추구하는)
(C) sought   (D) be sought

해설 Non-Governmental Organizations의 관계절인 'that seek the world peace'를 분사 형태로 간단히 바꾼 것으로, 선행사인 Non-Governmental Organizations가 seek의 주체이므로 ~ing 형태를 취합니다.

★ **celebrity** 유명인사

7 은행에서의 견제와 균형 체계는 정부의 한 부서가 너무 강력하게 _________ 예방합니다.

(A) to become
(B) becoming
(C) become
(D) from becoming (되는 것을)

★ **checks and balances** 견제와 균형 / **department** 부서, 과 / **prevent (keep) A from B** A를 B하는 것으로부터 막다, 예방하다

8 심리학자들은 무의식의 세계를 시험하는데, _________ 중요한 상징이라고 _________.

(A) which language they believe
(B) they believe its language
(C) whose language they believe (그들은 무의식의 언어가 ~믿습니다)
(D) they believe what language

해설 선행사인 the unconscious가 관계절에서 language를 꾸미는 소유격으로 쓰이고 있습니다.

★ **the unconscious** 무의식

9 Michael은 파란 눈과 금발 머리를 가진 그의 아버지와 _________ 을 가지고 있습니다.

(A) very stronger resemblance
(B) a much stronger resemblance (훨씬 더 강한 유사성)
(C) strongly resembles
(D) resemble much stronger

해설 비교급의 강조는 much, still, even 등을 사용합니다.

★ **have (a) resemblance to ~** ~와 유사성을 가지다

10 국제연합은 _________ 의무와 기회를 모두 가지고 있습니다.

(A) to help defeat deadly diseases (죽음의 질병들을 굴복시키는 것을 도울)
(B) help defeating deadly diseases
(C) helping to defeat diseases deadly
(D) helped defeat diseases deadly

해설 help의 목적어로 원형부정사나 to부정사를 취할 수 있습니다.

★ **defeat** 처부수다, 지우다 / **deadly** 죽음의, 치명적인 / **obligation** 의무

11 최근의 부모들은 아이들을 충분히 만져주고 안아주면서 _________ 을 더 주려고 노력합니다.

(A) 촉각적 자극   (B) 미각기관
(C) 청취 가능한 책   (D) 시각적인 형태

해설 cuddling과 touching을 통해 촉각에 관련된 것임을 추측합니다.

12 몇몇의 현대적 가족들은 아이들을 입양하거나 부모와 합가하는 등의 방식으로 _______ 가족으로 변형되고 있습니다.

(A) 핵   (B) 축소된
(C) 확장된   (D) 편부모

★ **adopt** 입양하다 / **transform** 변형시키다

13 북미에 사는 사람들은 뉴욕이나 로스엔젤레스, 토론토와 같은 _______ 밖으로 이사하기를 열망합니다.

(A) 도시 외곽의 삶   (B) 바쁜 도시 지역
(C) 편안한 분위기   (D) 시골의 평온함

★ **be eager to** ~하기를 열망하다 / **tranquility** 평정, 평온

14 정상 회담의 결과는 세계 경제에 엄청나게 긍정적인 영향을 주고, 그것은 금융 위기로부터의 회복을 _______ 도울 것입니다.

(A) 간신히, 가까스로   (B) 간신히, 겨우
(C) 방대하게   (D) 단지, 그저

★ **summit talk** 정상회담 / **tremendously** 엄청나게, 거대하게 / **financial crisis** 금융위기

15 간헐적 취업이라고도 지칭되는 _______ 은 날씨나 계절에 의존하는 실업상태를 의미합니다.

(A) 구인전략   (B) 불공평한 해고
(C) 계절적인 실업   (D) 직업 안내

★ **refer to** ~라고 지칭하다 / **periodic** 주기적인, 간헐적인 / **employment** 취업 / **unemployment** 실업 / **seasonal** 계절적인, 주기적인

16 Teresa 수녀는 인도 국적의 가톨릭 수녀였습니다. 그녀의 삶은 그녀가 죽는 순간까지 45년간 말 그대로 가난한 자들과 아픈 사람들, 그리고 고아들을 돌보는 데 헌신되었습니다. 그녀는 100개국 이상에서 600개 이상의 선교활동을 수행했습니다. 그것은 병원과 에이즈환자를 위한 시설, 그리고 고아학교를 포함했습니다. 그녀는 1979년에 노벨평화상을 받았습니다. 그녀의 위대한 업적에도 불구하고 어떤 사람들은 그녀가 가졌던 '고통'에 대한 철학에 대해 비판합니다. 그녀는 '고통'이 그녀의 신인 예수에 더 가까이 가는 방법이라고 생각했습니다. 그녀의 생각은 여전히 논란거리이지만, 그녀가 사회적 약자들을 돕는 위대한 사람들 중의 하나라는 점은 의심할 여지가 없습니다.

★ **citizenship** 시민권, 국적 / **literally** 말 그대로 / **devote** 헌신하다, 바치다 / **minister** 관할하다 / **award** 수여하다 / **accomplishment** 업적

Q: Teresa 수녀에 대해 사실이 아닌 것은 무엇입니까?

(A) 그녀는 인도 여성이었습니다.

(B) 그녀는 약자들을 돕기 위해 45년을 보냈습니다.
(C) 아무도 고통에 대한 그녀의 철학에 의심을 가지고 있지 않습니다.
(D) 그녀는 에이즈 환자들을 위한 병원과 시설, 고아들을 위한 학교를 운영했습니다.

해설 Teresa 수녀의 위대한 업적에도 불구하고 그녀의 '고통'에 대한 철학은 논란거리였습니다.

17 쓰나미는 엄청난 양의 물과 높은 에너지를 가진 거대한 물결입니다. 그것은 종종 지진, 화산분출, 수심폭발 등의 결과일 수 있습니다. 파도의 높이는 많은 경우 100미터 이상입니다. 파도의 속도는 시간당 600에서 800킬로미터에 범위에 있습니다. 80%의 쓰나미가 태평양에서 일어나는데, 이것은 가끔 일본 동부해안이나, 북미의 서부해안과 같은 지역에 파괴적인 손상을 입힙니다. 쓰나미로 인해 피해를 입는 것으로부터 해안지역을 보호하기 위하여, 사람들은 해안에 홍수림이나, 산호초, (인공)숲과 같은 자연적인 방어막을 설치하는데, 이것은 그 지역에 피해를 덜 주는 것으로 증명되었습니다.

★ **gigantic** 거대한 / **immense** 엄청난 / **eruption** 분출 / **devastating** 황폐시키는, 파괴적인 / **barrier** 울타리, 장벽, 방어막

Q: 쓰나미의 피해를 최소화하기 위해 사람들은 무엇을 합니까?

(A) 해안가로부터 피합니다.
(B) 자연적인 방어막을 세웁니다.
(C) 숲을 파괴합니다.
(D) 지역을 떠납니다.

[18-19]
도넛은 전형적인 미국 간식입니다. 그것은 기름에 튀겨진 작은 동그란 케이크로, 전형적으로 고리모양을 하고 있습니다. 그것은 밀가루 반죽을 기름에 튀긴 것으로 보통은 달콤합니다. 그것은 때때로 중간에 구멍이 없이 크림치즈와 같은 속재료(충전물)를 가지고 있기도 합니다. 역사에서 그것은 미국에 살던 네덜란드 이민자에 의해 개발되었다고 알려집니다. 도넛이란 이름은 네덜란드말로 '기름진 케이크'란 뜻입니다. 최초의 도넛 기계는 1920년 Adolph Levitt이라는 러시아 망명자에 의해 뉴욕에서 개발되었습니다. Levitt의 도넛 기계는 큰 히트를 쳤고, 도넛의 인기의 증가를 이끌었습니다. 1934년 시카고에서 있었던 세계박람회에서 도넛은 '세기의 진보음식'으로 선정되었습니다. 기계가 자동적으로 도넛을 만들어내는 것을 보면서 사람들은 뭔가 미래적인 것을 느꼈음에 틀림없습니다. 도넛은 간식으로서 미국의 주류 음식이 되었습니다. 오늘날 미국에서만 백억 개가 넘는 도넛이 매년 만들어지고 있습니다.

★ **typical** 전형적인 / **deep-fried** 기름에 튀겨진 / **progress** 진보 / **automatically** 자동적으로 / **mainstream** 주류 / **futuristic** 초현대적인

18 본문은 무엇에 관한 것입니까?

(A) 도넛의 영양성분
(B) 도넛이 만들어지는 방법
(C) 미국의 러시아난민들의 삶
(D) 미국 도넛의 역사

19 본문을 통해 알 수 없는 것은 어느 것입니까?

(A) 도넛 기계는 네덜란드 사람들에 의해 수입되었다.
(B) 어떤 도넛은 반죽 안에 속재료(충전물)를 가지고 있다.
(C) Adolph Levitt은 러시아 출신이다.
(D) 많은 미국인들에 간식으로 도넛을 즐긴다.

해설 도넛 기계는 네덜란드 사람에 의해 만들어졌지만, 수입된 것이 아니라 미국에서 개발한 것입니다.

[20-21]

'10월의 축제'를 의미하는 옥토버페스트는 5백만명 이상의 사람들이 참가하는 가장 유명한 행사들 중 하나입니다. 옥토버페스트는 독일 Munich에서 2주 이상 매년 개최되는데, 늦은 9월에서 10월의 첫 주말까지 계속됩니다. 옥토버페스트의 하이라이트는 전통의상과 총잡이들의 퍼레이드입니다. 독일 문화의 이 다채로운 전시는 옥토버페스트의 첫 일요일 아침에 있습니다. 옥토버페스트에는 30개 이상의 맥주 천막이 있고, 전화나 메일, 팩스로 미리 테이블을 예약할 수 있습니다. 옥토버페스트는 오늘날 실용적인 이유에서 9월에 시작합니다. 독일의 날씨는 9월이 더 낮고, 밤에도 그렇게 춥지 않습니다. 역사적으로, 옥토버페스트의 마지막 주말은 10월에 거행되며, 이 전통은 오늘날까지 계속되고 있습니다. 옥토버페스트는 맥주를 마시는 것 이상입니다. 어른들뿐만 아니라 아이들도 즐길 수 있는 재미난 놀이기구와 대관람차, 롤러코스터, 음악과 퍼레이드를 포함합니다. 사람들은 그들의 아이들과 함께 여기에 옵니다. 아이들도 맥주 천막에 들어올 수 있지만, 저녁 8시 이후에는 6세 이하의 어린이는 천막을 떠나야 합니다. 옥토버페스트를 방문하는 아이들에게 최고의 시간은 주중 오후 5시 이전입니다.

★ annually 매년 / rifleman 소총 명사수 / in advance 미리, 사전에 / practical 실용적인 / reservation 예약

20 본문은 무엇에 관한 것입니까?

(A) 아이들이 옥토버페스트에 허락되지 않는 이유
(B) 미리 옥토버페스트를 예약해야 하는 중요성
(C) 옥토버페스트에서 제공되는 맥주의 종류
(D) 가장 유명한 독일 페스티벌들 중 하나인 옥토버페스트

21 옥토버페스트에 대해 사실이 아닌 것은?

(A) 축제는 2년에 한 번씩 열립니다.
(B) 팩스로 테이블을 예약할 수 있습니다.
(C) 아이들은 롤러코스터를 즐길 수 있습니다.
(D) 아이들은 맥주 텐트에 들어올 수 있습니다.

해설 옥토버페스트는 매년마다 개최되는 행사입니다.

[22-23]

몸짓(제스처)은 구어체 언어의 전형적인 요소입니다. 하지만, 만약 몸짓만을 가지고 사람들과 의사소통을 해야 한다면 당신은 엄청난 문제를 갖게 될 것입니다. 수화는 뜻을 전달할 때, 소리의 형태 대신에 시각적으로 전달되는 신호의 형태를 사용하는 언어입니다. 수화는 화자의 생각을 표현하며 손의 형태와 손의 움직임 또는 몸과 얼굴의 표정을 동시에 결합시킵니다. 수화는 청각 장애인들이 존재하는 지역에서 발전합니다. 수백 가지의 수화가 전 세계적으로 사용되고 있습니다. 수화는 특정한 것들을 표현하기 위한 그것들만의 신호형태를 가지고 있는데, 이것은 '지문자(손가락으로 문자를 표현하는 것)'를 제외하고는 일반적으로 문어체계에 의존하지 않습니다. Fingerspelling이라고도 불리는 '지문자'는 문어체계에서 차용된 전문적인 어휘를 위해서만 주로 쓰입니다. 예를 들면, 청각 장애인들은 'love'를 수화로 표현할 때, '지문자'로 L, O, V, E의 알파벳을 하나씩 나타내는 대신에, 주먹을 쥔 손에서 엄지, 검지, 새끼손가락을 폅니다.

★ tremendous 엄청난 / transmit 전달하다 / simultaneously 동시에 specialized 전문적인 / describe 묘사하다

22 '지문자'는 무엇을 위해 사용됩니까?

(A) 신호형태와 소리형태
(B) 문어체계에서 온 전문적 어휘
(C) 손 또는 몸의 움직임
(D) 생각을 전달하기 위한 얼굴표정

23 수화에 대해 사실이 아닌 것은 무엇입니까?

(A) 의미를 전달하기 위해 소리 형태를 사용합니다.
(B) '지문자'는 문어에 의존적입니다.
(C) 청각장애인을 위해 주로 쓰입니다.
(D) '지문자'는 단어의 각 문자의 모양을 만드는 것을 의미합니다.

[24-25]

심리학자들은 사람의 출생 순서가 그들의 성격에 직접적인 연관이 있다는 것을 보여줍니다. 부모들은 출생 순서에 따라 아이들을 이해하고 그것은 아이들의 미래를 설계하는 데 도움이 될 수 있습니다. 한 연구에 따르면, 첫째 아이들은 집단의 우두머리가 되고 활동적으로 일을 하는 경향이 있습니다. 믿든 믿지 않던 간에, 전세계의 첫째 아이들은 유사한 성격적 특징을 함께 가지고 있습니다. 첫째 아이는 보통 자기에게 집중되는 최대의 관심을 받고 자란 아이입니다. 이들의 두 가지 전형적인 특징이 있는데, 그것은 순종적인 것과 공격적인 것입니다. 순종적인 첫째 아이들은 사람들을 기쁘게 하고 다른 형제자매들에 대해 책임감을 느끼며, 호감의 지도자로서의 역할을 합니다. 공격적 성향을 가진 첫째 아이들은 완벽주의자로, 지배하려고 들며, 집단의 활동을 장악하려는 경향이 있습니다. 그들은 주로 자기 방식대로의 일을 원합니다. 이것에도 불구하고 첫째 아이들은 높은 수준의 자신감과 인내심, 집중력을 가지고 있습니다. 그들은 매우 잘 조직화되어 있으며 집중되어 있습니다. 그러므로 그들은 보통 법조계, 의학계, 컴퓨터 설계 혹은 건축과 같이 높은 수준의 정확성을 요구하는 직업을 주로 선택합니다. 그들은 종종 사장으로서 한 회사를 경영하고 관리합니다.

★ similar 비슷한, 유사한 / siblings 형제, 자매 / compliant 순종적인, 고분고분한 / favorable 호감의 / concentration 집중 / organized 정리된, 조직화 된 / precision 정확도 / administer 관리하다 / high degree of 고난도의 ~

24 본문은 무엇에 대한 내용입니까?

(A) 첫째 아이의 성격적인 특징
(B) 장래의 직업을 정하는 것의 중요성

(C) 출생순서가 아이의 인내심에 영향을 끼치는 방식
(D) 첫째 아이를 위한 부모의 역할

25 첫째 아이에 대해 사실이 아닌 것은?

(A) 그들은 집단의 지도자인 경향이 있습니다.
(B) 그들 중 몇몇은 공격적인 성격을 가지고 있습니다.
(C) 그들은 자신감 부족을 겪습니다.
(D) 그들은 좋은 인내심을 가지고 있습니다.

[26-27]

약 30년 전, 하버드의 연구자들은 커피 섭취와 암의 관계에 대해 발표했습니다. 그 결과는 잘못되었음이 증명되었음에도 불구하고, 커피는 그 때 이후로 건강하지 않다는 이미지를 가지게 되었습니다. 하지만 커피는 사실 암에는 아무 책임이 없습니다. 커피는 지방이나, 소량의 탄수화물과 단백질도 포함하고 있지 않습니다. 커피 안의 카페인은 각성의 일시적 증진을 이끌어 내는 두뇌 자극제입니다. 최근 밝혀진 사실에 따르면, 커피는 알츠하이머병, 당뇨병, 피부암 등의 특정 질병을 치료하고 예방하는 데 도움을 줄 수 있다고 합니다. 커피는 담석이 발생하는 위험을 줄여주고, 결장암의 발생을 약화시켜주며, 인지적인 기능을 증진하고, 간질병에 취약한 사람들의 간 손상의 위험을 줄여주며, 파킨슨병의 위험도 줄여준다고 합니다. 커피는 또한 장기간의 신체활동에서의 참을성을 증진시켜주는 것으로 나타났습니다. 커피는 사실상 수십만의 사람들이 규칙적으로 섭취하는 가장 건강한 음료들 중에 하나입니다.

★ consumption 섭취 / conclude 결론짓다 / contain 포함하다 /
awareness 각성 / carbohydrate 탄수화물 / temporary 일시적인 /
diabetes 당뇨병 / gallstone 결석 / colon 결장 / cognitive 인지적인 /
endurance 참기. 인내 / long–duration 장시간의

26 본문은 무엇에 관한 것입니까?

(A) 커피를 마시는 것의 이로운 효과
(B) 커피가 암에 미치는 부정적 영향
(C) 카페인이 몸에 흡수되는 방식
(D) 지방 관련 질병에 대항하여 싸우는 방법

27 카페인은 어떤 작용을 합니까?

(A) 탄수화물과 단백질 제공   (B) 당뇨병 유발
(C) 뇌 자극   (D) 근육 완화

[28-29]

자연 친화적으로 사는 것이 최근 많은 사람들에게 화젯 거리로, 그것은 사람들이 뒤뜰에 정원을 갖는 것을 고려하게 만듭니다. 그들은 매일의 식사에 먹을 채소나, 집을 장식할 식물을 키우는 것이 쉬울 거라고 믿습니다. 하지만, 정원일은 많은 에너지와 노력을 필요로 합니다. 사람들이 식물과 농사에 대해 충분한 지식을 가지고 있지 않을 때, 그들은 채소를 경작하고 식물을 돌보는 데 심각한 어려움을 경험합니다. 무엇보다 먼저, 사람들은 무엇을 키울 것인지, 언제 씨를 뿌려야 하는지, 언제 수확하는지 등에 대한 정보를 가져야 합니다. 이 정보들이 완전히 이해가 되면, 사람들은 정원에 자신의 노동력을 줄 준비를 해야 합니다. 규칙적으로 정원에 물을 주는 것이 채소와 식물의 성장에 요구되는 가장 중요한 것입니다. 가끔씩, 사람들은 유망한 작물의 성장을 돕기 위해 나머지 것들을 솎아내야 할 필요도 있습니다. 마지막으로 중요한 것은 식물과 채소들을 애정으로 돌보고, 주의 깊게 그들을 재배하려고 노력해야 한다는 점입니다.

★ cultivate 경작하다 / seed 씨 / require 요구하다 / sort out 솎아내다

28 본문은 무엇에 관한 것입니까?

(A) 정원을 성공적으로 유지하는 법
(B) 자연 친화적인 삶의 이점
(C) 정원을 가지는 것의 신비
(D) 좋은 정원사를 고용하는 방법

29 좋은 정원을 갖는 데 필요한 것이 아닌 것은 무엇입니까?

(A) 애정   (B) 노동
(C) 정보   (D) 매일의 식단

[30]

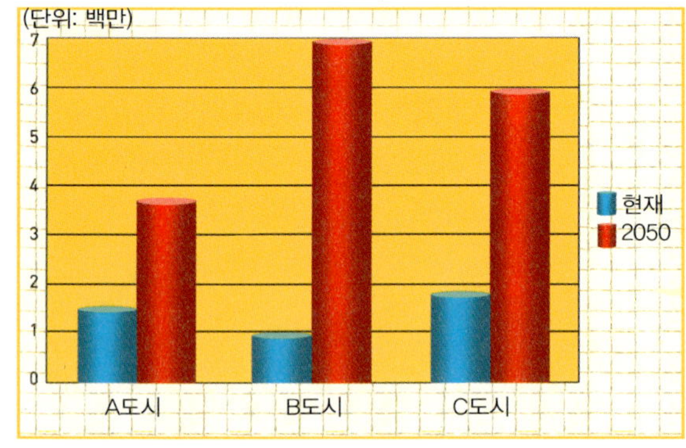

30 차트로부터 추론할 수 있는 것은 무엇입니까?

(A) A도시의 인구는 5백만에 도달할 것이다.
(B) 세 도시 모두에서 2050년까지 인구가 증가할 것이다.
(C) B도시의 인구는 2050년에 두 배가 될 것이다.
(D) C도시는 현재와 2050년 사이에 가장 큰 증가를 보일 것이다.

[31- 34]

세계가 점점 가까워짐에 따라, 국제 언어의 필요성이 최근 높아지고 있습니다. 그것(국제어)은 사람과 국가들이 각 문화를 더 잘 이해하고 정확한 방식으로 의사소통하는 것을 돕습니다. 두 나라가 경제에 대한 협정이나 동의를 이끌어 낼 때, 각 언어의 차이는 특정 단어의 오해를 일으킬 수 있고, 그것은 두 국가 간의 충돌을 유발할 것입니다. 덧붙여, 잘못 번역된 서류는 다른 국가의 무역회사들의 금융 상태에 손상을 입힐 수도 있습니다.

★ treaty 협정 / conflict 충돌. 마찰 / financial 금융의. 금전적인 / status 상태

요약: 국제어는 각 문화의 더 나은 이해와 의사소통의 32. ____⑦____ 을

위해 꼭 31.　　⑥　　것입니다. 언어의 차이는 두 나라 간의 충돌과
33.　　③　　를 유발할 수 있습니다. 이와 비슷하게, 무역회사들은
34.　　①　　방식으로 번역된 서류 때문에 금전적 손해를 경험할 수
도 있습니다.

① 잘못된　　② 경제　　③ 오해　　④ 번역
⑤ 금전적인　　⑥ 필요한　　⑦ 정확성　　⑧ 서류

[35- 40]

최근 미국에서는 호랑이 엄마가 논쟁거리입니다. 호랑이 엄마는 아이
들의 삶을 완벽하게 통제하는 것으로 알려져 있습니다. 그들은 아이들
에게 시험 준비를 위해 밤늦게까지 공부하기를 강요합니다. 그들은 밖
에서 놀거나, 친구 집에서 잠을 자고 오거나, 학교 연극에 참여하는 것으
로부터 아이들을 단념시킵니다. 그들은 그들에게 아이들을 안내할 의
무가 있다고 믿습니다. 이런 엄마들의 많은 수가 사실상 그녀의 아이들
을 사회에서 성공시켜내고 있습니다. 그러나 호랑이 엄마가 아이를 키
우는 방식에 대하여 들은 어떤 사람들은 이것이 학대의 일종이라고 생
각하며, 이 생각에 반대합니다. 그들은 엄마는 아이들을 친근한 방식으
로 대해야 하고, 이것이 아이들이 한 사회의 개인으로서의 정신적인 성
숙에 영향을 끼친다고 생각합니다. 그들은 또한 호랑이 엄마들이 아이
들의 자연적인 요구들을 억압할 지도 모르며, 궁극적으로는 사고의 심
리학적 과정에도 손상을 줄 것이라고 생각합니다.

★ controversial 논쟁의 / sleepover 친구 집에서 함께 자며 노는 파티 / be
obliged to ～할 의무가 있다 / oppose 반대하다 / ultimately 궁극적으로

A학생의 의견: 위의 본문에 대하여, 나는 엄마들이 아이들이 받아들일
수 있는 방식으로 행동하는 것을 돕기 위해 35.　　⑥　　해야 한다고
믿습니다. 아이들은 미래를 위해 지금 무엇을 해야 하는지 정확히 알지
못합니다. 엄마들은 결국 아이들의 37.　　⑦　　삶을 확신할 수 있는
방식으로 안내해야 할 36.　　⑧　　있습니다.

B학생의 의견: 위의 본문에 대하여, 나는 엄마들이 아이들에 대한 모든
38.　　③　　을 가져야 한다고 생각하지 않습니다. 아이들도 사회의
39.　　②　　구성원으로서 자라야 할 그들만의 권리를 가지고 있습니
다. 부모의 40.　　①　　의 필요성에도 불구하고, 부모는 조정자가 아니
라 조력자여야만 합니다.

① 안내　　② 독립적인　　③ 권한　　④ 논쟁
⑤ 친근한　　⑥ 엄격한　　⑦ 성공적인　　⑧ 의무를 지고

Memo